RESEARCH IN MARITIME HISTORY
NO. 35

MAKING GLOBAL AND LOCAL CONNECTIONS: HISTORICAL PERSPECTIVES ON PORTS

Edited by
Tapio Bergholm,
Lewis R. Fischer and M. Elisabetta Tonizzi

International Maritime Economic History Association

St. John's, Newfoundland
2007

ISSN 1188-3928
ISBN 978-0-9738934-5-8

Research in Maritime History is available free of charge to members of the International Maritime Economic History Association. The price to others is US $25 per copy, plus US $5 postage and handling.

Back issues of *Research in Maritime History* are available:

No. 1 (1991)	David M. Williams and Andrew P. White (comps.), *A Select Bibliography of British and Irish University Theses about Maritime History, 1792-1990*
No. 2 (1992)	Lewis R. Fischer (ed.), *From Wheel House to Counting House: Essays in Maritime Business History in Honour of Professor Peter Neville Davies*
No. 3 (1992)	Lewis R. Fischer and Walter Minchinton (eds.), *People of the Northern Seas*
No. 4 (1993)	Simon Ville (ed.), *Shipbuilding in the United Kingdom in the Nineteenth Century: A Regional Approach*
No. 5 (1993)	Peter N. Davies (ed.), *The Diary of John Holt*
No. 6 (1994)	Simon P. Ville and David M. Williams (eds.), *Management, Finance and Industrial Relations in Maritime Industries: Essays in International Maritime and Business History*
No. 7 (1994)	Lewis R. Fischer (ed.), *The Market for Seamen in the Age of Sail*
No. 8 (1995)	Gordon Read and Michael Stammers (comps.), *Guide to the Records of Merseyside Maritime Museum, Volume 1*
No. 9 (1995)	Frank Broeze (ed.), *Maritime History at the Crossroads: A Critical Review of Recent Historiography*
No. 10 (1996)	Nancy Redmayne Ross (ed.), *The Diary of a Maritimer, 1816-1901: The Life and Times of Joseph Salter*
No. 11 (1997)	Faye Margaret Kert, *Prize and Prejudice: Privateering and Naval Prize in Atlantic Canada in the War of 1812*
No. 12 (1997)	Malcolm Tull, *A Community Enterprise: The History of the Port of Fremantle, 1897 to 1997*

No. 13 (1997) Paul C. van Royen, Jaap R. Bruijn and Jan Lucassen, *"Those Emblems of Hell"? European Sailors and the Maritime Labour Market, 1570-1870*

No. 14 (1998) David J. Starkey and Gelina Harlaftis (eds.), *Global Markets: The Internationalization of The Sea Transport Industries Since 1850*

No. 15 (1998) Olaf Uwe Janzen (ed.), *Merchant Organization and Maritime Trade in the North Atlantic, 1660-1815*

No. 16 (1999) Lewis R. Fischer and Adrian Jarvis (eds.), *Harbours and Havens: Essays in Port History in Honour of Gordon Jackson*

No. 17 (1999) Dawn Littler, *Guide to the Records of Merseyside Maritime Museum, Volume 2*

No. 18 (2000) Lars U. Scholl (comp.), *Merchants and Mariners: Selected Maritime Writings of David M. Williams*

No. 19 (2000) Peter N. Davies, *The Trade Makers: Elder Dempster in West Africa, 1852-1972, 1973-1989*

No. 20 (2001) Anthony B. Dickinson and Chesley W. Sanger, *Norwegian Whaling in Newfoundland: The Aquaforte Station and the Ellefsen Family, 1902-1908*

No. 21 (2001) Poul Holm, Tim D. Smith and David J. Starkey (eds.), *The Exploited Seas: New Directions for Marine Environmental History*

No. 22 (2002) Gordon Boyce and Richard Gorski (eds.), *Resources and Infrastructures in the Maritime Economy, 1500-2000*

No. 23 (2002) Frank Broeze, *The Globalisation of the Oceans: Containerisation from the 1950s to the Present*

No. 24 (2003) Robin Craig, *British Tramp Shipping, 1750-1914*

No. 25 (2003) James Reveley, *Registering Interest: Waterfront Labour Relations in New Zealand, 1953 to 2000*

No. 26 (2003) Adrian Jarvis, *In Troubled Times: The Port of Liverpool, 1905-1938*

No. 27 (2004) Lars U. Scholl and Merja-Liisa Hinkkanen (comps.), *Sail and Steam: Selected Maritime Writings of Yrjö Kaukiainen*

No. 28 (2004) Gelina Harlaftis and Carmel Vassallo (eds.), *New Directions in Mediterranean Maritime History*

No. 29 (2005) Gordon Jackson, *The British Whaling Trade*

No. 30 (2005) Lewis Johnman and Hugh Murphy, *Scott Lithgow: Déjà vu All Over Again! The Rise and Fall of a Shipbuilding Company*

No. 31 (2006) David Gleicher, *The Rescue of the Third Class on the Titanic: A Revisionist History*

No. 32 (2006) Stig Tenold, *Tankers in Trouble: Norwegian Shipping and the Crisis of the 1970s and 1980s*

No. 33 (2007) Torsten Feys, Lewis R. Fischer, Stéphane Hoste and Stephan Vanfraechem, *Maritime Transport and Migration: The Connections between Maritime and Migration Networks*

No. 34 (2007) A.B. Dickinson, *Seal Fisheries of the Falkland Islands and Dependencies: An Historical Review*

Research in Maritime History would like to thank Memorial University of Newfoundland for its generous financial assistance in support of this volume.

Table of Contents

Part I: Port Case Studies

Part II: Port Systems

ABOUT THE EDITORS

TAPIO BERGHOLM <tberghol@mappi.helsinki.fi> is Senior Lecturer at the University of Helsinki. His research interests include the history of industrial relations and transport - especially port - history. He has published articles and books, mainly in Finnish but also in international and Scandinavian publications. He is a Vice President of the International Commission for Maritime History and Overseas Corresponding Member for the Society for Nautical Research.

LEWIS R. FISCHER <lfischer@mun.ca> is Professor and Graduate Coordinator of History at Memorial University of Newfoundland, where he serves as Editor-in-Chief of the *International Journal of Maritime History* and Series Editor of *Research in Maritime History*. He specialises in the international economic and social aspects of maritime history.

M. ELISABETTA TONIZZI <tonizzi@unige.it> works in the Department of European Research at the University of Genoa, where she teaches contemporary history and the history of globalisation. She has published extensively on the industrial and maritime economy of Genoa in the nineteenth and twentieth centuries. Her recent publications include "Economy, Traffic and Infrastructure in the Port of Genoa, 1861-1970," in Gordon Boyce and Richard Gorski (eds.), *Resources and Infrastructures in the Maritime Economy, 1500-2000* (St. John's, 2002), 119-140; and "Recent Maritime Historiography on Italy," in Gelina Harlaftis and Carmel Vassallo (eds.), *New Directions in Mediterranean Maritime History* (St. John's, 2004, with Michela D'Angelo), 55-82.

CONTRIBUTORS

MARC BADIA-MIRÓ <mbmiro@tinet.org> is a Lecturer in the Department of Economics and Business at the Universitat Oberta de Catalunya. He is completing a PhD thesis which examines the long-term concentration of economic activity in Chile.

HUBERT BONIN <h.bonin@sciencespobordeaux.fr> is Professor of Modern Economic History at the University of Bordeaux 4. He is a specialist on the history of service companies and French banking history. His recent publications include *Contrebande, fraude et contrefaçon, de l'Antiquité à nos jours* (Genève, 2007, edited with with Gérard Béaur and Claire Lemercier); *Histoire de la Société générale. Vol. I: 1864-1890. Naissance d'une banque* (Genève, 2006); and "The Compagnie du Canal de Suez and Transit Shipping, 1900-1956," *International Journal of Maritime History*, XVII, No. 2 (2005), 87-112.

EDOUARD GUIONNET <edouardguionnet@wanadoo.fr> has taught at the University of Avignon and Rheims Polytechnic and is now at the University of Paris XIII. His research focuses on the cotton trade of Lancashire as well as its major merchants. He is also interested in the cotton lobby's influence on imperial policy at the end of the nineteenth century.

HULYA GUNAYDIN<ghulya@bilkent.edu.tr> lectures in Political Science at Bilkent University in Turkey. An expert on privatisation, she has advised the Turkish government on this issue. Her lengthy list of awards includes grants from the Fulbright Foundation, Deutsches Akademishes Austauchdienst and the Kokkalis Foundation.

STÉPHANE HOSTE <Stephane.Hoste@UGent.be> is a doctoral student at the University of Ghent where he is preparing a PhD thesis on "The European 'Bunge Group:' Aspects on the Primacy of Port-related Entrepreneurship, 1870-1970." He has published on the nineteenth- and twentieth-century maritime and the business history of the port cities of Amsterdam, Antwerp and Rotterdam.

CHIH-LING LIN <al393939@dragon.nchu.edu.tw> is Assistant Professor of History at the National Chung Hsing University in Taiwan. He is currently conducting research on the liner service from Taiwan to Australia after the 1960s.

REGINALD LOYEN <reginald.loyen@mow.vlaanderen.be> received his doctorate in economic history from the University of Leuven in 2003 for a dissertation on functional shifts in the port of Antwerp in the twentieth century. He has published widely on the economic history of the ports of Antwerp and Rotterdam in the nineteenth and twentieth centuries. His research interests include port competition, port performance indicators and port governance.

BRUNO MARNOT <bmarnot@u-bordeau3.fr> is Assistant Professor at the University of Bordeaux. He is currently writing a book on the modernisation of the major French ports in the nineteenth century. His recent publications include *Les migrations internationales en Europe et aux États-Unis des années 1840 à 1940* (Neufchâtel, 2006); and *Guerre et économie dans l'espace atlantique du XVIe au XXe siècles* (Bordeaux, 2006, edited with Silvia Marzagalli).

JERONIMO G.R. MONTEIRO <jgrm@ewdiffmail.com> is Lecturer in Economics at Goa University and a research scholar at the University of Mumbai. He has presented many papers at both local and international seminars.

AMÉLIA POLÓNIA <Amelia.polonia@netc.pt> is Associate Professor in the Faculty of Arts at the University of Porto, where she is a researcher in the Institute of Early Modern History; a member of the editorial board of the *Revista da Faculdade de Letras – História*; and a member of the governing board of the Masters degree in Local and Regional Studies. She is also a member of the editorial board of the *International Journal of Maritime History*. A specialist in the social and economic history of early modern Portugal, she has a special interest in seaports. Her publications include "Dinâmicas comerciais e interacções sociais: os portos de Lisboa e Porto nos séculos XVII e XVII," in *La ciudad portuária atlântica en la Historia. Siglos XVI-XIX* (Santander, 2006); "De Portugal a espaços ultramarinos. Inclusão e exclusão de agentes femininas no processo de expansão ultramarina (Século XVI)," in Dora Davila Mendonza (ed.), *Historia, Género y Familia en Iberoamérica,. Siglos XVI-XX* (Caracas, 2004); and *A expansão Portuguesa numa perspectiva local O Porto de Vila do Conde no século XVI* (Lisbon, 2007).

KARI TERÄS <kteras@utu.fi> is Senior Lecturer in the Department of Finnish History at the University of Turku. He has published several books and articles in the fields of business, labour and maritime history.

MALCOLM TULL <m.tull@murdoch.edu.au> is an Associate Professor of Economics in the Business School at Murdoch University. An editor of the *International Journal of Maritime History*, he has published widely in the field of maritime studies. Malcolm is a Senior Editor of Oxford University Press' four-volume *Encyclopedia of Maritime History* (New York, 2007), a Principal Investigator for the History of Marine Animal Populations (HMAP) activities in Asia and a past President of the Australian Association for Maritime History.

STEPHAN VANFRAECHEM <stephan.vanfraechem@alfaportantwerpen.be> wrote a PhD thesis at the University of Ghent (2002) on labour relations in the port of Antwerp, 1880-1972. His post-doctoral research focused on the impact of labour-conditions and wages on inter-port competition in the Hamburg-Le Havre range. He is currently working as a senior policy advisor for Alfaport Antwerp, the federation of port companies and logistic service providers in the port of Antwerp.

Introduction

Tapio Bergholm, Lewis R. Fischer and M. Elisabetta Tonizzi

Maritime history in general is an international or, even better, a "global" enterprise, as ships, cargoes and seamen travel continuously around the world. Ports are focal nodes of this competitive, global activity: at the same time, they are tightly connected to local political, social, industrial and transport networks. Port history therefore sits, uncomfortably at times, at the crossroad of international, national and even local historiography.

On a warm, sunny day in June 2004 several port historians met on the island of Corfu, the site of the Fourth International Congress of Maritime History, sponsored by the International Maritime Economic History Association (IMEHA). During this congress a number of papers were presented on various aspects of port history that raised questions and methodological issues which begged for further elaboration and collegial discussion. This was when the idea of organising a special conference on port history arose. As we discussed this notion further, a number of researchers from around the world expressed an interest in participating. Doing something which involved the Fourteenth International Congress of Economic History, scheduled for Helsinki in August 2006, increasingly seemed to make sense. As a result, the editors of this volume submitted a proposal to the International Economic History Association for a special port history session that would have both global and local components. The aim was to address the complex interplay between global market forces, technological innovations and national transport systems, on the one hand, and local social and economic relations on the other.

When our proposal was accepted, and we issued a call for papers, it quickly became apparent that interest outstripped the number of papers which could be accommodated during the main conference. As a result, we decided to organise a dual conference, combining a session in Helsinki with a three-day workshop in Kotka, an important port town located about two hours away. The Kotka portion of this conference quickly received the support of the IMEHA. The combined conference, entitled "Making Global and Local Connections: Historical Perspectives on Port Economics," was held in Kotka, 18-20 August 2006, and, within the framework of the Fourteenth International Congress of Economic History, in Helsinki on 21 August. During these four days a total of twenty-one papers, exploring a vast range of topics and spanning four continents (even though Europe was over-represented) were presented and discussed. Ideas, debates and arguments during those days provided a unique opportunity to delve deeply into the very heart of "global" port history. The editors wish to extend their gratitude to the Palmenia Centre for Continuing Education and the City of Kotka, as well as the organizers of the larger congress in Helsinki, for providing an international panel of experts with excellent working accommodations and wonderful hospitality, a further demonstration of the importance of combining global concerns with local interests.

This volume contains revised and edited versions of ten of the papers presented at the two meetings. Although we would have liked to publish more of them, space limitations forced us to make some difficult choices. While we extend our gratitude to all the participants, in order to achieve a certain degree of coherence we have selected the essays that follow and have structured them into two sections.

The first part features six case studies on European, Asian and Australian port history. All the essays focus on the nineteenth and twentieth centuries, sometimes even extending the analysis into the early years of the new millennium. This relatively short time span, during which the first (1840-1914) and second (from the mid-1970s) waves of globalisation occurred, was a period of rapid and sometimes disturbing economic transformation which had explosive effects on two key facilitators of the process: ports and shipping. If the interaction, in both historical and contemporary terms, between ports and globalisation is clear, it is equally apparent that global processes impact differently at the local level. In other words, "global pressure" and "local action" are inextricably linked. Therefore, the specialisations and unique qualities retained by each port have led the editors to place papers concerned with local issues in the first section of the book.

In the opening essay Bruno Marnot and Hubert Bonin question some important facets of the well-established historiography on the port of Bordeaux. According to the traditional view, the port's "golden age" was followed in the nineteenth and twentieth centuries by a period of decline within a new and unfavourable international commercial environment. After considering a multitude of factors – investments in maritime and transport facilities; quantitative and qualitative trends; shifts in international trade; connections between trade and business cycles; and ambitions by Bordeaux merchants to maintain an international role for their port – Marnot and Bonin argue for the need to replace the notion of "decline" with that of adaptability to changes in the world and regional economies.

The rise of Manchester to become Great Britain's fourth largest port by 1913 was due almost entirely to the opening of the Manchester Ship Canal in 1894. Lancashire cotton merchants, threatened by heightened international competition and discontent with the poor performance and what they viewed as the onerous charges imposed by the port of Liverpool, played a crucial role in lobbying for the canal. Edouard Guionnet assesses the impact of this waterway on the cotton trade through the 1920s. Adopting a unique perspective from which to approach the role of the cotton lobby, the author devotes the bulk of his essay to an analysis of the rhetoric and promotional discourse used by key figures to promote the idea of the canal and the port. He shows convincingly that the arguments revolved around a demagogic and populist comparison of the liberal and competitive attitude of Manchester with the monopolistic practices of Liverpool.

Jeronimo G.R. Monteiro provides an overview of the history of the port of Mormugao, the "golden gateway" to Goa, a centuries-old port city and, since 1961, a tiny but flourishing state within the union of India. In his useful essay, which stretches chronologically from the sixteenth century to the present, the author focuses on some of the variables which have contributed to the port's development: a strategic location in the network of international maritime trade routes; a hinterland rich in mineral resources and commercial products; an active and helpful local government, particularly after the establishment of the Port Trust in 1963; and structural upgrades of infrastructure that were well timed to correlate with the increase in throughput. The locally-determined aspects are singled out as determining factors in the success of the port.

Port competition results from the interaction of many economic, political, cultural, financial and technological factors. Stéphane Hoste, Reginald Loyen and Stephan Vanfraechem shed new light on competition between Antwerp and Rotterdam during the third quarter of the twentieth century. In the thirty years after the end of World War II, Rotterdam expanded much more rapidly than Antwerp: by 1973, the former handled four times the latter's seaborne throughput, even though Antwerp ranked first in terms of value-added. The authors apply to the analysis of both ports the well-known and widely-used "Porter's diamond" model of competition, a holistic approach to understanding the competitiveness of national industries. Five parameters are discussed: seaborne cargo flows; composition of throughput; port labour; ship-handling costs; and, last but not least, maritime access, which in the authors' opinion was the most important factor in Rotterdam's leadership. Hoste, Loyen and Vanfraechem conclude by stressing the importance of theory while also underlining some weak points in the model, especially its tendency to ignore key factors, such as tradition, personal contacts and individual perceptions.

Ports and their related activities are voracious consumers of land and sources of serious environmental problems. While these problems are generated globally, their impacts are often felt most acutely on the local level. Rising environmental costs can generate conflicts with local communities and ultimately can lead to the "de-maritimisation" of port cities. Unfortunately, their impact on the environment has received almost no attention from environmental and maritime historians, who might have been expected to examine the issue. Malcolm Tull takes the port of Fremantle as a case study and uses it as a first step in measuring the long-run environmental impact of Australian ports. Starting from the 1850s, when there was no clear evidence of port-related environmental degradation, and going up to the 2000s, when the Fremantle Port Authority adopted sound environmental management strategies, the author focuses on the varied and constantly changing sources of environmental pressure. Given the proximity of ports and densely populated cities, the temporal interval used by Tull probably does not fit Europe. In Genoa, for instance, the pollution of port sea water was a great danger to public health and has been a deep concern for port managers since the early nineteenth century. As a result, by the 1880s measures were adopted to improve the quality of water in the port. Nonetheless, in a useful conclusion Tull challenges the stereotype of ports as enemies of the environment and suggests that they be considered "check points" rather than "hot spots." In this way, he suggests a realistic approach to restoring harmony between ports and local interests.

The first part on the volume closes with Chih-lung Lin's concise examination of the "policy for survival" adopted between 1949 and 1957 by the Port Authority of Kaohsiung, Taiwan's biggest port. Since 1949, after a long period of material destruction and socio-political instability, Taiwan was separated from China, its most important mainland market. The import-substitution policy adopted by the authoritarian Kuomintang government, involving a host of rules and regulations and heavy tariffs on imports, had detrimental economic effects. Aid from the United States after the outbreak of the Korean War rescued both the Kaohsiung Port Authority and Taiwan as a whole.

The second part of the book features four papers which discuss the change and development of port systems from national perspectives. The interplay of international and global forces, as well as local geographic and political peculiarities, is taken into taken into account by all the authors.

Maritime expansion and trade have been essential components of the histories of Great Powers. Naval strength and overseas colonies made Portugal, England and The Netherlands significant nations in the early modern period. Amélia Polónia use theoretical ideas from the "Histoportos" project in her essay on the evolving seaport system in Northwest Portugal during the sixteenth, seventeenth and eighteenth centuries. She discusses how Porto and smaller ports in the region were connected to each other and to the dominant national port, Lisbon. Polónia describes the interplay of international, national and local forces in determining the success and failure of the ports and shows how clearly the fortunes of the satellite ports were connected to economic conditions in the major centres. The development of smaller ports was also related to other factors. During the expansion of Portuguese overseas trade, new opportunities opened for smaller ports. When the redevelopment of port infrastructure became essential, political decisions concerning state funding became crucial. When inappropriate choices were made, the success of the sixteenth and seventeenth centuries was transformed into decline in the eighteenth.

The second paper is especially timely because 2006 was the fiftieth anniversary of the introduction of container traffic. Although Finland was not in the vanguard of the container revolution, Kari Teräs shows how technological innovations were debated quite early in Finldand by official committees and port and transport professionals. He also demonstrates how in the 1960s and 1970s Finland underwent an "unitisation revolution" without containers, as wrapped timber, special systems for paper exports and ro-ro traffic were introduced. Even though the formal introduction of containerisation was delayed on the northern shores of the Baltic, Teräs concludes that a consensus over a national containerisation strategy was created through discussion. The goal was to reach transport parity with other industrial countries. The Finnish debate over the need to adopt the new technology helped to achieve this aim.

The next essay also examines a regional port system over a considerable period of time. Due to the geographic peculiarities of Chile, maritime transport - and hence ports - were essential for Chilean economic development. Marc Badia-Miró looks more closely at the thirty-four ports of northern Chile, where first nitrate and later copper exports were particularly important. He analyses the interplay between the main economic activities and changes in port traffic, with a special emphasis on the importance of the shift from labour-intensive nitrate exports to capital-intensive copper mining. These shifts in industrial structure and port traffic contributed to both the development of port networks and a significant demographic transition.

Maritime transport and ports are essential for trade and industry. This was also the case in Turkey. Globalisation, economic liberalisation and pressures to adapt to frameworks specified by the European Union were major factors in Hülya Günaydin's analysis of the introduction of privatisation, commercialisation and competition to the ports of Turkey. She shows that the conversion from a "public goods" approach to privatisation in the ports was complicated, creating new regulatory responsibilities for state authorities. Günaydin uses Alfred Baird's port privatisation model to shed light on the privatisation process. Her analysis shows that up to 2006 privatisation has been limited; to the extent that it has occurred, this has mainly been due to the need for extensive investment in infrastructure.

All the contributors to this book, while naturally adopting individual approaches, have delivered useful descriptions and insightful analyses on the historical development of ports and port systems in many parts of the world, framing their investigations within an international and global perspective. They have also tested the explanatory effectiveness of models, gauged the role of local port governance and human cultures, questioned accepted wisdom and added new themes to the research agenda of port historians. Despite the array of international case studies presented, which reflect fairly accurately the state of the field, there is a clear European bias, and comparison is almost totally lacking. Nevertheless, the importance of local factors to a better understanding of the extremely complex global situation is confirmed. It is also clear that the relation between global and local conditions is symbiotic, and that ports are ideal locations from which to monitor the historical evolution of these processes.

We hope that this collection of essays will be regarded as a first step upon which port historians can build. For those interested in global phenomena, it may be a second step, coming as it does a decade after David J. Starkey and Gelina Harlaftis' edited collection, *Global Markets: The Internationalization of the Sea Transport Industries since 1850* (St. John's, 1998). We hope it will encourage historians to conduct further research and provide even more useful insights on these important, and still little understood, issues.

The International Scope of Bordeaux Port: Logistics, Economic Effects and Business Cycles in the Nineteenth and Twentieth Centuries

Bruno Marnot and Hubert Bonin

By contrast with the brilliant eighteenth century, the prevailing view in the literature is that Bordeaux in the nineteenth and twentieth centuries was a declining port. Nonetheless, most of the city's merchants never abandoned hopes of maintaining an international scope for their port, despite a new economic environment which appeared unfavourable to their interests. That is why it is useful to survey the international involvement of the port and its capacity to adapt to major maritime revolutions over two centuries. In this study we will focus on some aspects of the evolution of the harbour, such as the structure and features of Bordeaux's trade; the pattern of investments and their influence on the growth of trade; the logistic development of the port and connections with the hinterland; the relationship between foreign trade and industrial or business cycles; and links with France's constricting colonial empire. We also intend to place the port within an international and national framework of production, transport and logistics and examine how this affected Bordeaux's competitive position. After the Napoleonic wars, the nineteenth century was marked by a lengthy effort to re-establish trade links using traditional expertise and local comparative advantages. Despite an increasingly peripheral location in the twentieth century, the port tried to maintain its role as an international entrepôt, especially in passenger traffic, and strengthened its colonial ties until the 1960s. In the last three decades of the century the port had to adjust to radically different national and international commercial climates.

International Links and Nineteenth-Century Port Modernisation

After two decades of war the trade of the port of Bordeaux, as elsewhere in Europe, was stagnant in 1815. Its activities during the Continental Blockade (1806-1814) were maintained only by neutral US vessels and the "regime of licences."[1] The city's merchants were no longer in touch directly with overseas

[1]Paul Butel, "Guerre et commerce: l'activité du port de Bordeaux sous le régime des licences, 1808-1815," *Revue d'histoire moderne et contemporaine*, XIX (1972), 128-149; and Silvia Marzagalli, "Guerre et création d'un réseau commercial

markets. After these dark years, they had to face two challenges: to revive the former trading ties that had generated so much prosperity in the eighteenth century and to adapt to a new maritime environment dominated by British shipping. Since the merchants knew that it was impossible to restore all of Bordeaux's trading patterns, finding new markets was crucial if it was to remain among the main ports of France and Europe.

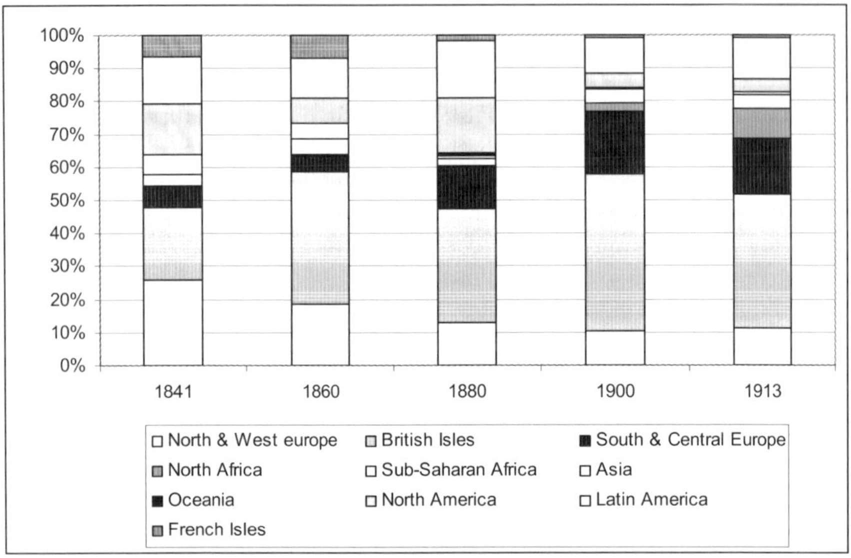

Figure 1: Bordeaux's Foreland, 1841-1913

Source: *Tableau général du commerce de la France avec l'étranger et ses colonies* (Paris, various years).

Statistical data for a seven-decade period show three main changes in the structure of Bordeaux's trade (see figure 1).[2] First, trade with Britain in-

entre Bordeaux et les Etats-Unis, 1776-1815. L'impossible économie du politique," in Marzagalli and Bruno Marnot (eds.), *Guerre et économie dans l'espace atlantique du XVIe au XXe siècles* (Bordeaux, 2006), 375-393.

[2]There are no data available before 1841 in the *Tableau général du commerce de la France*. The three years 1860, 1880 and 1900 were arbitrarily chosen to assess changes in Bordeaux's overseas trading partners in the long run. These are in fact aggregate data resulting from the addition of every country which had commercial links with Bordeaux. The same arduous analysis was performed for the other fifteen major French ports. "North and West Europe" includes Russia; "Latin America" includes South and Central America and non-French isles in the Caribbean.

creased substantially, a fact which confirms the nodal role played by the UK in European seaborne trade. At the same time, there was a more-or-less continual decline in commerce with northern and western Europe. Second, although almost a third of its trade in 1880 was with the Americas, this proportion was reduced sharply by 1913. This was largely due to a sharp fall in Bordeaux's trade with North America, since trade flows with Latin America were fairly constant. Finally, from the 1850s onwards, and especially after the 1880s, it became obvious that Bordeaux could not maintain a substantial flow of traffic with ports in the North Atlantic. This was potentially damaging, since this was by far the most rapidly growing trade zone in the period. The decline in North Atlantic trade was also symptomatic of Bordeaux's increasingly peripheral geographic location. In view of this, the merchants of Bordeaux had to seek new overseas markets to avoid the cut-throat competition in the North Atlantic.

To understand the traditional propensity of the Bordeaux merchants we can examine trade with the "sugar islands," especially Martinique and Guadeloupe. This commerce accounted for 6.75 percent of the volume of total trade in 1860, but owing to the nature of the goods its value was considerably more important. In fact, the importance of this trade decreased constantly thereafter, at least in part because of the rising shares accounted for by other regions. The close commercial links between Bordeaux and the Caribbean were significant only in the first two-thirds of the nineteenth century. Indeed, an examination of the port's trading partners shows both the rise of southern and eastern Europe and closer relations with Latin America and Africa (13.6 percent of total trade in 1913 was with northern and sub-Saharan Africa). Conversely, the role of Asia and Oceania constantly decreased.

The international trade of the port was finally reorganised along three different lines. First, Bordeaux was traditionally known as a "colonial port" in the nineteenth century.[3] A strong eighteenth-century colonial network was strengthened during the nineteenth century, and the port's business cycle was based not only on Caribbean commerce but even more on trade with Indochina and the French colonies in North and West Africa. New Caledonia was also exploited to a lesser extent. From the 1880s, trade with Africa became more substantial than with East Asia in part due to competition from Marseilles. One of the characteristics of this colonial network was its family structure; family-owned businesses extracted raw materials, carried them to Bordeaux and dispatched them elsewhere. Value was sometimes added to the raw materials in a family plant built near the port.[4] Another feature of these networks was the

---

[3]See John D. Casey, *Bordeaux: Colonial Port of Nineteenth Century* (New York, 1981).

[4]See, for example, the work devoted to the Denis' story in Delphine Boissarie, "La maison bordelaise Denis Frères et l'Extrême-Orient, 1862-1954" (Unpublished MA thesis, University of Bordeaux-3, 2005).

sharing of colonial areas among families, such as Maurel and Prom in Senegal (peanuts), the Denis brothers in Indochina (rice) and Tandonnet and Ballande in New Caledonia (nickel).

Second, contrary to what John Casey has argued, the merchants of Bordeaux never stopped searching for spatial diversification.[5] As the commercial structure of foreign trade shows, the port maintained constant contact with Britain, northwest and Baltic Europe and North America. These trades depended on either short-sea or deep-sea shipping, but tramp rather than liner shipping always predominated. As early as 1827, however, British liner companies called at the port. In spite of requests from the merchants, the port failed to obtain a subsidised line to the US, even though the export of wine was as important in value as in volume.[6]

A third direction for Bordeaux's trade was South America. Trade with South America can usefully be conceptualised as comprising two periods. Until the mid-1850s, it was developed by traditional family concerns which established trading posts there, nurturing a sufficient flow of goods to justify the creation of a subsidised line in 1857. Thereafter, services to Brazil and Rio de la Plata were reinforced by the activities of the Compagnie générale transatlantique. As in other major ports of northwest Europe, Bordeaux shipping companies carried mail, goods and emigrants, and Bordeaux became the main French port of embarkation for immigration to South America.[7]

Bordeaux obviously had to improve its infrastructure if it wished to remain an international port. Indeed, continual modernisation became the rule for large ports in the nineteenth century. The modernisation of Bordeaux harbour was tied to its transatlantic ambitions and its increasingly problematic site on the River Garonne. The latter explains why local merchants and shipowners worried constantly about improving the accessibility of the port and handling the ever-larger ships of the nineteenth century. Investment for the modernisation of the port between 1814 and 1910 totalled sixty-three million *francs*.[8]

---

[5]Casey, *Bordeaux*, 55.

[6]Stéphane Herrero, "Le développement des relations maritimes entre Bordeaux et les Etats-Unis de 1815 à 1914" (Unpublished MA thesis, University of Bordeaux-3, 2005); and Gabrielle Cadier, "L'exportation des vins de France sous le Second Empire," *Bulletin du Centre d'histoire économique et sociale de la région lyonnaise*, No. 4 (1972), 10-21.

[7]Marthe Barbance, *Histoire de la Compagnie générale transatlantique. Un siècle d'exploitation maritime* (Paris, 1955); and Philippe Roudié, "Bordeaux, port d'émigration lointaine, 1865-1918," *Revue historique de Bordeaux*, XXX (1983-1984), 157-188.

[8]France, Ministère des Travaux publics, *Actes législatifs et dépenses concernant les travaux de navigation intérieure et maritime de 1814 à 1900* (Paris, 1902); and

Table 1 indicates the expenditures on Bordeaux's port facilities in each of the seven investment cycles.

Table 1
Investment in Facilities in the Port of Bordeaux (*francs*)

	1814-1830	**1831-1847**	**1848-1851**	**1852-1870**	**1871-1878**	**1879-1900**	**1901-1910**
Amount	0	1,476,019	1,230,100	10,070,575	10,938,059	16,939,115	10,043,632

Source: France, Ministère des Travaux publics, *Actes législatifs et dépenses concernant les travaux de navigation intérieure et maritime (1814-1910)* (Paris, 1912).

The interpretation of these data is difficult because of the unequal length of the cycles and because expenditures soared after 1852, a trend that was not unique to Bordeaux. The need for modernisation increased dramatically in every major European and North American port from the mid-nineteenth century due to the boom in maritime trade and the rapid structural changes in shipping. In terms of quality, there were two phases in the modernisation of Bordeaux's facilities. The first priority was to increase capacity by extending the quays and building a wet dock. Later in the nineteenth century this shifted to the improvement of navigation on the Gironde and Garonne; in the last twenty years of the century dredging proceeded under a law passed in 1880, and the Gironde's channel was deepened under a law enacted in 1910. Given the increasing problems of access for transatlantic steam liners, port authorities (in Bordeaux this was the Chamber of Commerce) decided to develop an "outer harbour" downstream at Pauillac.[9] But the equipment in this harbour was reduced to a single wharf on the eve of World War I.

Finally, we may compare the effects of these investments with the evolution of the port's foreign trade. We prefer *foreign* to *total* trade not only because the latter includes coastal shipping but also because from the nineteenth century onward the main changes in all large ports were determined by foreign trade. Investment also includes public funds for new works, but fortunately these are distinguished in French public accounting. Figure 2 shows two almost parallel curves during the first four cycles.[10] But this similar evolution

Actes législatifs et dépenses concernant les travaux de navigation intérieure et maritime de 1901 à 1910 (Paris, 1912). These are major sources for nineteenth-century port investments in France.

[9]Nathalie Cler, "Le port et la ville de Pauillac, 1880-1939" (Unpublished MA thesis, University of Bordeaux-3, 1992), 33-38.

[10]Since there are no data available for foreign trade before 1831 in the *Tableau general*, figure 2 omits the first trade cycle depicted in table 1.

disappeared during cycle 5 (1879-1900); this corresponds with the "*plan Freycinet*," usually considered the most important public effort to modernise French ports in the century. In the case of Bordeaux, the annual average investment paradoxically was weaker than in previous cycles, whereas the annual growth of foreign trade rose. Was the growth of foreign trade unrelated to investments between 1879 and 1900? On the other hand, was there was a link between the two variables before 1879? The answers are not obvious because the data do not allow the calculation of meaningful correlation coefficients.[11]

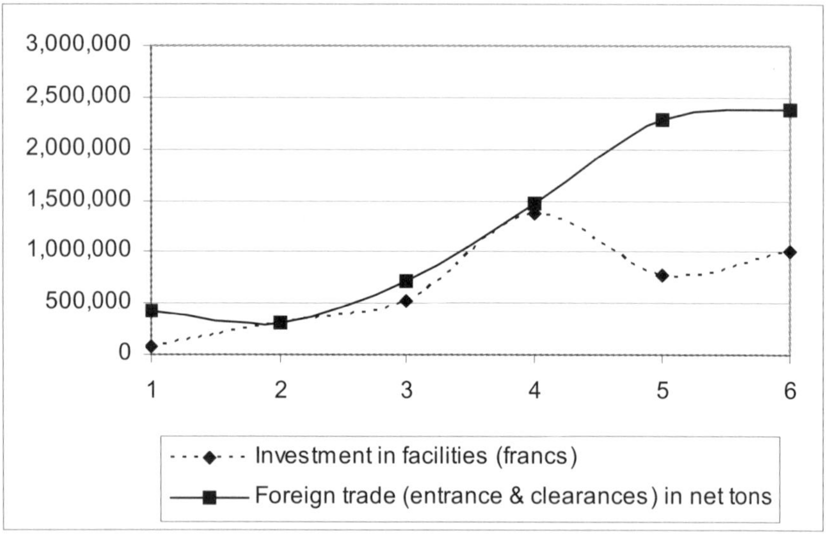

Figure 2: Annual Average of Investment and Foreign Trade in Bordeaux during Six Cycles

Source: See figure 1.

In addition, over time an efficient sea-land interface became an important criterion for port performance. Was Bordeaux's port well-connected to its hinterland? Was it able to extend this hinterland toward the "competition margins," as "functionalist theory" would predict? We know that these "competition margins" increasingly determined a port's competitiveness, which can be defined as its capacity to attract and forward goods and passengers over long distances. Ever since François Crouzet's seminal article, many historians have

[11] *Actes législatifs et dépenses* provide figures for the investment by cycles rather than by year. If it is impossible to calculate relevant correlation coefficients, it is also impossible to see whether investment in facilities was the only variable which determined the growth of foreign trade and, if so, the length of the time lag.

debated the "remoteness" of Bordeaux from the rest of France.[12] Regardless, the efficiency of its interconnections can be assessed on two different scales. On a regional scale, the port was well connected to its primary hinterland thanks to a good network of rivers, notably the Garonne and the Dordogne. These natural connections were improved by the Bordeaux-Toulouse-Sète rail line, partly opened in 1855, which belonged to the Compagnie du Midi.

But the real challenge for the port was its integration into the national market. On this score, the port could potentially expand its reach into three areas: central France and beyond toward Lyon and Switzerland; the Mediterranean; and the Paris region. Among the three, the latter was preferred by local merchants because the capital was obviously the biggest market in France. In 1837 a local businessman, Alexandre Corréard, launched the first, if unsuccessful, project to build a rail line between Bordeaux and Paris via Angoulême, Poitiers, Tours, Chartres and Versailles. The Bordeaux merchants quickly grasped the advantages of this new means of transport, not least because it promised to overcome the problem that the two main rivers flowed in the "wrong" direction. In view of both declining coastal shipping and poor road transport, the creation of a rail line seemed the only solution. In this respect, however, Bordeaux was at a disadvantage compared with French Atlantic ports such as Le Havre, Rouen or even Nantes, all of which were nearer Paris. In 1842 the government decided to construct a "star network" around Paris to enable each main French main port to be served by a railway line. The first were built to link the Channel harbours to Paris. The remote location of Bordeaux partly explains its late connection with the capital compared with railway lines to Rouen (1843), Le Havre (1847) and Dunkerque (1848).

Bordeaux businessmen looked forward to obtaining a link with Paris, but they had to wait until 1855.[13] The delay caused great damage to the port because it allowed competitors to secure important market niches. Bordeaux, for example, was unable to dispatch the "articles of Paris" to England and America or to supply the capital with bulk goods, especially coal. Such traffic remained the prerogative of Channel harbours like Le Havre, Rouen and Dunkerque. But even when the line to Bordeaux was completed, railway tariffs worked against the port. The Chamber of Commerce complained constantly

---

[12]François Crouzet, "Les origines du sous-développement économique du Sud-Ouest," *Annales du Midi*, No. 45 (January 1959), 71-79; André Armangaud, "A propos des origines du sous-développement industriel du Sud-Ouest," *Annales du Midi*, No. 49 (January 1960), 75-81; and André Charles, "L'isolement de Bordeaux et l'insuffisance des voies de communication en Gironde au début du Second Empire," *Annales du Midi*, No. 49 (January 1960), 59-73.

[13]On this debate, see Florian Druon, "La contribution de la Compagnie du chemin de fer du Paris-Orléans au développement industriel de l'agglomération bordelaise" (Unpublished MA thesis, University of Bordeaux-3, 2000), 28-31.

about what it considered "unfair practices" by the railway. Many goods produced in Bordeaux's hinterland were diverted because of arrangements between the Compagnie du Paris-Orléans, which had a connection with the town, and other rail operators. For example, this company agreed with the Compagnie du Nord to ship Mazamet's wool to Dieppe, Rouen and Dunkerque, despite the much longer distances.[14] As a result, while Bordeaux remained an important regional hub, sufficiently equipped with transport facilities, the port suffered because of its peripheral location; the main flows of goods and passengers were increasingly concentrated on the North Atlantic and along the Milan-London axis.[15] That is why Bordeaux, like Nantes or La Rochelle, exemplified a peripheral model of growth in the nineteenth century based upon its traditional primary hinterland, on the one hand, and foreign trade with Africa, South America and central and southern Europe, on the other.

Foreign Trade and Industrialisation

The quality and density of transport facilities were not the only reasons for the underdevelopment of southwest France in the nineteenth century. The delay in industrialisation must also be taken into account. Yet the slow pace of industrialisation in Aquitaine does not necessarily imply retardation for the port. The core of the problem is to know whether the port's trading activity could spark industrialisation. At the end of the French wars, Bordeaux had a set of industrial facilities processing foodstuffs, even if its refineries and distilleries suffered from a "real weakening of the re-exportation trade towards Northern Europe."[16] Moreover, a group of industries grew during the nineteenth century as business recovered; these included sugar refineries, flour mills, tobacco factories (reorganised since 1811), liquor distilleries, oil mills (based mainly on the import of peanuts), chocolate factories and canning facilities. Last but not least, a biscuit industry developed in the last third of the century based on modern technologies, and for a period Bordeaux became the main centre of biscuit production. We can also add the concentration in Bordeaux in the sec-

[14]The role of private railway companies was probably a major factor in the competition between seaports. It would be interesting to assess their real effects on the growth of each port, but such studies are lacking for France, particularly for Bordeaux.

[15]For further details, see Bruno Marnot, "Bordeaux au XIXe siècle: un port isolé des axes de circulation?" *Revue d'Histoire de Bordeaux et de la Gironde*, Nos. 7-8 (2005), 79-89.

[16]Jean-Pierre Poussou, "Le Sud-Ouest de la France est-il au XIXe siècle une région sous-industrialisée et sous-développée?" in *L'économie française du XVIIIe au XXe siècles. Mélanges offerts à François Crouzet* (Paris, 2003), 649.

ond half of the nineteenth century of the cod fishery, an industry which became "the single supplier in southern France and the colonial Empire."[17]

Besides the food industries, which drew their raw materials from the hinterland and the colonies, the civilian shipyard was the second pillar of Bordeaux's industrial economy. Its main prosperity and technological peak were reached between 1850 and 1865 when builders like Arman, Chaigneau and Bichon built sailing ships and excellent clippers used mainly in the South Atlantic. The shipyard sector spurred the development of thirteen foundries and forges in the town.[18] In addition, Bordeaux was an important railway node in the late nineteenth century thanks to the presence of two big companies whose needs for coal generated a substantial flow of imports. As result, a coal port was established, and coal imports continued to rise into the 1920s.[19]

In spite of these activities, which were dominated by small- or medium-size firms, Bordeaux was not a true industrial city. The industries that did exist, however, were adapted to the economic strengths of the port, which even nurtured "high-tech" industries like shipbuilding. Indeed, except for Marseilles, the industrial culture of Bordeaux was as important as in the other major French ports.[20] As with most of its competitors, the port enjoyed a surge of industrialisation from the 1880s onwards, with funds provided mainly by outside capitalists. The new age was characterised by the establishment of modern iron and mechanical industries (railway workshops and motorcar firms), chemical plants and shipyards downstream from the port. Florian Druon has shown the major role of the Compagnie du Paris-Orléans in this process of developing the so-called "north bank."[21]

---

[17]Jean Dumas, *Les activités industrielles dans la communauté urbaine de Bordeaux. Etude de géographie économique et socio-politique* (Bordeaux, 1980), 357.

[18]*Ibid.*, 240.

[19]According to the figures given by Pierre Guillaume, "Bordeaux, port charbonnier," *L'archéologie industrielle en France*, No. 15 (1987), 68, the maximum importation was in 1928 with 1,831,000 tons.

[20]For further comparisons, see Jacques Fiérain, *Les raffineries de sucre des ports de France, XIXe-début XXe siècles* (Paris, 1975); Jean-Louis Maillard, "La Révolution industrielle au Havre, 1860-1914" (Unpublished PhD thesis, University of Rouen, 1978); Emile Thelliez, "Les industries de l'agglomération dunkerquoise," *Revue du Nord*, No. 155 (July-September 1957), 13-49; Christian Borde, *Calais et la mer, 1814-1914* (Villeneuve d'Ascq, 1997); Georges Oustric, *Le port de Boulogne-sur-Mer au XIXe siècle* (Boulogne, 1995); Marthe Barbance, *Saint-Nazaire. Le port, la ville, le travail* (Marseille, 1979); and Olivier Pétré-Grenouilleau, *L'argent de la traite. Milieu négrier, capitalisme et développement: un modèle* (Paris, 1996).

[21]Druon, "La contribution," 84-107.

Table 2

Annual Average Growth Rate of Foreign Trade per Five-year Period (net tons)

Five-year Periods	1835/ 1830 *	1840/ 1835 **	1845/ 1840 ***	1850/ 1845	1855/ 1850	1860/ 1855	1865/ 1860	1870/ 1865	1875/ 1870	1880/ 1875	1885/ 1880	1890/ 1885	1895/ 1890	1900/ 1895	1905/ 1900	1910/ 1905
Bordeaux	+0.80	-10.78	-0.06	+2.66	+8.51	+6.63	+4.84	+6.41	+4.38	+9.37	+1.56	+0.76	-6.02	+4.21	-1.94	+8.38
Average Rate of Annual Growth of Major French Seaports	+4.37	-11.03	+4.53	-0.03	+10.38	+3.24	+3.71	+6.09	+4.51	+8.43	+1.12	+2.50	-0.95	+7.23	+2.89	+6.17

Notes : *Includes Bordeaux, Dunkerque, Le Havre, Marseille, Nantes, Rouen, Bayonne, Boulogne, Brest, Cherbourg and La Rochelle La Pallice. **Includes fifteen ports (the eleven previous previous ports plus Caen, Calais, Sète, Dieppe, La Rochelle). ***Includes sixteen ports (the fifteen previous ports plus Saint-Nazaire).

Source: See table 1.

Did Bordeaux's industrialisation have positive effects on the foreign trade of its port? We can measure this, at least indirectly, by comparing the annual average rate of growth of Bordeaux's foreign trade with other major French seaports. Table 2, which shows the pattern of foreign trade for five-year periods, reveals that the growth of Bordeaux's foreign trade was constantly better from 1855 to 1885 - except for 1870-1875 - than the annual average growth of the major French ports taken together. The Second Empire and early Third Republic were the most dynamic phases for Bordeaux's foreign trade. The greatest growth corresponded with the peak of the "traditional industrial cycle" (foodstuffs industries and sail shipbuilding). Conversely, the growth of Bordeaux's foreign trade was lower than the annual average growth of the sixteen ports in each period between 1885 and 1905: the most important industrialisation phase of the port (1880-1913) did not improve the poor performance of foreign trade (measured in tons). It appears that the new industrial enterprises established in the port had no positive impact on its foreign trade until at least 1905. In fact, the meaning of the last positive period (1905-1910) is not obvious. Can we conclude that the intense industrialisation of the port in the late nineteenth century began to generate positive effects on foreign trade, or was it simply a local reflection of the strong general growth that marked the prewar years? It is hard to answer to answer this conclusively.

Bordeaux Harbour in the Twentieth Century

The evolution of Bordeaux harbour relied on its integration into the national and international division of production and therefore rested on transport and logistics. Like all important ports, it had ambitions to become a key node for international exchange, either on a European or a transoceanic level. Bordeaux's memory is still of its great past, when the quays had been impressively large; this was enhanced, at least up to the 1970s, by the fact that a large part of the town lived near the port, before recent expansion in the new service and industrial zones shifted much activity to the suburbs. The history of Bordeaux harbour in the twentieth century is encapsulated in the struggle against imminent decline and a desire to retain traditional sources of employment. This required adaptation until the 1990s, when Bordeaux was finally forced to admit that its harbour was no longer a transoceanic hub.

The failures of Bordeaux's maritime sector were not due to weaknesses in entrepreneurship, because important investments to improve the port were made constantly by the state and the Chamber of Commerce; since 1925, they have been made by the Port autonome de Bordeaux, a mixed company combining state and mercantile institutions. Before World War I, the channel was dredged to accommodate larger vessels, and in the interwar years the Bassens quays and warehouses were developed on the right bank of the Garonne. Later, more modern storage facilities were built on the left bank (some of them by the Germans alongside the Dawes Plan's Repairs). In the 1950s and 1960s new cranes and cold stores were installed, and an outer harbour was inaugurated in 1976 at Le Verdon at the entrance to the Gironde to avoid dependence on tides. Finally, the facilities were adapted to containerisation (Bordeaux Fret). But these investments did not staunch the increasing competition from other ports.[22] We will examine this effort at adaptation on three levels: attempts to attract international (European and global) maritime traffic; efforts to take advantage of the expansion of the imperial economy; and the regional basis of the port's activity.

The Dream of an International Port

On the Atlantic coast, Bilbao, Nantes-Saint-Nazaire, Le Havre, Dunkerque and the Belgian and Dutch ports competed to become regional gateways for international maritime traffic. Bordeaux had a comparative advantage in controlling the hinterland of southwest France and was well positioned as a transhipment port for Atlantic trade, although Cherbourg and Le Havre were perhaps even better situated. Moreover, Bordeaux was well placed to become a transfer point for lines to South America because passengers could easily join a ship in Bordeaux by train from southern Europe or Paris (see table 3). Downstream, the Pauillac concrete wharf, with direct access to the railway, was opened in 1929 to accelerate this process, and the first Verdon terminal was conceived later to serve the same purpose, although it was destroyed by bombing in 1944. Italian emigrants regularly used Bordeaux, and middle-class passengers and businessmen bound for Chile or Argentina also were key customers.

Table 3
Passenger Traffic through Bordeaux Harbour in 1920

Total	Latin America	North America	West Africa	Morocco
57,598	17,035	6454	10,581	23,363

Note: Passengers travelling with Chargeurs réunis and Sud-Atlantique and Compagnie générale transatlantique only.

Source: Figures of the Port autonome de Bordeaux.

---

[22]Robert Chevet, *Le port de Bordeaux au* XX*e siècle* (Bordeaux, 1995); Paul Butel (ed.), *Histoire de la Chambre de commerce et d'industrie de Bordeaux* (Bordeaux, 1988); and Antoine Lebègue, "La stratégie du port de Bordeaux, projets novateurs et poids des traditions," in Hubert Bonin, Sylvie Guillaume and Bernard Lachaise (eds.), *Bordeaux et la Gironde pendant la Reconstruction (1945-1954)* (Pessac, 1997), 47-60. US troops built the first facilities at Bassens during World War I when Bordeaux was a key port for Allied forces in 1917-1919. In 1970, the harbour was equipped with 141 cranes on the quays, along with five floating cranes and a mobile aspirator for cereals.

Bordeaux harbour was in fact rarely used for international bulk traffic. Throughout the twentieth century, Le Havre-Rouen captured the majority of the commodity imports for French (and even Swiss) industries, such as cotton and North European wood, and it shared wool imports with Dunkerque. From the 1950s Le Havre and Dunkerque became the key Atlantic ports for petroleum imports for northern France, and especially Paris, and were joined by Nantes for liquid gas imports, especially once petrochemical plants were established all along the Seine valley (for Le Havre). Heavy industries prospered in Dunkerque from the 1950s, drawing coal, iron and aluminium imports. The key role of such northern ports in fostering national industries explains why they functioned as gateways for large and developed hinterlands; Bordeaux's hinterland was large but lightly industrialised.

Besides Ford cars between 1917 and 1923 – before the Bordeaux plant assembling Model-Ts was transferred to Asnières, near Paris – the only international flows were confined to wool, fish and wood. Wool was imported from Argentina to feed textile mills in the southwest which, from the 1840s until the 1960s, prospered in Castres, Mazamet and the Aude valley. Cod cargoes marked Bordeaux as a key worldwide port: its ships were active all over the North Atlantic employing thousands of fishermen and seamen (both generally coming from Brittany).[23] Dozens of fish plants, mainly in Bègles, in the suburbs of Bordeaux, transformed the catch into salt cod for shipment all over southwest Europe, where consumption was high in Spain, Portugal and Italy, as well as in southern France. The fishing fleets jammed Bordeaux harbour in the winter, giving it its "picturesque" appearance, but they also stimulated employment and production in shipbuilding, sail and motor works and maintenance facilities.[24] Fishing lasted into the 1960s before new patterns of consumption doomed the industry on the Gironde.

While cod fishing, processing and shipping helped to feed the working people of southern Europe, Bordeaux also exported huge cargoes of pine from the Landes forest to collieries in Britain, where they were used for pit props and railway sleepers. Wood exports through Bordeaux (supplemented by smaller flows through Bayonne) peaked in the 1920s (except in 1926 because of the general strike by miners in the UK) and again immediately after the Second World War. But the decline of British coal mining and the modernisation of propping techniques slashed demand in the 1960s, and wood shipments from Bordeaux disappeared soon thereafter.

---

[23]Philippe Fournet, "Redémarrage et renouveau de l'économie morutière bordelaise (1945-1955)," in Bonin, Guillaume and Lachaise (eds.), *Bordeaux et la Gironde*, 69-77.

[24]In 1931, the Bordeaux cod fishery was prosecuted by 123 vessels, among which were fifty-seven trawlers.

The best known specialty of the Gironde economy was Bordeaux wine, supplemented by a few spirits, such as anisette and rum distilled in Bordeaux with imported spices and alcohol.[25] While the main market for wine was domestic, a significant amount was exported; this continued even during US Prohibition in the 1920s when shipments went through Saint-Pierre-et-Miquelon and Canada. Most wine exports went by sea, providing a return cargo for ships carrying North European (wood, machinery, etc.), American (raw materials) or Asian specialties (silk, etc.). While wines and spirits did not provide full cargoes, their high values created an important business for forwarding agents and ship managers. The leading markets were Germany (more than a third of exports in the 1930s) and the UK, followed by the Baltic countries (although the Soviet Union disappeared from the list in the 1920s).

Table 4
Traffic through Selected French Ports and Their Competitors, 1970
(millions of tons)

France	219
Marseille	74
Le Havre	58
Dunkerque	25
Rouen	13
Nantes-Saint-Nazaire	11
Bordeaux	11
Antwep	78
Rotterdam	255

Source: See table 3.

The history of traffic through Bordeaux harbour until the 1970s is clear: its international trade was limited to only a few goods. It lacked the redistribution function of Belgian and Dutch ports or French harbours such as Dunkerque and Le Havre-Rouen; its industrial hinterland did not generate significant exports or require large volumes of imports (see table 4). Bordeaux was important mainly for cod, wool, wood, wine and alcohol. These were not large bulk cargoes, and most involved short-sea rather than deep-sea shipping.

The key question in recent times has been about the competitiveness of the port. A growing perception that something needed to be done led to the construction of an ocean cargo terminal at Le Verdon. It was opened in 1976, but outmoded rail and road links and high labour costs caused by restrictive labour laws limited its growth.[26] Although reforms were initiated, Bordeaux

---

[25]Hubert Bonin, *Marie Brizard (1755-1995)* (Bordeaux, 1995).

[26]A progressive social law in 1947 placed strict conditions on harbour activities without providing any flexibility to adapt to irregular shipping or to shorten delays

was unable to compete with alternative harbours. Even the Ford plants in Bordeaux-Blanquefort used Le Havre or Antwep to ship parts to the US.

Despite its modernisation, Bordeaux harbour was ousted from the worldwide sea lanes. It was unable to attract container lines; little international shipping called at Bordeaux once the classical bulk lines disappeared in the 1970s and 1980s. This explains why Bordeaux was reduced to being a secondary port, served once or twice a week by one or two "feeder" lines that collected cargoes for shipment through larger ports. Since 2005, special barges have used the port several times a month to carry parts for the Airbus A-380 from Pauillac to Langon before being moved by truck to the assembly plant in Toulouse. The state of the port is perhaps symbolised by its new role in the tourist industry: between twenty and forty cruise ships now call to allow wealthy passengers to tour the Gironde wineries.

From Reality to Legend: Bordeaux's Booming Imperial Functions

In the twentieth century the port of Bordeaux became a key player in the French imperial trading system, which was now extended to include Morocco.[27] This was a logical opportunity for Bordeaux entrepreneurs to grasp because several dozen large trading houses managed wholesale and retail commerce throughout sub-Saharan Africa (Maurel and Prom, Maurel Frères, Vezia, Buhan and Teisseire, etc.) and Indochina (Denis Frères). Moreover, these commercial activities were financed principally by Bordeaux banks or local branches of Paris concerns. But how much did these trading links actually stimulate traffic in the harbour? Although orders for exports were placed from Bordeaux, the vast majority of goods was sent through other French or foreign ports. And the same held true for commodity imports: while they were managed by the Bordeaux headquarters, a majority went to other ports without transiting through Bordeaux. These conditions explain why Bordeaux did not become a significant transhipment port like Liverpool or Hamburg, despite the fact that it had played such a role in the eighteenth century.

A majority of the activities of Bordeaux trading houses led to the expansion of trade in other ports. Indeed, African goods, such as cocoa, rum or

---

in the name of extensive employment rather than increased productivity and lower costs; large-scale strikes blocked each French port in the 1970s, 1980s and 1990s while reforms were being implemented.

[27]Jean-Claude Maillard, "Du repli impérial à l'ouverture européenne. Les relations économiques de Bordeaux avec l'outre-mer, Bordeaux," *Cahiers d'outre-mer*, No. 200 (December 1997), 338-393. See also Hubert Bonin, "La construction d'un système socio-mental impérial par le monde des affaires ultramarin girondin (des années 1890 aux années 1950," in Bonin, Catherine Hodeir and Jean-François Klein (eds.), *L'espirit économique imperial (1830-1970)* (Paris, 2007).

groundnuts, largely bypassed Bordeaux. On the other hand, Bordeaux drew many goods for export from local and hinterland producers, including metal building equipment; shoes, hats and clothing; pumping facilities; agricultural tools and machines; tinned food (a Bordeaux specialty); and alcohol, spirits and middle-range wines. Factories producing cement or equipment made from it also contributed to exports to Africa. This led to special lines, mainly Compagnie générale transatlantique and Chargeurs réunis from Paris, but also Delmas-Vieljeux from La Rochelle and Compagnie nantaise de navigation from Nantes, picking up cargoes in Bordeaux for shipment to Africa and sometimes to South America.[28]

Table 5
Coffee Imports, 1927 (hundred kgs.)

	Total Imports	Imports from the Empire
Bordeaux	78,208	2874
Le Havre	1,266,908	41,739
Marseille	222,295	13,388

Source: Annuaire économique colonial (Marseille, 1929).

A fierce competition developed between Le Havre, Nantes and Bordeaux for control over the Caribbean trade. Although Bordeaux played a key role for products, such as rum and sugar from the French Antilles and gum from Senegal, Le Havre handled two-thirds of rum imports in 1929 and half of Antilles rum in 1950. And Bordeaux was not a leader in national cocoa imports despite the existence of the large Touton trading firm. Moreover, it was surpassed by Le Havre and Marseille for coffee imports (see table 5).

Bordeaux was unable to become the French gateway for tropical products; its imports were dedicated to southern France only (see table 6). The four sugar refineries in 1903 – Abribat-Bordes (later Saint-Rémi), Tessandier (later Sainte-Croix), Bertault-Tivoli and Frugès – were reduced to only one by the 1930s (Say, which produced a record 87,000 tons in 1977 before its closure in 1984). It was a similar story for the factories (Grande Huilerie bordelaise, Huilerie franco-coloniale, Astra-Calvé-Unilever, Maurel frères and

---

[28]Philippe Fournet, "Bordeaux, capitale française du négoce et de l'industrie du rhum," in Alain Huetz de Lemps and Philippe Roudié (eds.), *Eaux-de-vie et spiritueux* (Bordeaux, 1982); Yves Péhaut, "Le commerce et l'industrie du rhum à Bordeaux," *Cahiers d'outre-mer* (1953), 352-363; Hubert Bonin, "L'industrie agro-alimentaire du grand Sud-Ouest (XIXe-XXe siècles). Un renversement historique du positionnement dans les flux économiques," in Jacques Marseille (ed.), *Les industries agro-alimentaires en France. Histoire et performances* (Paris, 1997), 121-160; and Élie Desplats and Jacques Quénivet, *Les compagnies maritimes à Bordeaux* (Bordeaux, 1993).

Maurel et Prom) that processed African groundnuts to produce oil.[29] The two still active in 1970 produced fourteen percent of French oil and found outlets only in southwest and central France (see table 7). The dozens of tiny coffee roasters and merchants in Bordeaux also were confined to local sales. The key Paris market was barely reached by these companies. Even for wood from Central Africa, where some Bordeaux businessmen invested in plantations or wholesale trading, the outlets were merely regional; Rouen, for instance, imported many more logs for building or furniture than Bordeaux (see table 8).

Table 6
Imports from the French Empire through Bordeaux, 1929 (tons)

Phosphates (North Africa)	173,700
Groundnuts (sub-Saharan Africa)	137,000
Woods	38,450
Cereals (from North Africa)	20,300
Flour and semolina from Algeria and Morocco	3350
Indochina rice	18,000
Rums	19,000
Spirits from Algeria	2100
Raw sugar from Antilles	10,000
Bran and rush (Morocco)	6000
Vegetables and fruits from North Africa	5600
Bananas from Guinea	2300
Coffee and cocoa	1700
Wools and skins	2000
Cork	2000
Gums and rubber	1200
Total (for a value of 750 million *francs*)	580,000

Source: See table 3.

Table 7
Imports of Oils in France, 1932 (tons)

Bordeaux	142,000
Marseille	642,000
Dunkerque	252,000
Le Havre	84,000
Nantes	16,000
Total	1,205,000

Source: Claude Malon, *Le Havre colonial de 1880 à 1960* (Le Havre, 2005), 106.

The same conclusion holds true for phosphates from North Africa, which were used in fertiliser plants for regional agriculture. Except for Arabic

[29]Philippe Terrasson, *L'industrie huilière en France et en Aquitaine, de 1945 à 1993* (Bordeaux, 1995).

gums, Bordeaux harbour did not play a national role (see table 9). Although local plants were responsible for a huge traffic with Africa (reaching 580,000 tons of African imports in 1929 and generating 220,000 tons in exports, fifteen and twenty-five percent of ship entrances and clearances and twenty-five percent of the value of freight), African trade was not responsible for any major expansion of international or even nationwide trade. Bordeaux continued to lag behind Marseille and Le Havre for the traffic to and from sub-Saharan Africa.

Table 8
Destinations of Okoume Logs from Gabon, 1937 (tons)

Bordeaux	5110
Le Havre	195,198
Hambourg	48,849
Rotterdam	48,438
Antwerp	15,946
Bremen	11,818
Rochefort	22,842
La Rochelle-La Pallice	6740
Dunkerque	6687

Source: Malon, *Le Havre colonial*, 138.

Table 9
Traffic with Africa, 1927 (French *tonneaux* [half-tons])

Coming into	**From West Africa**	**From Central Africa**	**From Madagascar**	**Total from sub-Saharian Africa**
Bordeaux	98,967	12,771	0	111,738
Marseille	161,188	12,735	38,751	212,674
Le Havre	53,523	74,416	54,115	182,054
Coming out	**To West Africa**	**To Central Africa**	**To Madagascar**	**Total to Africa**
Bordeaux	46,357	27,064	1050	74,471
Marseille	12,994	218,375	11,618	242,987
Le Havre	31,950	49,652	34,113	115,715

Source: *Tableau général de la navigation* (1927), cited in Malon, *Le Havre colonial*, 152.

In short, in trade with North Africa Bordeaux lost out to its Mediterranean rivals (Marseille, Sète and even Port-Vendres). Its main strength rested with phosphates for its fertiliser plants and the agriculture of its hinterland (see tables 10 and 11). The percentage of traffic with West Africa through Bordeaux reached a peak of thirty percent in 1954, before dwindling to eight percent (814,000 tons) by 1982. While African trade remained viable, it was always for regional consumption.[30]

Table 10
North African Imports through Bordeaux, 1931 (tons)

	Algeria	Tunisia	Morocco
Phosphates	17,444	79,173	9250
Wine	13,680	2027	
Cereals	1023	4320	18,103
Flour and semolina	2583		1681
Woods			2180
Rush	2167		

Source: See table 3.

Table 11
Exports for North Africa through Bordeaux, 1931 (tons)

	Algeria	Tunisia	Morocco
Wood for building	11,666		3052
Refined sugar	2988	3895	3101
Cars, cycles, railway cars, etc.			4066
Machines, metal Equipment	3699		1927
Fertilisers	2412		
Paper, cardboard	2586		

Source: See table 3.

Of course, the imperial function of Bordeaux was a reality through the location in the city of the headquarters of large trading houses, but its national importance has always been more of a legend. Fundamentally, it was (and remained) a regional port. Nonetheless, this legend has been sustained by intensive campaigns promoting economic pride through local magazines; an annual fair; and numerous speeches by ministers and local officials. Owing to local businessmen's associations and the Chamber of Commerce, a well-structured identity was constructed (and revived in the 1950s) that insisted on the role played by "the great Bordeaux harbour." Indeed, an official publication in 1984 still wrote about "Bordeaux, the metropolis of Africa."[31] In the 1960s, Bordeaux firms were displaced by large Parisian wholesalers and transit and

---

[30]Jean Touton, *et al.*, *Le négoce bordelais des denrées tropicales* (Bordeaux, 1996), 30.

[31]*Bordeaux-Le Verdon. Gazette du port, Revue du Port autonome de Bordeaux*, No. 69 (February 1984), 9 and 16.

ship-handling companies in the trade with sub-Saharan Africa. As a result, Bordeaux harbour lost its role as a gateway with Africa and Indochina, which led to the closure of most local trading houses and banking units involved in these trades. In the 1970s, the port was increasingly excluded from regular national or international flows linking "South" and "North" by sea. Only occasional ships called when local branches of national forwarding agents, such as SDV and SDV Bolloré, manage to attract a sufficient number of containers.

The Regional Functions of Bordeaux Harbour

The above discussion suggests that the port of Bordeaux was essentially sustained by its regional functions. We shall not repeat our points about the sugar and oil industries, but it is important to note that the same business model was followed by the flour plant (Grands Moulins de Bordeaux), which was built in the 1920s to serve markets primarily in southwest France. Wood from northern Europe was consumed regionally, as was coal from Great Britain. More recently, imports of petroleum followed the same pattern. The first refinery, Raffineries de pétrole de la Gironde, was established in 1929-1931 with US investments; the apex was reached in the 1960s with two such plants: Esso, which opened in 1959, and Raffinerie des pétroles de la Gironde-Caltex, which dated from the 1920s. There was also Elf at the Bec d'Ambès, downstream from Bordeaux, and Shell in Pauillac, close to the Rothschild vineyard.[32] Their function was to provide oil products to southwest France, which explains their limited production (five percent of the national total in 1970). Chemical plants were discussed in the mid-1970s, and some plans were even drawn up, but none eventuated. As well, some local politicians argued at the end of the 1970s for a Rotterdam-style development at Le Verdon or Bec d'Ambès. But Bordeaux harbour never reached such national or European levels. Indeed, the four oil refineries closed in the 1980s, and the port became a mere importer of refined products transported by tramp ships from Saint-Nazaire, Dunkerque, Antwep or Rotterdam. This minor role was confirmed in 2006 when a project to provide imported gas to southwest France was announced.

As far as heavy industries were concerned, coal, steel or iron ingots and bars were imported for local and regional plants. The main customers were regional shipyards which had been unsuccessful at challenging their counterparts in Nantes-Saint-Nazaire, the Basse-Seine or Dunkerque. In fact, the Forges et Chantiers de la Gironde failed twice in the 1880s and the 1920s

[32]Christophe Briand, "Le développement d'une économie des hydrocarbures en Aquitaine au cours des trois premiers Plans (1947-1962)," in Christophe Bouneau (ed.), *Nouveaux regards sur l'histoire économique de l'Aquitaine* (Pessac, 2003), 277-298.

before resuming its activities thanks to public orders and grants, and except for luxury boats the entire industry closed at the beginning of the 1970s.[33]

This large range of regional functions was in fact shaped by economic cycles which explain the demise of the local sugar, oil and metal industries in the 1960s, 1970s and 1980s. As the Bordeaux industrial platform dwindled, so did the links between the port and the Aquitaine economy. Containerisation and the growing use of lorries for domestic and European freight transport at the expense of railways and ships allowed forwarding agents to search for lower fees and more convenient access to worldwide sea-lines, both of which disadvantaged Bordeaux. Despite important investments to modernise the facilities at Bassens, Bordeaux remains a marginal port.

Table 12

Transit Imports through Bordeaux, February 1939 (tons)

Coal	59,752
Petroleum	56,383
Cereals	5590
Sugar	4609
Pyrites	4193
Wool and hides	2115
Bananas	1725
Coffee	1505
Northern wood	1500
Cocoa	459
Rubber	441

Source: See table 3.

During the interwar period regional industries contributed to the port's life mainly through their imports of raw materials, while energy remained the basis of the transit (see table 12). These developments left only a few market opportunities for the port. One involved the transit of bulk agricultural products: wheat for the flour plant; soya cake for the plant specialising in animal food; paper rolls for the printing unit of the local daily *Sud Ouest*. In addition, fertilisers, cement and various bulk cargoes are still imported for local consumption. From the 1960s, exports included greater quantities of corn (of

[33]Jean Dumas, *Les activités industrielles dans la Communauté urbaine de Bordeaux. Étude de géographie économique et socio-politique* (Bordeaux, 1980); Roger and Christian Bernadat, *Quand Bordeaux construisait des navires. Histoire de la construction navale à Bordeaux* (Camiac-et-Saint-Denis, 2006); and Hubert Bonin and Olivier Pétré-Grenouilleau, "Deindustrialisation and Reindustrialisation: The Case of Bordeaux and Nantes," in Franco Amatori, Andrea Colli and Nicola Crepas (eds.), *Deindustrialization and Reindustrialization in 20th Century Europe* (Milan, 1999), 233-262.

which Aquitaine became a French specialist) to other European countries, such as Italy; flour to Africa; some specialty wheats for Africa; and low-range wines to Africa or North America. Since the 1980s, unlike Marseille, Le Havre and Dunkerque, Bordeaux harbour has become increasingly dedicated to local functions. This explains its recent stagnation, as yearly traffic fell from fourteen million tons in the 1980s to about eight million in the 2000s, almost to the level of La Rochelle-La Pallice.

Conclusion

The history of Bordeaux harbour has always been characterised by a combination of fact and myth. The "glorious" history of the seventeenth and eighteenth centuries and the reputation of Bordeaux wines presented an image of global importance, although the reality was quite different. Since port and maritime history cannot be isolated from general economic and business history, the reality of what happened to the harbour is far from what the myths suggest.

On the other hand, historians benefit from hindsight while merchants do not. Despite the obstacles, Bordeaux merchants did not stop trying to maintain an international role for their port. Some have managed, at least on a small scale, to reshape Bordeaux's international foreland, retaining old markets while seeking new ones. Traditional industries, such as foodstuffs and shipbuilding, supported the growth of trade until the late nineteenth century. When this pattern of growth disappeared, it marked the beginning of a new era.

To realise these ambitions, the port was constantly modernised: warehouses in the 1820s-1840s, quays and berths in the 1860s-1880s, modern warehouses in the 1920s and cranes in the 1950-1970s. Nonetheless, the port failed to maintain its position. The history of the port of Bordeaux is not merely one of decline but, more important, of adaptability to change in the world economy and its regional environment, especially the impact of the conquest (and then independence) of a colonial empire, the role of commodity trades during the first wave of global expansion (from the 1880s to the 1950s) and the involvement of local industries (groundnut oil, petroleum oil, chocolate, coffee, cod, etc.). But its merchants and trading houses were far more important and internationalised than the port because they often acted as intermediaries for other harbours which handled goods in parallel with Bordeaux.

We can conclude, then, that the "decline" was not real. Rather, the highs and lows of trade marked an adaptation to economic trends and commercial flows. The harbour depended on outlets abroad and on the redeployment of local industries. The port could not benefit from a large industrialised hinterland, such as Barcelona or Calais-Dunkerque, or from a transit function from or to industrialised areas. It had therefore to rely on the portfolio of skills of its wholesale traders and shipowners – that is, on an "immaterial" knowledge which was the key to competitiveness.

The Lancashire Cotton Lobby and the Making of the Manchester Ship Canal from 1883 to the Interwar Period

Edouard Guionnet

This study focuses on the influence of the Lancashire cotton lobby in the creation and development of a port at Manchester for ocean-going ships. On the surface, the idea seems paradoxical on several grounds. Manchester was not far from Liverpool, England's second port, a city connected to every part of the world, dealing with the world's leading exchanges, and with docks able to berth and unload the largest steamers and sailing vessels. Moreover, Manchester and other Lancashire industrial towns were served by an extensive railway and canal network. Finally, to turn a city situated thirty-six miles from the sea into a seaport involved digging a canal from the Mersey estuary that was navigable by deep-draught ships. The idea was not new, and several schemes had been proposed (and rejected) previously. But the issue came to a head at the beginning of the 1880s when British manufactures (especially cotton products) began to face intense international competition. In this context, the recent slump in the traffic of Liverpool pointed out by the local mercantile community and a general discontent with the slow pace in improving the situation revived the idea of a canal. Debates over the construction of such a waterway opened in Parliament in 1883. The bill was finally approved in 1885, and the canal opened in 1894.

At the outset, the scheme was promoted by a provisional committee, but after the bill received Royal assent the Ship Canal Company (SCC) was created. Lancashire cotton men played prominent roles in both these bodies. Their leader until 1887 was Daniel Adamson, an engineer who also chaired the board of a Manchester spinning concern. He was assisted by a number of other prominent spinners and manufacturers, including Edward Walmsley and Joseph Leigh. Both were Stockport spinners, but their influence was much broader: the former presided over the Cotton Spinner's Association, while the latter was Mayor of Stockport on several occasions and was also Adamson's son-in-law. Another prominent supporter was William Richardson, who was not a spinner but represented Platt Bros. and Co., a firm which made cotton processing machinery.[1] The board of the SCC also included J.K. Bythell. Before becoming the board's chairman and vice-president of the Manchester Cotton Association in 1894, Bythell had been resident partner in India for Gaddum and Co. and chairman of the Bombay Chamber of Commerce.[2]

In Parliament, the promoters of the scheme included cotton industrialists such as John Fielden and Reuben Spencer (the manager of John Ryland's mills), along with John Slagg and Jacob Bright, two MPs for Lancashire who were closely linked to the trade.[3] At a lower level, cotton operatives were also committed, including men such as Thomas Ashton and James Mawdsley, the secretaries of the Oldham Spinners and the Amalgamated Operative Cotton Spinners Association, respectively. In other words, cotton men from every trade and social level boosted the project. All aimed to divert both the imports and exports of cotton from Liverpool to Manchester. But how could they hope to bypass the UK's leading exporting port?[4] This paper first explores how cotton men justified their scheme and promoted it to the people. Second, we will assess how the canal affected the cotton trade through the interwar years when Manchester became the country's fourth busiest port.

To justify the new waterway, the cotton lobby based its rhetoric on what its members argued was a choking monopoly held by a few commercial organisations in Liverpool. Lancashire cotton men also spoke with a single voice in attacking the railways which carried raw materials from the port of Liverpool to Manchester and transported manufactured products in the opposite direction for export. Railways were blamed for impeding trade in a variety of ways, but the main grievance was about what users viewed as artificially high rates.[5] For example, Marshall Stevens argued that railway companies created comparative disadvantages by charging differential rates between Liverpool and various centres, noting that it cost three shillings and four pence per ton-mile to carry raw cotton from Liverpool while from Hull, a journey three

---

[1]Manchester Central Library (MCL), F86 M85, Manchester Ship Canal (MSC), Provisional Committee, 1887.

[2]Douglas A. Farnie, *The Manchester Ship Canal and the Rise of the Port of Manchester, 1894-1975* (Manchester, 1980), 18.

[3]Slagg owned a successful cotton firm, while Bright's father and brother were cotton manufacturers.

[4]Francis E. Hyde, *Liverpool and the Mersey: An Economic History of the Port, 1700-1970* (Newton Abbot, 1971), 98 and 139.

[5]Cottonopolis, *Manchester Ship Canal. Is It Wanted? And Will It Pay?* (Manchester, 1882), 11.

times as long, transport costs were only one shilling and nine pence.[6] He also noted that Fleetwood, Garston and Barrow were favoured by railway rates at the expense of Manchester. Manchester manufacturers resented the reluctance of the railway companies to abide by what they saw as basic market principles and simple laws of supply and demand. Liverpool's geographic position and its proximity to the main manufacturing district encouraged spinners and manufacturers to believe that they were entitled to lower rates.[7]

There were three main reasons, though, why the railway rates to Manchester was so high. The first was that railway companies controlled rates jointly, which interfered with normal market forces. Henry Coke argued that "when the Midland Company wanted to come into Liverpool, promises were held out that the competition would reduce our charges. When their act was obtained, the Midland united with the other companies to charge conference rates."[8] The second was that the railways held a virtual monopoly on transportation (including waterways) in the region. The cotton lords were fond of citing the case of the Bridgewater Canal, which had been purchased by a firm acting for the Manchester Sheffield and Lincolnshire and the Midland Railway companies.[9] But most important, railways developed port ventures on their own.

> The railway companies practically own the port of Barrow, and they have constructed the docks there at a cost including their investment in steamers, of £2,000,000 sterling. The Lancashire and Yorkshire Railway Company have constructed docks and warehouses at Fleetwood. And they have a large sum of money invested in Hull.[10]

---

[6]Liverpool Record Office (LRO), Hq386.4700037(7)MAN, Manchester Ship Canal Bill, evidence and proceedings in the House of Commons, 8 July 1884.

[7]Great Britain, Parliament, House of Commons, *Parliamentary Papers* (*BPP*), Select Committee on Railways, "Report," evidence of Henry Harrison, 7 April 1881; and evidence of Benjamin Walmsley, 29 June 1881. Henry Harrison was not only Mayor of Blackburn but also a spinner and manufacturer. Walmsley was a Preston spinner and manufacturer.

[8]LRO, H387.109 CHA, Liverpool Chamber of Commerce (LCC), Manchester Ship Canal Bill, summary of the evidence given on behalf of the principal mercantile associations of Liverpool, evidence of Henry Coke, 5 October 1885. Henry Coke managed the Liverpool branch of the firm David Sassoon and Co., East India and China merchants. Its business was principally in cotton.

[9]Cottonopolis, *Manchester Ship Canal,* 23.

[10]*BPP*, evidence of W.B. Forwood, 31 March 1881.

Relying on regional monopolies, railways aimed to stimulate their own port investments by overcharging on the established routes in order to divert traffic. For cotton men, this strategy acted as a tax on the cotton trade and its consumers:

> practically Liverpool is the milch cow of the railway companies; they get a large profit out of their Liverpool traffic which they expend in developing ports...they know that they have a strong head of trade in Liverpool, and therefore they put an extra charge on our traffic.[11]

The cotton interest therefore decried the lack of competition in railway transport. As Samuel Andrew insisted before the House of Commons, Manchester producers were dependent on railways that declined to compete.[12]

This situation placed Lancashire at an even greater disadvantage because of the numerous transhipments involved. Henry Harrison explained the process:

> In the first instance, the cotton leaves Liverpool for the great spinning centre, Oldham and the neighbourhood. Then after it is spun into cotton yarn it goes to Manchester for distribution and sale; it then goes from Manchester to the centres of manufacture, say to Blackburn; and then when manufactured, back from Blackburn to Manchester; and afterwards from Manchester to Liverpool or London.[13]

Such descriptions underscore the increasing emphasis on distribution and related costs, highlighting Manchester's evolution from a manufacturing to a commercial centre.

In the eyes of the cotton masters, the second set of impediments stemmed from the port of Liverpool and its related activities. The first problem was linked to the dock and town dues. The cotton men considered that the harbour was abusing its geographic situation. It was deprecated as the toll barrier of the Mersey because of its "unreasonable" and "unjustified charges" compared with other ports. Marshall Stevens provided the select committees with some comparisons (see table 1).

---

[11]*Ibid.*, 98.

[12]LRO, Hq386.4700037(7)MAN, Manchester Ship Canal Bill, evidence and proceedings in the House of Commons, evidence of Samuel Andrew, 29 May 1883.

[13]*Ibid.*, evidence of Henry Harrison, 7 April 1881.

Table 1
Dock and Port Charges on Raw Cotton, 1884

	Liverpool	**Glasgow**	**Hull**	**Newcastle**	**London**
Dock Dues per Ton	3s	2s	6d	5d	3s 9d
Total Charges (including Dock Dues)	6s 5 1/4d	3s 4d	2s 6d	...	5s 6d

Source: Liverpool Record Office (LRO), Hq386.4700037(7)MAN, Manchester Ship Canal Bill, 8 July 1884, table 13.

Because Liverpool's docks had begun as a municipal undertaking, ships using the port were liable to both dock and town dues. But when the corporation was dispossessed of its docks, the port became a public trust. Although a dock board ran the port, it continued to raise money through town dues. This infuriated the outside mercantile community because the funds raised by the town dues were often used for the city rather than the docks. Moreover, the new port administration had to compensate the town for the estate and the powers it had acquired. For instance, it had to pay interest on the sum of £1,500,000 to Liverpool for relinquishing the town dues: "these charges have to be paid out of the current trade of the port. The interest is paid to the Liverpool Corporation and presumably spent for town purposes."[14] As well, the dock board had to repay its borrowings. In 1882, for example, the accumulated debts of the port amounted to £16,300,000 while the revenue for that year totalled £1,200,000; since expenditures were just over £1,000,000, this did not leave much to transfer to the sinking fund which was supposed to pay off the debts. Those who used the docks were therefore asked to service the debt at an annual rate of about four percent, which seemed to many of them too much to bear: "How long the trades of Lancashire will submit to be taxed for the benefit of over-mortgaged Liverpool remains to be seen."[15] As a result, canal promoters argued that the fruits of their trade were diverted to the city of Liverpool or to pay off the debts of its port.

Porterage was one of the port activities which infuriated the cotton men. It originally was initiated by the dock board and the shipowners to curb mercantile practices which delayed unloading and to speed up the discharge of cargo, thus decreasing the turnaround time of vessels. In the case of steamships, the master porter was nominated by the owner or consignee entitled to the largest portion of the cargo. But if the consignees did not agree on a nomination within an hour of the ship reporting at customs, the steamship owner

---

[14]*Manchester Guardian*, 24 October 1882.

[15]*Ibid*.

was given authority to make an appointment.[16] The first bone of contention arose from rates. E.H. Pember, assessing the advantages that would accrue to the cotton trade from the canal, characterised these as a "gross abuse" because of the aggregate charge of one shilling two pence per ton, which covered eighteen services.[17] Moreover, payment was compulsory even when all the services were not needed.[18] The canal promoters therefore highlighted the shipowners' vested interests in the present system, since they not only controlled freight rates but also managed to glean substantial revenues from porterage; according to Pember, "Mr. Squarey, the dock board solicitor, admitted in evidence in 1880 that it was a profitable business."[19]

Porterage also was a vexing issue because of mishandling. Cotton manufacturers (like cotton traders) complained about the damages to bales by dockers during discharge and about the losses incurred. A number of witnesses testified to these practices: "who has travelled the length of the docks in Liverpool has not noticed the thousands of bales lying on the quay exposed to the elements and soaking in that moisture."[20] One of the reasons cotton bales accumulated on the quayside was because cargoes were discharged too quickly since shipowners were desperate for a rapid turnaround. In addition, bales were spoiled by moisture after being tapped for samples and then made heavier by being soaked by rain. Bales were weighed and sampled twice: once for the purchaser's agent and a second time to check the quality after it was purchased by a spinner; the latter therefore lost a part of his cargo because of dampness and repeated sampling. This led manufacturers to refer to Liverpool firms as robbers: "sampling is a very serious matter in Liverpool. Lots of Liverpool firms make a fair share of their profits out of sampling." Criticisms in this regard focused even more on the brokers, who made "a considerable portion of their rents out of it." For spinners, shipping cotton direct via the canal would reduce handling and transhipments:

> cotton would go right up to Manchester, and on unloading from the docks the lorries would take it straight to the mills. At Liverpool cotton is unloaded in the docks, then loaded on

---

[16]Hyde, *Liverpool*, 128-129.

[17]E.H. Pember was a lawyer and counsel for the scheme in Parliament.

[18]LRO, Hq386.4700037(7)MAN, Manchester Ship Canal Bill, evidence and proceedings in the House of Lords, speech of E.H. Pember, 20 May 1884.

[19]*Ibid.*

[20]*Ibid.*, evidence of John C. Fielden, 12 March-7 May 1885.

> the wagons, and taken up to the railway and it is there unloaded again. There are three unloadings there.[21]

In other words, mishandling would be reduced. An added benefit would be to loosen the brokers' grip on sampling.

The Liverpool Cotton Association (LCA) and its brokers were also targets. Some Lancashire cotton men were long-time detractors of the LCA's domination over transactions in raw cotton. For instance, Fielden explained that "the Association injures the free sale of cotton. If a man passes by the association he is a black sheep for the future. That is why so small an amount of cotton is bought direct between the spinners and the merchants."[22] The LCA's by-laws prevented merchants who belonged to the association from allowing sales outside its control. Breaking the laws entailed fines and banishment.[23] In fact, what merchants and manufacturers wanted to avoid was the double brokerage charged on cotton by the buying and the selling broker. Double brokerage was deemed to be sheer robbery because this dual control was sometimes performed by the same broker. Quoting Samuel Andrew, Pember denounced "the same man very often acts the two parts - one broker acts the part of the buyers' and the sellers' broker receiving often payment from both sides." But charging only one fee for both transactions was not condoned. Pember recalled W.B Forwood's testimony that "the LCA fined a member £50 for acting alone between buyer and seller...namely acting for one fee." Directing trade to Manchester via a canal was the only solution to steer clear of the LCA's monopoly. Edward Walmsley boastfully endorsed this opinion, arguing that "I should get rid of both brokers, I should find plenty of merchants in Manchester who would show me samples, instead of merchants' brokers showing me them." According to the canal promoters, bypassing one brokerage would save six shillings a ton, or £152,000 per year.[24] But this total was contingent upon enticing at least seventy-five percent of Liverpool's cotton trade to the canal.

In short, Lancashire cotton men tried to present Liverpool as a port that strangled their interests with unrelenting corporatist practices and monopolistic designs. Liverpool was scorned as a port in decline where commercial

---

[21]*Ibid.*, 380 COT 5/1, Liverpool Cotton Association (LCA), 10 September 1883.

[22]*Ibid.*, Hq386.4700037(7)MAN, Manchester Ship Canal Bill, evidence and proceedings in the House of Lords, speech of Pember, 20 May 1884.

[23]*Ibid.*, LCA, by-laws, 1883.

[24]*Ibid.*, Hq386.4700037(7)MAN, Manchester Ship Canal Bill, evidence and proceedings in the House of Lords, speech of Pember, 20 May 1884.

organisations encouraged tolls, interruptions and diversions, clung to its vested interests and preferred inertia to competition. Whatever truth there may have been to some of these charges, it was hardly the complete view, if only because Liverpool continually invested in the construction of new docks, quays and larger entrances to handle the latest generation of steamers. This was especially true in the period that coincided with the debate over the canal. In 1881 the Langton and Alexandra docks were opened, followed by the Hornby Dock in 1884 and the Harrington and Toxteth docks in 1888, not to mention all the ancillary facilities.[25] The cotton men also presented a distorted picture because cotton manufacturers were themselves often on the side of empty cant and demagogy.

The promotion of the canal was encompassed in a trite comparison of the two cities. Manchester was praised as the champion of liberal virtues, of which the ship canal was an offshoot. The cotton men's rhetoric revolved around a correlation between liberalism and naturalism and was derived from the nineteenth-century liberal belief that competition is "natural;" what is natural is liberal in essence and therefore worth promoting. As a result, their first aim was to show that building a ship canal was congruent with this analogy. The natural legitimacy of the ship canal (as regards cotton) proceeded from its compliance with the natural laws of market economy:

> As to the question of the cotton market going to Manchester if the ship canal is made...it all depends upon whether the port is upon the line of business...and there is no doubt that if you open the ship canal to Manchester and put docks there, you are not putting them in an out of the way corner of the country, but you are putting them straight in the line of business, where the business is going.[26]

Because Manchester was the centre of the cotton textile trade, it was "natural" that it should engross the entire cotton trade and that the town should become a port.

The Lancashire cotton lords also highlighted a spurious dichotomy between the features of a canal and those of a railway. Canals were presented as natural means of transport while railways were associated with the unnatural deviation of trade:

---

[25]For a thorough discussion, see Hyde, *Liverpool*, chapter 7.

[26]LRO, Hq386.4700037(7)MAN, Manchester Ship Canal Bill, evidence and proceedings in the House of Lords, evidence of Fielden, 1885.

> I do say there can be no question that a water way is a far more natural road than a railroad...The wholesale interference with valuable property and the numberless crossings of roads and highways which such schemes imply, as compared with the simplicity and ease of partially following the course of a natural river...is sufficient to convince as to which plan offers the maximum advantage.[27]

It is ironic that a cotton manufacturer, Edward Hargreaves, should have been called by the Liverpool lobby to testify against the canal because his mill and estate were on the course of the canal and had to be expropriated for its construction.[28]

Even after the canal was completed, the promotional discourse still focused on its harmony with nature and the regeneration it brought to a region whose means of transport were affected adversely by the railway monopoly: "thoroughly incorporated with the scenery, all marks of newness or disturbance are buried beneath a radiant verdure, as might be in token of satisfaction at being thus raised from a sleepy and monotonous level to a position of usefulness and trust."[29] Conversely, talking about the Bridgewater Canal at a mass meeting organized by cotton men, Alderman Bailey launched into a metaphorical and satirical interpretation of the unnatural aftermath which the railway monopoly had generated in the region: "Something told me that the place was haunted. Yes, haunted by the evil spirits of monopoly, which created an artificial death on a waterway which ought to be the busiest in the world."[30]

Several paradoxes in this liberal rhetoric can be underlined. First, the discourse on the benefits of the canal was based upon a fundamentally altered vision of nature. While it associated the waterway with activity and vitality, nature was not seen as liberal, or unfettered, but was rather endowed with restraining qualities - hence, the oxymoron that presented the canal as "letting in a new saving vitality."[31] This formulation sprang from a professed (if untrue)

---

[27]Cottonopolis, *Manchester Ship Canal*, 15 and 20.

[28]LRO, Hq386.4700037(7)MAN, Manchester Ship Canal Bill, evidence and proceedings in the House of Lords, evidence of Edward Hargreaves, 21 June 1883.

[29]W. Burnett Tracy, "The Manchester Ship Canal," *Journal of the Manchester Geographical Society*, XIII (July 1897), 8.

[30]MCL, F386 M8, Manchester Ship Canal, "Great Meeting in the Free Trade Hall," 31 October 1883, 30.

[31]Tracy, "Manchester Ship Canal," 12.

contempt for profits. Moreover, for liberal stalwarts, the use of a totalitarian tone by some Lancashire cotton men seems strange. For the promoters, building the port of Manchester and luring raw cotton away from Liverpool was presented as the fulfilment of a Mancunian commercial manifest destiny. It was but a natural historical evolution; "a ship route was part of her commercial history," claimed the *Journal of the Manchester Geographical Society*, which went on to state that the first baronial residence in the area would have been located at the point of confluence of the Irk and Irwell at Hunt's bank, which just happened to be the limit of the proposed port of Manchester.[32] Conjuring up historical determinism sounds inconsistent with freedom and liberalism, since determinism bends people to its "law." History weighs on people's lives and in this case determines economic choices. In fact, the local parochial jingoism voiced by the promoters seemed nothing more than the ecstatic acknowledgment of this subservience. Speaking of the declining Bridgewater Canal, Alderman Bailey said that:

> I asked myself with dejection and humiliation, am I going from my imperial city? Is this the way from Manchester to the sea? Am I in the primacy of race, and a worthy son of the birthplace of freedom in trade? We must make ourselves worthy of our history.[33]

The proud advocate of freedom is thus diminished to being an agent of history and territory. Fielden brought this to a peak when he drew a comparison between the parallel increase of Lancashire's population and the imports of cotton bales:

> In the year 1861 the population of Lancashire seems to have been 2,400,000...and the import was 2,600,000 bales. In the year 1881 the population was 3,400,000 and there was [sic] 3,600,000 bales imported, or an increase of 1,000,000 in both cases.

He later concluded that "Manchester is like a sun in the midst of a constellation of towns." Such comparisons embrace the people in a totalitarian cosmological vision in which Lancashire is regarded as the *cosmos* and the cotton trade as the *logos*, thereby endorsing any step in its favour, even to the extent of stripping Liverpool of its trade in raw cotton. When asked if he wanted "to

---

[32] *Ibid.*, 1.

[33] "Great Meeting," 30.

turn Manchester into a commercial port instead of Liverpool," Fielden replied that "we think it would be a very great advantage to the community."[34]

To arouse enthusiasm in this community about the canal, Lancashire cotton men and promoters engaged in local propaganda. Their early strategy relied on cross-class cooperation and loyalty of place, but most of all on demagogy and populism. The idea was to drum up investors from among people of slender means (especially cotton workers) and the middle class. To convince them, mass meetings were organised, financed by the manufacturing interests represented by Reuben Spencer.[35] Several arguments were posited to win the attendees over, but an effective one was to disparage speculation. This idea sprang from the hackneyed opposition between the nefarious nature of business transactions and the virtuousness of production. A moral hierarchy was established, with production at the top and business transactions merely derived from it. Hence, it was necessary to transform Manchester into a port to remove its dependence on Liverpool, which was described as unnatural and immoral:

> Liverpool produces nothing. Lancashire...produces all things, or at all event is capable of producing almost all things. I draw a distinction between business that is merely transacted and the industry which actually produces. The business that Liverpool can do are [sic] secondary. Liverpool is the tradesman, Lancashire the producer and the consumer. I say that the tradesman exists for the two latter, and not the two latter for the former.

Later in his speech Pember denounced Liverpool as a lair infected by a plague of middleman and praised Manchester as an incorrupt Elysium of industrial activity: "a parasite would have no chance of growing in what I would call the healthy atmosphere of Manchester."[36] This idea was in its turn related by the working class, cotton workers in particular, and Jim Mawdsley, one of their leaders.[37] The result was a condemnation of illegitimate profits and speculative designs. It also explains Fielden's emphasis on the savings derived from eco-

---

[34]LRO, Hq386.4700037(7)MAN, Manchester Ship Canal Bill, evidence and proceedings in the House of Commons, evidence of Fielden, 29 May 1885.

[35]*Manchester Guardian*, 15 November 1882; "Great Meeting;" and *Manchester Examiner and Times*, 21 September 1885.

[36]LRO, Hq386.4700037(7)MAN, Manchester Ship Canal Bill, evidence and proceedings in the House of Lords, evidence of Fielden, 29 May 1885.

[37]*Justice*, 3 December 1882.

nomical Mancunian management. When asked about potential profits in the millions of pounds for the canal, Fieldin denied saying this, stressing instead savings of this magnitude "to the community."[38]

This line of reasoning underpinned Adamson's promotional strategy to raise funds, which denounced the rich and praised the working class: "London and large capitalists should not be asked to find the money for us – or they will get the just fruits of our labour."[39] For the promoters, the investments had to be local. In their speeches, the moneyed classes were not financiers but those who owned the means of production. When asked how funds were raised to build the cotton mills in Oldham, Jacob Bright replied that it was "the work-people of Oldham, the work people of every grade and every class...who have chosen to subscribe for shares. The truth is there has been among us a silent revolution."[40] Although Bright implied that such capital had been raised from among the working classes, few cotton operatives were shareholders, and the structure of share ownership in Oldham did not change as radically as Bright seemed to suggest.[41] Yet he went on to argue that these same cotton operatives would buy shares in the proposed canal company. To encourage contributions, a shilling coupon system was introduced. The coupons were transferable for shares, and a one shilling weekly collection was also established.[42] The trouble was that working-class funds did not flow in, despite the urgent need for investment capital.

As a result, in 1887 the SCC's new board of directors had no other choice but to turn to financiers and London banks: £1,500,000 was provided by Rothschild, Barings and Morgan and Co.[43] In other words, the incorporation of working men through the ownership of small shareholdings collapsed, and the scheme was rescued by those who had previously been pilloried. To cap it off, the city of Manchester provided £3,000,000 in 1891 and £2,000,000 more two years later.[44] The campaign against speculation did not keep profit

---

[38]LRO, Hq386.4700037(7)MAN, Manchester Ship Canal Bill, evidence and proceedings in the House of Lords, evidence of Fielden, 1885.

[39]*City News*, June 1887.

[40]"Great Meeting," 23.

[41]Roland Smith, "A History of the Lancashire Cotton Industry between 1873 and 1896" (Unpublished PhD thesis, University of Birmingham, 1954), 182-195.

[42]*Manchester Guardian*, 22 November 1882.

[43]*Ibid.*, 2 June 1886.

[44]J.R. Galloway, "The Municipalities of Manchester and Hamburg," *Transactions of the Manchester Statistical Society* (8 December 1887), 60-61.

seekers from investing, although it did cement cooperation between cotton operatives and manufacturers. For employers, it was easier to focus attention away from the priorities and processes of production that could arouse frictions, such as technological improvements; using Liverpudlians as scapegoats and focusing on distribution instead of production was far more consensual. On the other hand, trade unions were going through difficult times financially and were in no position to sustain strikes. Besides, they were concerned with their image among employers and were seeking respectability.[45]

To arouse enthusiasm among the populace the promoters also had to provide an exhilarating depiction of the project. But this, too, was often based on empty rhetoric and descriptions of seemingly affordable mirages, thereby creating an aura of tractable gullibility. One such device was to compare the canal to other successful schemes. The promoters tried to project a spectacular picture of the canal's potential. To do this they sent deputations to sites where similar ambitions had been fulfilled, as on the Tyne and the Tees. In the reports of their visits they focussed on how Mancunian emulators could do better than the "northern men" at a lower cost. The reports were often filled with spectacular accounts of how the past was transformed by the emancipating power of modern technology:

> At Bill Point, until recently, a rocky cliff stood 72 ft above high water. This has been taken away, and in its place, a channel formed from 20 to 22 ft at low water and 35 to 37 at high water. The removal of this obstruction to navigation was affected by combining blasting with dredging.[46]

The dredging of a channel in the Mersey was planned along the same lines, which explains the beguiling figures used by Bright. But in the end, the dredging was limited to twelve feet to prevent the silting of the bar and modifying the currents of the estuary.[47]

Figures also projected a spectacular perspective on the canal. This technique was fundamental to quantify the benefits of the project. But most of

---

[45]Alan Fowler and Terry Wyke (eds.), *The Barefoot Aristocrats: A History of the Amalgamated Association of Operative Cotton Spinners* (Littleborough, 1987), 75 and 86.

[46]MCL, F386 M8, Manchester Ship Canal, "Visit to the Tees and Tyne," 31 October 1883.

[47]LRO, H387.109CHA, LCC, Manchester Ship Canal Bill, summary of evidence given on behalf of the principal mercantile associations of Liverpool, 5 October 1885.

the time they turned out to be quite delusive. For instance, these were the estimates of the savings to be generated by the canal:

> on the supposition that we only charge 5s. on canal toll and wharfage, it would be a saving of 1s. a ton, and it would give us an extra £25,440. Then there is the avoidance of one brokerage, 6s a ton, £152,000 – lower charges for dock quay services; then those charges at Liverpool say 6d; average saving per ton, 14s. 6d., making a total of £387,887.

Those were the estimated savings for imports; with the predicted savings on exports, the total amount saved by the cotton trade reached £508,035.[48]

The convincing power of these figures came from an accumulation of apparently meticulous calculations or from experts' numerous testimonies; Reuben Spencer thought his savings would amount to £2500 to £3000 a year.[49] These estimates were the results of complicated, rational-looking calculations and many a squabble (over the number of spindles used in Lancashire, the quantity of cotton each spindle used, etc.). Yet their relevance and accuracy can easily be challenged since they were based upon sheer speculation and witnesses' extremely subjective expertise.

Indeed, all the calculations were first contingent upon the amount of cotton reaching Manchester via the canal. The promoters assumed that this would be about seventy-five percent, which was quite optimistic. Fielden's testimony illustrates the nature of the cotton pundits' fanciful and unreliable declarations. In May 1883, he could hardly conceal the difficulty of trying to estimate the quantities of cotton that might be delivered via the canal; "that must be a very problematical question," he admitted. Yet five months later he was convinced that the canal would convey 500,000 tons of cotton. And two years later, Fielden's estimates were even more inflated: "I have no doubt whatever that 9-10ths of the cotton trade will be brought by this canal. I have watched the course of trade... [which] is going to leave Liverpool." A second assumption concerned freight. Again, faith, belief and wishful thinking prevailed. Asked if "you are going to get the shipowners to do the work of carrying your goods the forty miles between Liverpool and Manchester for nothing?" Fielden replied "certainly; that is quite certain."[50] But the promoters

---

[48]Liverpool Record Office, Hq386.4700037(7)MAN, Manchester Ship Canal Bill, evidence and proceedings in the House of Lords, speech of Pember, 20 May 1884.

[49]*Ibid*.

[50]*Ibid*., Hq386.4700037(7)MAN, Manchester Ship Canal Bill, evidence and proceedings in the House of Commons, evidence of Fielden, 29 May 1883, 396; and evidence and proceedings in the House of Lords, evidence of Fielden, 1 August 1883.

ignored the strong opposition to the canal in Liverpool, and they forgot the monopolies exerted by conferences and shipping rings, which was at the core of their complaints.

In the end, though, it all boiled down to faith in the promoters' words: "I believe we shall have brighter business times again. I believe in your success, just as Mr Adamson believes in it, and I believe in it, because I believe in the enterprise of Lancashire men." If Jacob Bright was a harbinger of better days, Adamson came up as a doomsayer: "if [we] did not make the canal, disaster would happen in consequence. It would be brought about by the absence of employment. There might be a civil war and bloodshed." This was a frightening prophecy as revelation replaced argument. In fact, an entire cult was built out of the canal in which local economic loyalty flirted with pious wishing and religious devotion. This cult had its patriarchal figures, and among its apostles, Adamson and Bright were prominent. Concluding his journey to the Tyne and Tees, Bright declared that "We shall go back in the spirit of a missionary, as Mr Adamson has said, spreading the information we have gained, and so increasing the volume of opinion in favour of the great project which he leads."[51] These men were proselytising, preaching the gospel of technology and the miracles it could accomplish. Their dogma praised the Victorian values of obduracy and perseverance and generated commandments presented as self-evident economic laws, like "facilities beget trade"[52] or "wherever cheap facilities are afforded, trade is sure to go."[53] The offertory took the form of the weekly one shilling collection, and devotion was gauged by the subscriptions of people who "feel the necessity of doubling their subscriptions to the canal scheme, and of increasing their devotion four-fold."[54]

Yet on the whole this rhetoric was purely demagogic and populist, concerned with appealing to the desires of the masses, in particular their eagerness for cheap loaves: "The canal is as important for cheapening supplies of food as it is for cheapening the transport of goods."[55] When it came to finding money, Adamson was never at a loss to spin consensual stock phrases: "he would not in the future invest his money in works which were to compete against other works, but would invest it in works, that would confer hard bene-

[51]"Great Meeting," 6.

[52]Cottonpolis, *Manchester Ship Canal*, 24.

[53]LRO, Hq386.4700037(7)MAN, Manchester Ship Canal Bill, evidence and proceedings in the House of Commons, evidence of Fielden, 29 May 1883.

[54]"Great Meeting," 5.

[55]LRO, Hq386.4700037(7)MAN, Manchester Ship Canal Bill, evidence and proceedings in the House of Lords, evidence of Fielden, 1 August 1883.

fit upon all, and would injure none."[56] This kind of rhetoric ended up precisely in what it blamed. It extolled savings and penny-pinching devices and turned into a pound-foolish scheme of £15,000,000, although the cost was estimated originally at £5,000,000.[57]

Did the canal divert cotton from Liverpool as the promoters hoped? Table 2 presents the exports of cotton manufactures and the imports of raw cotton through Manchester and Liverpool. With regard to raw cotton, the take-off was slow during the first two years. At the peak of the first season, *Cotton* opined that "the port of Manchester had been available since the first day of last year, but only a very infinitesimal proportion of the cotton consumed by the spinners of American cotton had been brought direct to Manchester."[58] Over a thirty-year period, however, the canal gradually captured 1.7 percent to one-quarter of Liverpool's traffic in raw cotton, before reaching record levels in 1937 when Manchester successfully engrossed thirty-five percent of the trade.

Table 2
Imports and Exports of Raw and Manufactured Cotton, Liverpool and Manchester, 1894-1925

	Raw Cotton Imports (cwt.)		Yarn Exports (lbs.)		Exports of Piece Goods (yds.)	
	Liverpool	**Manchester**	**Liverpool**	**Manchester**	**Liverpool**	**Manchester**
1894	14,447,593	251,778	84,313,800	40,679,800	3,940,020,200	191,900,600
1895	14,394,006	466,799	76,502,500	56,351,500	3,195,717,300	612,756,900
1896	13,384,393	1,324,792	92,298,800	45,132,500	3,502,122,400	519,341,500
1897	12,964,990	1,488,593	88,987,500	39,054,500	3,191,212,800	491,302,300
1898	16,184,362	1,952,482	84,967,200	50,933,100	3,511,282,600	499,981,400
1911	16,847,884	3,929,336	65,104,000	57,229,000	4,281,613,600	918,659,600
1915	20,295,313	4,407,635	62,851,300	51,495,700	3,385,240,300	425,599,500
1925	15,218,036	3,518,066	34,944,400	63,968,900	2,851,496,900	659,197,200

Source: Great Britain, *Annual Statement of the Trade of the United Kingdom*, 1894-1925.

In cotton manufactures, Manchester managed to control an important part of yarn exports, reaching over three-quarters of Liverpool's share in 1915

[56]*Manchester Examiner and Times*, 27 June 1884.

[57]Galloway, "Municipalities," 60-61.

[58]*Cotton*, 5 October 1895, 2. *Cotton* was the weekly publication of the Manchester Cotton Association aimed at the promotion of the cotton market and the port of Manchester.

and even surpassing its rival in some years, as in 1925. But yarn exports were far less valuable than the market in cotton piece goods, which remained in the hands of Liverpool throughout the period. Nonetheless, the canal diverted between five and twenty-three percent of the local export trade in piece goods. Moreover, their shipments more than doubled the value of cotton manufactures exported and improved the status of Manchester from fifth to the second most important port after 1895, outstripping London, Southampton and Glasgow. Textiles accounted for the second largest export category between 1895 and 1914 but gradually fell to third between 1914 and 1924 and to fourth from 1925 to 1930. Their shipments accounted for the lowest rate of expansion of any of the main exports using the canal. Between 1895 and 1913 they expanded in volume at one-third the rate of both non-textile exports and raw cotton imports. And the direct exports of cotton manufactures during the same period comprised less than half the expected quantity.[59] Indeed, bearing in mind Stevens or Fielden's buoyant expectations, these results fell short of the original hopes for the canal. Why? How was it hindered or encouraged? How did the cotton lobby try to develop cotton traffic at the port of Manchester?

In spite of the canal, Liverpool's attractiveness and reputation as the principal depot for the world's cotton crop could not be challenged as easily as the promoters had anticipated. Spinners kept paying weekly visits to Merseyside, and this remained a necessity because of the wide choice Liverpool offered. Moreover, the dependence of spinners upon Liverpool was reinforced by a forty-three percent decline in cotton prices between 1890 and 1895. That deflation encouraged spinners to reduce their stocks to the minimum and to replenish them only when necessary. This was all the easier because American exports were expanding rapidly.[60] As a result, spinners did not need to make large purchases but preferred to increase their reliance upon the Liverpool market and its large warehouses.[61] As well, secular relationships united the spinner to his Liverpool broker, making their links difficult, if not impossible, to sever. These bonds were based on established connections, family ties, the extension of credit by brokers and on brokers' investments in spinners' limited-liability companies. Reporting a spinner's words, *Cotton* testified to this attachment: "Mr Emmot's own Liverpool cotton brokers were personal friends, and the connection dated back to fifty years. That was a tie which he would not gladly see broken." Further, cooperation between the LCA and its new competitor, the Manchester Cotton Association (MCA), was not encouraged. For instance, Mr. Boumphrey, a director of the MCA, was blackballed

---

[59]Farnie, *Manchester Ship Canal*, 104 and 110.

[60]LRO, MD 230, George Holt and Co, Records, Liverpool Cotton Brokers' Association Annual Circulars, 1890-1895.

[61]Smith, "History," 74-91.

when he claimed from the LCA the share of his deceased partner. This explains the fear of cotton merchants who were afraid of being boycotted by Liverpool if they applied for membership in the MCA: "there was an impression among some of the cotton importers that if they sent cotton to Manchester to be sold as 'spot' they would find that their samples of Liverpool 'spot' would not get out freely among buying brokers." Finally, the canal promoters had to come to terms with another problem: "strange to say, the cotton trade, which might have been expected to be the pioneer trade, has hitherto been the worst laggard." As Mr. Macara explained, this was apparently "due to the difficulty of obtaining rates of freight up to Manchester on a par with the rates of Liverpool."[62] Indeed, shippers would not send goods to Manchester for less than 1/32 over the Liverpool rates. The fact is that the shipowners and shippers of New Orleans had been closely linked to Liverpool since the 1820s by mutual interest and customary channels. Because cotton was shipped in bulk, while consignments to Manchester were small, freight rates were necessarily higher. Besides, during the 1895-1896 season, the charterers of steamers loading at American ports refused to book freight for Manchester unless merchants were prepared to offer large quantities of cotton to start each steamer, but the merchants would not offer cotton to spinners or brokers for shipment to Manchester unless they were certain of securing freight space at the same price as Liverpool. This occurred only if merchants ordered large quantities, which they could not really do once spinners began to reduce their stocks.[63]

What did the directors of the SCC do to overcome these setbacks? First, Lancashire cotton men tried to emancipate themselves from Liverpool and establish their own cotton market. Ironically, this emancipation looked a lot like mere duplication. For instance, the rules of the MCA were adapted from its Liverpool rival; it was considered "wise to assimilate the bye laws pretty closely to the Liverpool condition in the first instance." The MCA's practices were thus completely inspired by the LCA: "it was decided that the aim of the association should be to convince Liverpool and other cotton merchants that if they send cotton to Manchester, it will be dealt with in the same way as at Liverpool, and that no fancy experiments will be made." Even the location of the market was chosen to parallel its counterpart:

> I am requested to inquire whether the corporation would kindly permit the members of the M.C.A. to stand on the flags of the Victoria Arcade to transact their business in cot-

---

[62]*Cotton*, 1 June and 5 and 12 October 1895.

[63]*Manchester Chamber of Commerce Monthly Record*, 26 March 1895.

> ton in the same way as the members of the L.C.A. use the flags of the Liverpool Exchange. [64]

This progress towards independence was cramped to such an extent that the Manchester cotton market realized it could not do without the LCA and the good will of the brokers, whom they tried to cajole into cooperation. For instance, the MCA invited the Liverpool brokers to visit the port of Manchester via the canal. For the occasion, Macara, the president of the MCA, and Bythell distilled a rhetoric which both parties could not have seriously believed: "the L.C.A. was composed of cotton merchants and brokers, while the M.C.A...was mostly composed of cotton spinners. There could therefore be no rivalry between them. Indeed, there ought to be the very heartiest cooperation." Emancipation was turning into a desire for cooperation because the LCA's pressure would not go away: "the proper course to adopt in the interests of all concerned was to regard Liverpool and Manchester as one cotton market."[65]

Most of all, the SCC tried to ensure that the freights to Manchester would be reduced to Liverpool's level. Bythell embarked on an active policy of negotiations with shippers and charterers of US cotton to make sure that cotton would arrive regularly at Manchester. He also initiated a policy of independent chartering under which the SCC would be in charge of chartering steamers filled with cotton to Manchester. Despite immense difficulties, he successfully established a direct service from New Orleans and Galveston to Manchester.[66] Since Liverpool shipping rings would not let steamers sail to Manchester at equal rates, he also endeavoured to attract non-conference lines. From August 1894, Bythell undertook negotiations through the Hindu merchants of Bombay to secure Indian piece goods by the canal. On 29 December 1894, the Bombay contract was signed, with the conference lines providing that three steamers should load in Manchester each month. It was concluded for a year and reduced the through rate by ten percent.[67] Manchester retained this direct trade to Bombay until the depression of the 1930s.

Such achievements encouraged efforts to develop direct shipments to Bengal and China as well. But Manchester did not break the pressure exerted by the China and Calcutta conferences, so that after 1895 the city was temporarily excluded from the export trade in piece goods to the rest of Asia, espe-

---

[64]Manchester Archives, M26/1/1, Manchester Cotton Association Board, 18 January 1895.

[65]*Cotton*, 11 May and 28 September 1895.

[66]*Ibid.*, 5 October 1895.

[67]*Manchester Chamber of Commerce Monthly Record*, 26 March 1895.

cially the rapidly-expanding East Asian markets, and even from Africa. Yet when the services to Calcutta and Cape Town were started in 1920 in 1924, exports of cotton manufactures were boosted to their peak levels in 1925, when they accounted for 17.8 percent of the national volume and fourteen percent of the value. Twelve years earlier, exports of piece goods had reached their apex; the beginning of direct services to Australia in 1904 and to the Levant in 1910 certainly contributed to this. The maximum level for yarn exports was reached by 1922, mainly because freight rates were reduced much more than on piece goods – they had already been reduced by thirty-seven percent for exports to the continent, and freight to Bombay was further trimmed to a level twenty-two percent below that of 1894. On the whole, for the first twenty years of the canal's operation, cotton manufactures dominated Manchester exports in value (sixty-nine percent). But after 1930 they provided less than half, and by 1928 had been outclassed in value by raw cotton imports. Still, those imports never dominated the traffic of the canal in volume, receding to sixth place in 1914. These exports retained their primacy in volume until 1952.[68]

[68]Farnie, *Manchester Ship Canal*, 81, 100, 110-111 and 117.

Mormugao Port:
The Golden Gateway to Goa

Jeronimo G.R. Monteiro

Introduction

Ports are engines for the economies they serve. The development of modern ports is the result of a variety of factors. This essay focuses on some of the variables which have contributed to the success and development of the modern port of Mormugao, the "golden gateway" to Goa. Some of the factors behind the growth of Mormugao are clear. First, Goa is endowed with many mineral resources, especially iron ore in the hinterland, which was discovered in the 1950s by private entrepreneurs. Second, this port on the west coast of India is strategically located to cater for the traffic not only of Goa but also of the neighbouring states and indeed the world. Finally, since the port achieved its greatest success after the establishment of the Port Trust in 1963, it is obvious that this form of organisation has enabled Mormugao to function well. The growth of the port continues in the era of increased globalisation and heightened competition. Indeed, it is even taking part in the container revolution.

Goa has a rich heritage. It was referred to in ancient Hindu mythology and has been ruled by many dynasties, such as the Bhojas, Konkan Mauryas, Goan Silharas, Kadambas and Vijaynagaras. Empires rose and fell in Goa, but in its long history the port city of Goa, and later the port of Mormugao, has withstood the test of time.[1] The origin of the modern port, however, derives from the Treaty of Lisbon signed in 1878 between Britain and Portugal.[2]

Goa, the twenty-fifth state of the union of India, is a tiny, scenic place which has been variously known as the "Tropical Paradise of Tourists," "Golden Gateway of Commerce and Trade," "Pearl of the Orient," "Rome of the East" and "*Kashi* of the *Konkan*."[3] It is situated between the slopes of the Western Ghats to the east and the Arabian Sea in the west. It has an area of

---

[1]Amaro A. Pereira, *History of Mormugao Port* (Goa, 1981), 1-4.

[2]Mario Cabral e Sa, *Song of the Golden Gateway* (New Delhi, 1985), 1-8.

[3]Pratima P. Kamat, "Historical Geography and Natural Resources," in Teotonio R. de Souza (ed.), *Goa through the Ages, Vol. II: An Economic History* (New Delhi, 1990), 1-36.

3701 sq. km. and stretches for sixty km. in an east-west direction and about 105 km. from north to south.

Mormugao, a rapidly expanding port and a "gateway" to a growing industrial complex in the hinterland, is situated on the west coast of India at the mouth of the Zuari River.[4] It is an open harbour protected by a breakwater and a mole. More than a century ago Mormugao port had a commendable draft of nearly twenty-five feet.[5]

Historically, ports have played a crucial role in regional economic development. Mormugao Port, which has made the export of iron ore from Goa possible, has been instrumental in enhancing the prosperity of the state and its people.[6] By the end of the sixteenth century, Goa had reached the zenith of glory and prosperity, and it came to be called "*Goa Dourado*" (Golden Goa). Its flourishing harbour, military strength and ecclesiastical power were the main causes for this prosperity.[7]

Ports are gateways to a country's international trade and are thus vital catalysts for social and economic development in any maritime nation.[8] A port is essentially an economic entity which, through its infrastructure, serves the coastal and overseas traffic of a region. Ports are crucial links in the transport network which links producers and consumers.[9] This is particularly true in India, where about ninety-five percent of the volume and seventy percent of the value of the country's foreign trade is carried by maritime transport.[10]

India has an extensive coastline of 7517 km. along the states of Gujarat, Maharashtra, Karnataka, Goa and Kerala on the west coast, and Tamil Nadu, Andhra Pradesh, Orissa and West Bengal on the east coast. These nine states have twelve major and 187 minor and intermediate ports. The major ports on the west coast are Kandla, Mumbai, Jawaharlal Nehru (near Mum-

---

[4]V.T. Gune (ed.), *Gazetteer of the Union Territory, Goa, Daman and Diu* (2 vols., Panaji, 1979), I, 1-1023.

[5]Cabral e Sa, *Song,* 8.

[6]Prabhakar S. Angle, *Goa: An Economic Update* (Mumbai, 2001), 1-150.

[7]Pereira, *History,* 1-6; and K S. Mathew, "Trade and Commerce in Sixteenth Century Goa," in de Souza (ed.), *Goa through the Ages*, II, 140.

[8]United Nations Conference on Trade and Development (UNCTAD), *Development of Ports* (New York, 1969), 4-9.

[9]Buddhadeb Ghosh and Prabhir De, "Indian Ports and Globalisation: Grounding Economics in Geography," *Economic and Political Weekly*, 25 August 2001.

[10]India, Ministry of Shipping, *Draft Policy for Maritime Sector* (New Delhi, 2004), 1-60.

bai), Mormugao, New Mangalore and Cochin; on the east coast are Tuticorin, Chennai, Vishakapatnam, Paradip, Calcutta/Haldia and Ennore. Four of the major ports - Calcutta, Mumbai, Chennai and Mormugao - are more than 100 years old (Mormugao celebrated its centenary in 1985). The cargo handled at Indian ports has increased from 19.38 million tonnes in the major ports in 1950-1951 to around 500 million tonnes in all the ports by 2004-2005.[11]

Ports in India are classified as major and minor ports. Major ports are under the control and supervision of the central government and are placed in the Union List of Schedule VII of the Indian Constitution. They come under the purview of the Major Port Trusts Act of 1963 and the Indian Ports Act of 1908. Minor ports and others are placed in the Concurrent List of Schedule VII of the Constitution and are therefore controlled and operated by the respective state governments subject to some national legislation.

The findings and analyses in this paper are based on archival sources, Portuguese documents, annual administration reports of Mormugao Port Trust (MPT) and secondary works related to this port and other ports in general. The databases of the Centre for Monitoring the Indian Economy (CMIE) and the Indian Ports Association were also used extensively.

Having discussed the histories of Goa and Mormugao Port, the essay next looks at the development of trade, commerce and the ports up to 1961, along with the building of a rail line to Goa's hinterland. A British company constructed the port of Mormugao and the railway line simultaneously. The construction of the port and railway line marked the turning point for the expansion and growth of this region. The third section examines developments after Goa became part of India in 1961. During this period the port expanded further due to the exploitation of rich deposits of natural resources in the hinterland and rose to become one of the four most important harbours in India. The final section contains some concluding remarks about the port.

Port City of Goa to 1961

Goa has a long historical involvement with seaborne commerce. Its earliest trading port was at Chandrapur.[12] The maritime history of coastal Goa can be traced from the period of the Indian Emperor Ashoka when trade was conducted with distant lands.[13] Commerce with Arabia, Persia and Turkey continued by land as well as by sea. Seaborne trade, however, played an increasingly

[11]India, Ministry of Finance, *Economic Survey 2006* (New Delhi, 2006).

[12]Varsha Kamat, "Trade and Commerce under Yusuf Adil Shah," in S.K. Mhamai (ed.), *Goa: Trade and Commerce through the Ages* (Panaji, 2000), 43-55.

[13]V.T. Gune, "Goa's Coastal and Overseas Trade: From the Earliest times til 1510 A.D.," in de Souza (ed.), *Goa through the Ages*, II, 117-136.

important role in medieval India when the port of Goa was visited by merchants of all nationalities.[14] Indeed, Goa was one of the principal trading emporia on the west coast of India and attracted people of various races, cultures and creeds from all over Asia.[15] The presence of rich merchants of all nationalities added to its greatness. Magnificent edifices, residences, mansions and buildings adorned Old Goa.

As Tome Pires observed in 1511, Goans were known for their skill in shipbuilding, and the availability of timber and excellent craftsmen gave it a fine reputation for quality vessels.[16] At any given time more than twenty vessels were generally constructed in the port and were kept ready for sale. New docks were built for the construction of large ships to trade with other parts of India. Moreover, the area's seamen were known for their skills and bravery.

The city of Goa grew in importance because of the trade in horses imported from Persia, Arabia, Hormuz and Cambay (Gujarat). Besides horses, Goa also traded in betel, areca, calico, fine muslin, rice, velvets, satin, damask and chinaware. In the sixteenth century there was an annual trade of about 2381 horses. Over time, Goa developed contacts with other parts of India and especially with Malabar in the south. Pepper, ginger and other spices were traded by Goa to these new markets.[17] Mormugao port played a crucial role in Goa's trade in the years of growth and development.

The area now known as Old Goa, situated on the banks of the Mandovi River, was a flourishing trading centre before the Portuguese came to India. During the period of the sultanate of Yusuf Adil Shah of Bijapur, exports far exceeded imports, and Goa maintained a favourable balance of trade.[18] The port of Goa came under foreign rule after Afonso de Albuquerque, sent by Portugal as Goa's Governor General, defeated Adil Shah in 1510. As K.S. Mathew has noted, trade in the Portuguese period was not only confined to West Africa but also extended to coastal India, Southeast Asia and Western Europe. The inland and local trade swelled to keep pace with external commerce. After 1530 Goa became the permanent headquarters of Portuguese India. Trade received an unprecedented fillip, and Goa became a kind of storehouse, sending many commodities to factories elsewhere.

---

[14]Mathew, "Trade and Commerce," II, 137-144; and Kamat, "Trade and Commerce," 44.

[15]Kamat, "Trade and Commerce," 47-48.

[16]Mathew, "Trade and Commerce," 139.

[17]*Ibid.*, 139-142.

[18]Kamat, "Trade and Commerce," 47.

Historians believe that the Portuguese *Estado da India* and its capital of Goa entered a period of decline early in the seventeenth century.[19] Due to the lack of economic opportunities, many inhabitants migrated, mostly to British India, East Africa and later to the Gulf. Goa's decline was also due to the failure to maintain its foreign trade, since the authorities in Goa for at least three centuries ignored opportunities to develop major export markets based on local products. The principal potential export was iron ore, although the area also had rich deposits of manganese, aluminium and mica.

As Goa's trade declined its great merchants moved to Indian port cities like Bombay and Madras, where the British-dominated economies were prospering. Economic historians posit two principal reasons for Portuguese decline. First, there was the isolation of Portuguese India due to the lack of a railway line to connect it to the vast rail network of British India. Second, there was the flourishing trade in Bombay. Goods from central and southern India were diverted through Bombay because it offered a convenient exit point. Some historians also attribute the decline of Portuguese India to mistakes made in Lisbon, especially the decision to cede Bombay to the British in 1661.[20]

Goa's earliest port was shifted from Chandrapur to Old Goa and then to New Goa (Panaji) in 1818.[21] But these three earlier ports were insufficient to serve international trade and could not handle large vessels. In addition, they had navigation problems. It was later discovered that the mouth of the Zuari River was an excellent sit at which to construct a full-fledged port, and the Portuguese enlisted British aid to build Mormugao Port.[22]

Mormugao Port owed its origin to the Treaty of Lisbon signed in 1878 between the British and Portuguese governments. An agreement was then signed with the West of India Portuguese Guaranteed Railway Company (WIPGR) for the construction, operation and maintenance of the port and its

---

[19]Celsa Pinto, *Trade and Finance in Portuguese India: A Study of the Portuguese Country Trade 1770-1840* (New Delhi, 1994), 29-60.

[20]This treaty was signed by the Portuguese to give Bombay (now Mumbai) as a dowry to Charles II of Great Britain, who married Infanta Catherine of Portugal. The decline of Portuguese India may in part be attributed to this treaty. Satkartar Batra, *Port of Bombay* (Kandla Adipur, 1967).

[21]Chandrapur and Old Goa were also important cities some centuries ago because both possessed excellent hinterlands.

[22]Goa's port was shifted over time from Chandrapur to Old Goa and then to Panaji. The Portuguese shifted this to Mormugao, where a new port was to be built by a British company. At one time Mormugao was known as "the pearl necklace" and also "the village of pearls" because it was surrounded by many islands and a string of volcanic rocks which looked like a necklace around the neck of "golden Goa." See Cabral e sa, *Song*.

railway line in 1881. Mormugao was virtually gifted by the Portuguese administration to the WIPGR. This treaty, *inter alia,* was for the purpose of having a union of commercial interests between India and Goa. The port was to provide adequate accommodation for all the trade of the surrounding districts and was to function in exactly the same manner as a transit port.[23] This was the turning point in the expansion of business and industry, as well as the overall growth of Mormugao Port. While the construction of these large projects was underway, in April 1885 the twenty-five-foot draught SS *Westbourne* sailed into Mormugao.[24] The port and its rail connection as far as Castle Rock commenced operations in 1888, the year that Bombay's prestigious Victoria Dock was constructed. Mormugao Port was soon described as one of the world's best all-weather natural harbours.

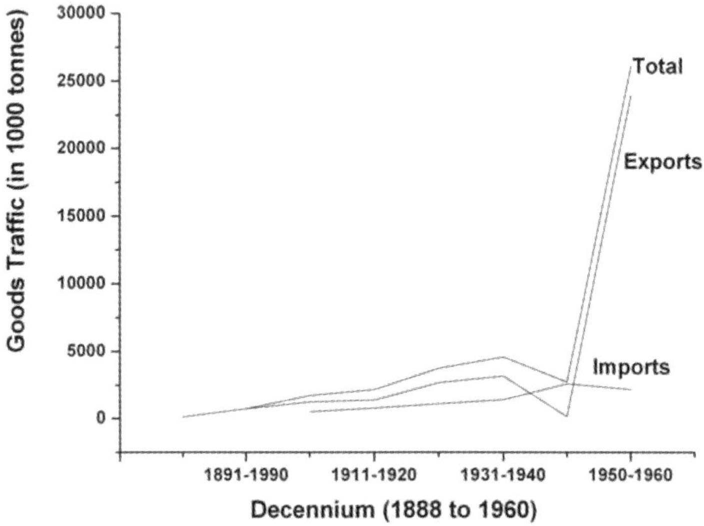

Figure 1: Imports and Exports through Mormugao Port, 1888-1960

Sources: Amaro A. Pereira, *History of Mormugao Port* (Goa, 1981); Mario Cabral e Sa, *Song of the Golden Gateway* (New Delhi, 1985); and Mormugao Port Trust (MPT), *Annual Administrative Reports*, various years.

[23]Gune (ed.), *Gazetteer*, 669.

[24]Cabral e Sa, *Song,* 8.

While the maritime history of Goa was being shaped, ports such as Panaji, Colvale, Betul and Talpona were used as feeders for the coastal and inland trades, while Mormugao Port was used to accommodate cargo steamers and passenger ships plying between Mumbai and East African harbours. Figure 1 presents the goods traffic handled by Mormugao from 1888 to 1960. It shows the trends in exports and imports for the last seventy years or so of the Portuguese occupation of Goa. Mormugao Port was in the forefront in those years, providing easy accessibility for its local and international trade. The figure shows a substantial increase in goods handled over the period. This may be attributed to the fact that the variety of exports increased to include areca, betel, spices, cotton and minerals. The prosperity of the hinterland contributed to the supply of these goods to the port. On the other hand, imports were mostly petroleum, oil and lubricants; food grains; and iron and steel machinery. Overall exports in each decade between 1901 and 1960 were, on average, about two and one-half times greater than imports. It may be noted that exports drastically decreased from 1940 due to World War II. But exports, especially of iron ore, increased sharply in the 1950s as private investors developed the mining industry to take advantage of incentives provided by the Portuguese administration.

Mormugao Port Trust after 1961

The port of Mormugao entered a new era in early 1961. Many developments took place with regard to the port and the railway line. The Indian economic blockade of the 1950s, likely designed to induce the Portuguese to leave Goa, had a severe impact in the early 1960s. Due to the closure of the India-Goa border there was a sudden change in the administration of Mormugao Port and the railway. Indeed, the Southern Railway, which was operated and managed the port railway, ceased all its operations in Goa. In April 1961, an autonomous body called the Junta Autonoma dos Portos e Caminhos de Ferro (Autonomous Commission for Ports and Railways) was created to replace the WIPGR and took over the Port and the Railway Administration.[25] This occurred before 19 December 1961 when Goa became part of India. With this, the Administration of the Port and its railway link were taken over by the Indian government through the appointment of an Administrative Officer on 8 January 1962.

Like other major ports, the port of Mormugao came under the direct control of the Ministry of Transport in November 1962. The railway section from Vasco da Gama to the border of Goa was transferred to the Southern Railway in May 1963. The Indian Ports Act, 1908 was extended to Mormugao, and on 2 December 1963 the Ministry of Transport declared Mor-

[25]Gune (ed.), *Gazetteer,* 670.

mugao the country's seventh major port. Thereafter, the Major Port Trust Act, 1963 became applicable and a Board of Trustees was appointed on 1 July 1964. When Goa became part of India the port had seven berths with a breakwater of 2500 feet. Since then, the facilities at Mormugao have been increased to comprise twelve berths, a traffic management system, a twenty-four-hour signal station, tractor tugs, a mechanical ore-handling plant and a variety of other equipment to handle containers, oil and general cargo.

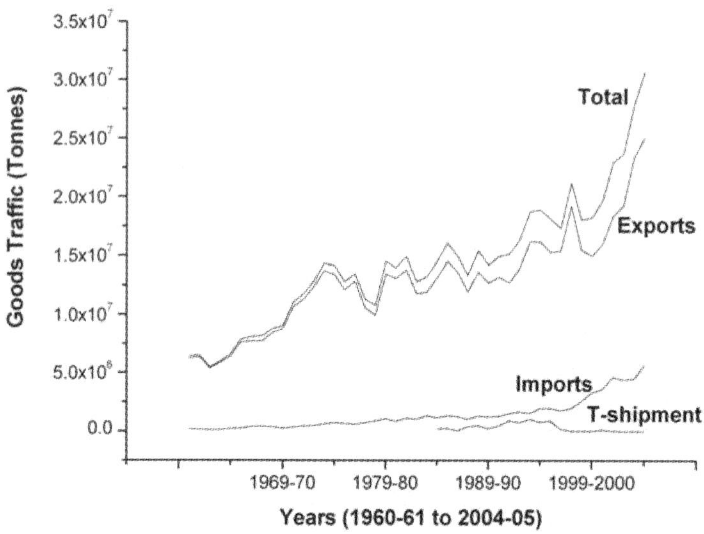

Figure 2: Variations in Imports, Exports and Transhipment Cargoes after 1960

Source: MPT, *Annual Administrative Reports*, various years; *Goa Gazetteer*, 1979; Centre for Monitoring the Indian Economy (CMIE), database; Indian Ports Administration (IPA), database; and India, Ministry of Shipping, *Basic Port Statistics*, various years.

India at present is ranked as the world's seventeenth most important maritime nation based upon the volume of tonnage entering and clearing its ports.[26] Situated at the confluence of the Arabian Sea, Indian Ocean and Bay of Bengal, it also has a locational advantage.[27] Mormugao is part of this. The

[26]India, Ministry of Shipping, *Draft Policy*, 1-60.

[27]Government of India, Seventh Lok Sabha, Estimates Committee (1981-1982), 32nd Report, 1-2; and Arun Prasad Sen, "Some Aspects of Calcutta Port" (Discussion Paper No. 12, Centre for Urban Economic Studies, Department of Economics, University of Calcutta, 1993), 6-7.

port is the country's premier iron ore exporter with an annual throughput of around thirty million tonnes, which accounts for about forty percent of India's iron ore exports. The most important factor contributing to the rapid growth of traffic is the excellent inland waterway system based upon the Zuari and Mandovi rivers and the Cumbarjua Canal. This system has been used to bring ore economically from the mines to the harbour. Though Mormugao's massive cargo-handling capacity has put it on the map, Goa is not free from problems, especially regarding health. There are high incidences of skin infections and lung problems in the mining areas of Goa. There are also problems with dust pollution and other environmental hazards due to mining.

There is a high correlation between cargo handled and health and environmental hazards. Figure 2 shows that most of the cargo handled in the post-Portuguese was exports, except in 1999-2000 when exports decreased by 3.43 percent while imports increased by twenty-nine percent over the previous year. The fall in export traffic was attributable to a drop in iron ore exports due to a lack of overseas demand. A noteworthy feature in figure 2 is that after the 1990s imports increased while transhipment cargoes disappeared after 2002-2003. The new development at Mormugao is that vessels of 70,000 deadweight tons (dwt) and above could now be berthed. This is the result of a continuous increase in the quality of port services in recent years.

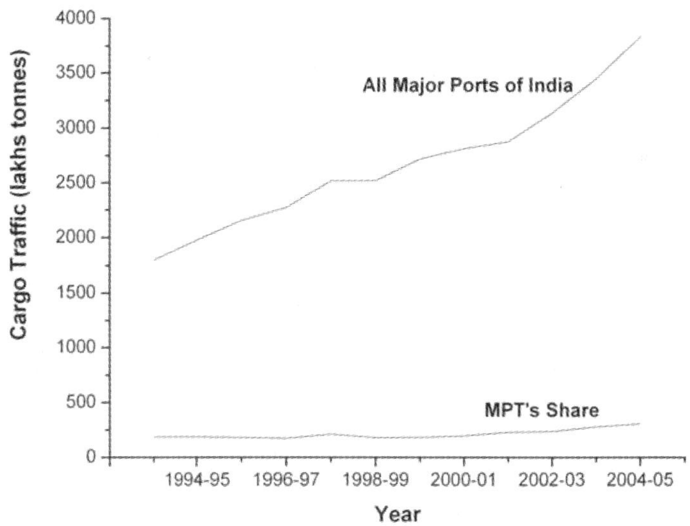

Figure 3: Cargo Handled at the Major Ports of India and at Mormugao, 1901-2001

Source: MPT, *Annual Administrative Reports*, various years; and IPA, database.

The major ports of India have accounted for the bulk of cargo traffic. In the 1960s the major ports handled about eighty-five percent of the traffic; this figure has risen to about ninety-five percent in the 1990s. Figure 3 shows the absolute growth of cargo handled by all the major ports in India and Mormugao's share of total cargo handled. The overall cargo handled by the major ports in 1993-1994 was on the order of 1792.60 *lakh* tonnes.[28] This increased to 1972.62 *lakh* tonnes in 1994-1995, a growth of 10.04 percent. When tonnage handled reached an all-time high of 3836.25 *lakh* tonnes in 2004-2005, growth increased to 11.26 percent. Mormugao's share over the years increased from nearly 187.17 *lakh* tonnes to 306.59 *lakh* tonnes. A noteworthy development for the MPT was that almost forty percent of the exports was comprised of iron ore.

At present the bulk of cargoes is handled by the country's five major ports: Mumbai, JNPT, Vishakhapatnam, Chennai and Kandla. Vishakhapatnam has maintained its premier position among Indian ports since 2001-2002. The commodities handled at the major ports has undergone a substantial change over the years. Petroleum and petroleum products have accounted for the major portion.

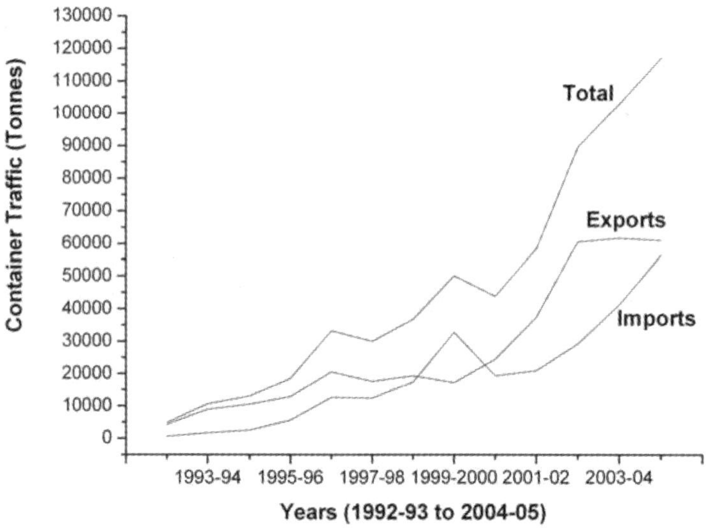

Figure 4: Container Traffic Handled at Mormugao, 1992/1993-2004/2005

Source: MPT, *Annual Administrative Reports*, various years.

[28]A *lahk* tonne is equal to 100,000 tonnes.

The commodities that comprised imports and exports in Mormugao were different than during the Portuguese era. Imports used to comprise lubricants, food grains, cement, mineral oils and fertilizers, while exports consisted of iron ore, manganese, oil cakes, bauxite and general cargo. The composition of trade after 1961 has changed significantly due to Goa's increased exploitation of mineral resources.[29] The port also began to serve other regions outside of Goa. In terms of export tonnage, Mormugao assumed second place among all the major ports, wresting this position from Calcutta in 1968-1969. The rise in container traffic has been particularly noticeable in recent years. Since 1992, there has been a regular container feeder service from the port. Figure 4 shows the rise in container traffic. In the container sector, exports have exceeded imports except in 1999-2000.

Table 1

Average Pre-Berthing and Turnaround Time at MPT, 1994/1995-2002/2003

Year	Average Pre-Berthing	Average Turnround Time
1994-1995	2.98	6.61
1995-1996	2.78	6.29
1996-1997	2.17	6.28
1997-1998	1.87	5.60
1998-1999	1.40	4.81
1999-2000	1.09	3.21
2000-2001	1.32	2.93
2001-2002	1.74	2.90
2002-2003	1.92	2.79

Source: MPT, *Annual Administration Reports,* various years; and CMIE database.

Table 1 shows performance of MPT with regard to pre-berthing and average turnaround time for the period 1994-1995 to 2002-2003. By both measures the port improved its performance over the period. Average preberthing time, which was 2.98 days in 1994-1895, declined to 1.09 days in 1999-2000 before rising again to 1.92 days in 2002-2003. With regard to average turnaround time, it was 6.61 days in 1994-1995, declining to 2.79 days in 2002-2003. Mormugao has the lowest figures on both these performance indicators among the major ports of India. Average ship berth output per day is also on the rise for the MPT. It was 16,746 tonnes for the year 2003-04. The productivity and efficiency of this port is increasing, enabling it to meet the competition in the new global world.

A study of the growth in the port and other aspects of its performance in the decade after December 1961 shows that the number of ore vessels and

[29]Goa's mineral resources were exploited over the years by entrepreneurs like V.M. Salgaocar, V.D. Chowgule and V.S. Dempo. Goa's mineral resources are privately owned by these three individuals, among others.

the tonnage increased considerably (see table 2). The growth was especially notable among the largest ships that visit regularly to load iron ore, Panamax vessels of about 70,000 dwt, but in recent years bigger vessels have called at the port. The total number of ore vessels has risen from 421 in 1962-1963 to 501 in 1970-1971, an increase of nineteen percent. The installation of the mechanical ore-handling plant has enhanced productivity. On 11 April 2006 MV *Goan Pride*, a new generation of modern technology with a storage capacity of 123,000 tonnes and a loading rate of about 75,000 tonnes per day, was installed, giving the MPT a new edge.[30]

Table 2
Numbers of Ore Vessels Calling at MPT by Tonnage Class, 1962/1963-1970/1971

Year	Up to 15,000 dwt	15,001-20,000 dwt	20,001-25,000 dwt	25,001-30,000 dwt	Over 30,000 dwt	Total No. of vessels
1962-1963	345 (82)	37 (9)	36 (8)	3 (1)	-	421
1963-1964	317 (73)	48 (11)	59 (13)	3 (1)	10 (2)	437
1964-1965	375 (76)	60 (12)	47 (9)	5 (5)	9 (2)	496
1965-1966	455 (76)	63 (11)	62 (10)	10 (2)	4 (1)	594
1966-1967	339 (66)	84 (16)	43 (8)	20 (4)	29 (6)	515
1967-1968	252 (55)	65 (15)	70 (15)	15 (3)	54 (12)	456
1968-1969	223 (52)	46 (11)	41 (10)	22 (5)	93 (22)	425
1969-1970	197 (47)	46 (11)	48 (11)	24 (6)	103 (25)	418
1970-1971	226 (45)	61 (12)	43 (9)	58 (12)	113 (22)	501

Note: Numbers in parentheses are annual percentages.

Source: *Goa Gazetteer,* 1979.

From the foregoing discussion, two healthy trends can be discerned. The first is a tendency towards traffic diversification with a growing volume of non-ore traffic. The second is the expansion of Mormugao's service areas beyond Goa's borders. Mormugao today caters to a vast hinterland, which encourages the growth of diversified port services and reduces the undue dependence on a single commodity. The economic hinterland of the port comprises 57,400 square miles.[31]

Population is another indicator which is important for the socio-economic development of Goa, for it is related to the growth and development of the region. As the hinterland of Goa developed due to the presence of a

[30]*Herald* (Panjim Goa), 11 April 2006.

[31]The economic hinterland of Mormugao Port covers the entire territory of Goa and extends to the hinterland regions of three neighbouring states: southwest Maharashtra, north Karnataka and west Andhra Pradesh.

port, there was a tremendous influx of people and consequently heavy pressure on existing resources. As a result, Goa, and especially the port city of Vasco da Gama, encountered health and social problems.[32] Figure 5 shows the trends of population growth in Goa and Mormugao. Today Mormugao is the fastest growing *taluka* (section) of Goa. About seventy percent of all workers in the port are migrants. Eighty percent of the cargo-handling department of the port in 2005 was comprised of migrant workers. The growth of population in both Goa and Mormugao show substantial increases in the post-Portuguese era due to the much freer influx of people from neighbouring states on account of increased employment opportunities in the unskilled, semi-skilled and technical sectors. Goa has had an influx of around seven *lakhs* of population from the other states of India. This may be due to the fact that Goans are *sussegado* (the Portuguese word for "easy going") and do not wish to do the hard physical work which is often required in the port. The development of the port and its hinterland have had important roles to play in this economic development.

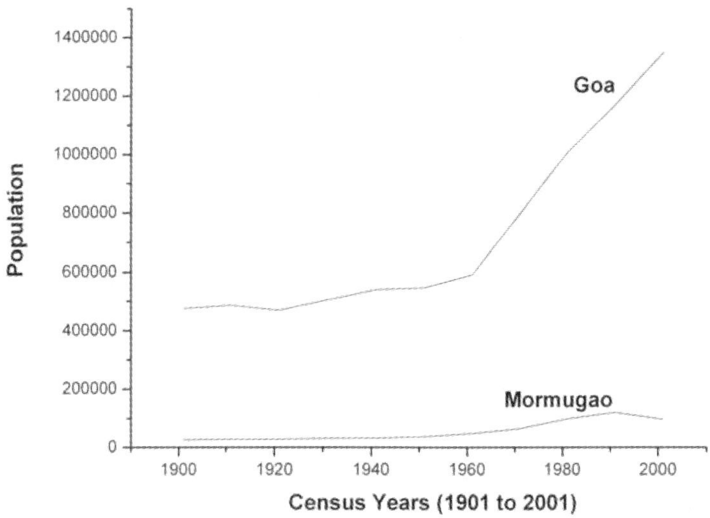

Figure 5: Population of Goa and Mormugao, 1900-2001

Sources: India, *Census*, various years; and Goa, Daman and Diu, *Statistical Packet Booklet*, various years.

[32]Goa today is experiencing a tremendous influx of population from the neighbouring states. This is helpful to Mormugao, which requires a good deal of physical labour. Goa has more than a *lakh* of its educated youth unemployed. This figure for a small state like Goa is very high compared to other states in India.

Conclusion

Mormugao Port has indeed been a "golden gateway" to Goa. The Luso-British Treaty of 1881 brought about sweeping changes in the Portuguese territory, and Mormugao has played a large role in many of these.

The port rose to prominence and became even more international after 1510. It was the first foothold for the Europeans on the lucrative spice routes. By the end of the tumultuous sixteenth century, Goa was one of the most dynamic cities in the world, larger than contemporary Paris or London and at the heart of a fabulously wealthy maritime empire that stretched from Japan to the southern coast of Africa. The Portuguese promoted Mormugao around the globe. The port has been well placed historically on important trade routes between East and West. It continues to be important in modern India as a facilitator of global trade. Almost forty percent of the iron ore of India is exported from Mormugao, largely due to improvements in infrastructure and an exceptionally good network of inland waterways, road and rail links. The success of this modern port is also due to the private mine owners who discovered and exploited important natural resources from the 1950s.

New Perspectives on Port Competition: Antwerp and Rotterdam, 1945-1975

Stéphane Hoste, Reginald Loyen and Stephan Vanfraechem

Introduction

In the Hamburg-Le Havre range of ports, Antwerp, Rotterdam, Hamburg, Bremen and Le Havre compete for market share. This competition is not based merely on cost or capacity; ports need to offer customers an attractive package. Accessibility, capacity, cost, flexibility, reliability and connections with the hinterland, among other factors, are important.

As authorities gear a port to meet the challenges of the twenty-first century, they often concentrate on infrastructure. Faced with increasing scale and growing demand for container-handling capacity, ports often push infrastructure as the dominant factor. To attract ever-larger vessels they need to offer both accessibility and sufficient capacity for rapid throughput. With charter prices between US $45,000 and $60,000 per day, "idle time" must be minimised. This puts upstream ports with longer sailing times, such as Antwerp, at a disadvantage. Investments in new deep-water container terminals in some ports in the Hamburg-Le Havre range (Port 2000 in Le Havre, Euromax in Rotterdam, Deurganckdok in Antwerp and Jade Weser Port in Wilhelmshaven, among others), and the effort that ports with limited natural draughts, such as Antwerp and Hamburg, are putting into improving accessibility show how port authorities and governments try to respond to the market. Yet infrastructure and port services need to be offered at a competitive price.[1] With declining freight rates, carriers increasingly are focusing on cost efficiency.

Carriers and shippers choose between ports on the basis of total costs. Although there are charges for port services, such as pilotage, towage and berthing – and while the costs of time and reliability should also be considered

[1]Hercules E. Haralambides and Albert W. Veenstra, "Port Pricing," in Costas Th. Grammenos (ed.), *The Handbook of Maritime Economics and Business* (London, 2002); and Haralambides, "Competition, Excess Capacity and the Pricing of Port Infrastructure," *International Journal of Maritime Economics*, IV, No. 4 (2002), 323-347.

– cargo handling comprises the bulk of port costs.[2] Labour costs account for between seventy and eighty percent of cargo-handling expenses, while the latter in turn represents seventy to eighty percent of total port costs. While it would be easy to assume that the port with the least expensive labour would attract more cargo, the level of service and the quality of investment also matter. Indeed, roughly twenty-five to thirty percent of total cargo-handling costs are related to the cost of investments.[3] On the other hand, costs and organisation are not the only issues carriers consider when analysing labour. With high fixed costs and charter rates, carriers will hesitate before sailing to a port with a reputation for labour unrest. A history of social peace may thus also be part of a port's marketing strategy. Ports are but one link in the supply chain. Freight forwarders examine the entire route from producer to consumer before deciding which port to use. Due to mergers, acquisitions and strategic alliances the savings on the seaborne leg are getting smaller, and the pressure to cut costs elsewhere is growing. Inland logistics is an area where savings can still be realised, since such transport often accounts for a much larger share of costs than vessel operations; its portion of total costs in container shipping ranges from forty to eighty percent. As a result, good hinterland connections are becoming more important. Since highways are becoming more congested, ports are seeking lower-cost alternatives to road transport.

In short, many factors influence port competition. To generate new insights scholars often turn to modelling to explain competitive performance. Recently, some factors mentioned above have been incorporated into a model based upon the well-known "Porter diamond." This essay tests whether such a model can be applied to the experiences of two northwest European ports notorious for their competition: Antwerp and Rotterdam. To what extent does this model explain the success of one port? Which factors determine the evolution of these ports? The discussion is limited to the expansionary postwar years. After defining port competition more precisely and introducing the model, we will examine inter-port competition at the commodity level to see which port dominated particular trades. The last sections examine the impact of some of the most important factors to try to explain this.

Port Competition

Port competition should be understood as a market phenomenon in which a port tries to devise an effective strategy in order to distinguish itself from its

---

[2]Jan O. Jansson and Dan Shneerson, *Liner Shipping Economics* (London, 1987); Jansson, *Transport System Optimisation and Pricing* (Stockholm, 1980); and Jansson and Shneerson, *Port Economics* (Cambridge, MA, 1982).

[3]European Union, Transport RTD Programme, *Analysis of the Cost Structures of the Main Ten Ports* (ATENCO) (Brussels, 2001), 145.

competitors. Competitiveness reflects the state of each port in a relevant market and the ability to retain old markets and to enter new ones. It results from the interplay among port authorities, terminal operators, labour and other service providers.

J.M. Verhoeff has discerned four interrelated levels of port competition. First, individual companies, such as terminal operators like ECT and DPWorld, compete for contracts. Second, port authorities compete with each other by offering enticing service packages in order to retain and attract customers (e.g., competition between the port authorities of Hong Kong and Shenzhen). A third type of competition exists between "port clusters," such as Antwerp/Rotterdam as opposed to Bremerhaven/Hamburg. A final level of competition is between "port ranges" with a more-or-less common hinterland, such as the Hamburg-Le Havre range versus Mediterranean ports.[4]

An increasing number of port economists, however, have rejected Verhoeff's schema for a model that stresses competition between logistical chains rather than ports.[5] As well as the classical transport links to the hinterland, this new approach also considers commercial and industrial services. It reflects the fact that total transport and handling costs have become increasingly important. These scholars discern three levels of competition. First, there is the rivalry between operators within a single port (intra-port competition) who try to acquire a certain cargo (an operator can handle more than one such flow and may operate in several ports simultaneously). A second kind of competition occurs between operators in different ports (inter-port competition). Finally, there is the struggle between ports on the policy level.[6]

---

[4]J.M. Verhoeff, "Zeehavenconcurrentie: een analyse van de aard dezer concurrentie," *Tijdschrift voor vervoerswetenschap*, IV (1977), 297-310; Verhoeff, "Zeehavenconcurrentie: overheidsproductie en havendiensten," in Verhoeff (ed.), *Vervoers- en haveneconomie: tussen actie en abstractie* (Leiden, 1981), 181-202; and Willy Winkelmans, *Elementen voor een havenbeleid* (Brussels, 1979), 179-217.

[5]Brian Slack, "Containerisation, Inter-port Competition and Port Selection," *Maritime Policy and Management*, XII, No. 4 (1985), 293-303; Yehuda Hayuth, "Port Competition and Regional Port Cooperation," in Gust Blauwens, *et al.* (eds.), *De dynamiek van een haven* (Kapellen, 1993), 210-226; Trevor D. Heaver, "The Implications of Increased Competition among Ports for Port Policy and Management," *Maritime Policy and Management*, XII, No. 2 (1995), 125-133; and Chris Coeck, *et al.*, "The Competitiveness of Seaports: Business and Government Agendas in Strategic Port Planning," in A.M. Goulielmos (ed.), *Essays in Honour and in Memory of Late Professor Emeritus of Maritime Economics Dr. Basil N. Metaxas* (Pireaus, 1997), 269-287.

[6]Marc Huybrechts, *et al.*, *Port Competitiveness. An Economic and Legal Analysis of the Factors Determining the Competitiveness of Seaports* (Antwerp, 2002), 9-13; and Elvira Haezendonck, *Essays on Strategy Analysis for Seaports* (Leuven, 2001), 12-17.

Thus, an analysis of port competition requires researchers to make choices, and we have done so here. Since our concern is to delineate the factors that influence the competitive advantage of one port over another - and because we are concerned that imposing a contemporary typology on historical data may distort reality - we have opted to use Verhoeff's model for our examination of competition between Antwerp and Rotterdam. Both ports, located close to each other and sharing almost identical hinterlands, have a strong tradition of competition. Since the nineteenth century each has been scrutinising the other's actions incessantly. But the two do not compete in a vacuum, since both need to fend off other competitors in the Hamburg-Le Havre range.

Port competition is determined by the interaction among a host of factors. Most experts include economic, political, financial, geophysical, technological, organisational, social and cultural elements but also refer to the quality and the cost of service within a regional, national and global context. Many scholars have attempted to integrate most or all of these factors in a model. Existing models, however, vary widely in scope, quality and explanatory power, and quite a few are unacceptable.

Without trying to create a typology of port models, the present article discerns two basic types. The first - "port range models" - explains the concentration of several smaller entities into one or two larger ports. This is mainly the purview of geographers and is often applied to ports in developing countries.[7] Many scholars have adapted this type of model or proposed extensions.[8] The second type - "single port models" - clarifies the expansion of a particular port. Apart from James Bird's renowned Anyport model, the UNCTAD model and the approach used by Arjen van Klink for Rotterdam are prominent examples.[9] This type of model clearly shows a port's different

---

[7]The best-known example is E.J. Taaffe, R.L. Morrill and P.R. Gould, "Transport Expansion in Underdeveloped Countries: A Comparative Analysis," *Geographical Review*, LIII (1963), 503-529.

[8]For example, see Peter J. Rimmer, "The Search for Spatial Regularities in the Development of Australian Seaports (1861-1961)," *Geografiska Annaler*, No. 1 (1967), 42-54; Yehuda Hayuth, "Containerisation and the Load Centre Concept," *Economic Geography*, LVII, No. 2 (1981), 160-188; and Brian Slack, "Intermodal Transportation in North America and the Development of Inland Load Centres," *Professional Geographer*, XLII (1990), 72-83.

[9]James Bird, *Seaports and Seaport Terminals* (London, 1971). This has been updated by Theo E. Notteboom and Jean-Paul Rodrigue, "Port Regionalisation: Towards a New Phase in Port Development," *Maritime Policy and Management*, XXXII, No. 3 (2005), 297-313; and United Nations Conference on Trade and Development (UNCTAD), *Review of Maritime Transport* (New York, 1993) 47-50. It has been criticised by Anthony K.C. Beresford, *et al.*, "The UNCTAD and WORKPORT Models of Port Development," *Maritime Policy and Management*, XXXI, No. 2 (2004), 93-107;

growth periods and - more important - offers an explanation for its development. Models like Anyport also include some attempts at generalisation towards other regional or international ports.

Generalisation and explanation are also key concerns of a new trend in the relatively novel sub-discipline of port competition. Verhoeff, writing in the early 1980s, was perhaps the first to discuss seaport competition in a comprehensive way. As competition between ports intensified due to containerisation, scholars have augmented their efforts to understand the phenomenon. Still, the literature remains scanty and methodologically unsound. Only a handful of studies have investigated the link between the package on offer and a user's final choice.[10] Very little theoretical research on port competition has been conducted. Indeed, even in the most recent research some authors examine "port competition," but not "port attractiveness," while others concentrate on "port-choice determinants" or on "intra-port competition." While all of these issues are related, there is a need for a comprehensive theoretical framework. The most that can be said of the literature at present is that it often features the well-known Porter diamond.[11]

Indeed, Elvira Haezendonck and her collaborators have designed a single-port model to explain a port's competitive position by applying the Porter diamond.[12] According to Porter, four variables determine the international success of nations or specific national industries. To relate this to ports, Por-

---

and H. Arjen van Klink, *Towards the Borderless Mainport Rotterdam: An Analysis of Functional, Spatial and Administrative Dynamics in Port Systems* (Amsterdam, 1995).

[10]Koi Yu Ng, "Assessing the Attractiveness of Ports in the North European Container Transhipment Market: An Agenda for Future Research in Port Compeittion," *Maritime Economics and Logistics*, VIII, No. 3 (2006), 238. Other such studies include Slack, "Containerisation and Inter-port Competition;" M.C. Willingale, "Ship-operator Port-routing Behaviour and the Development Process," in B.S Hoyle and David Hilling (eds.), *Seaport Systems and Spatial Change: Technology, Industry and Development Strategies* (New York, 1984), 43-59; Paul R. Murphy, James M. Daley and Douglas R. Dalenberg, "Selecting Links and Nodes in International Transportation: An Intermediary Perspective," *Transportation Research*, XXXI, No. 2 (1991), 33-40; Murphy, Daley and Dalenberg, "Port Selection Criteria: An Application of a Transport Research Framework," *Logistics and Transportation Review*, XXVIII, No. 3 (1992), 237-255; and Ximena Clark, David Dollar and Alejandro Micco, *Maritime Transport Costs and Port Efficiency* (Washington, DC, 2001).

[11]Ross Robinson, "Ports as Elements in Value-driven Chain Systems: The New Paradigm," *Maritime Policy and Management*, XXIX, No. 3 (2002), 241-255.

[12]Elvira Haezendonck, *et al.*, "The Competitive Advantage of Seaports," *International Journal of Maritime Economics*, II, No. 2 (2000), 69-81; and Michael E. Porter, *The Competitive Advantage of Nations* (London, 1990).

ter's original four features were extended to six.[13] On top of that, five geographic levels, ranging from regional to global, were brought in at each corner of the diamond.[14] In essence, the four original factors have been expanded to a set of thirty "potential influences" in the case of ports (see figure 1).

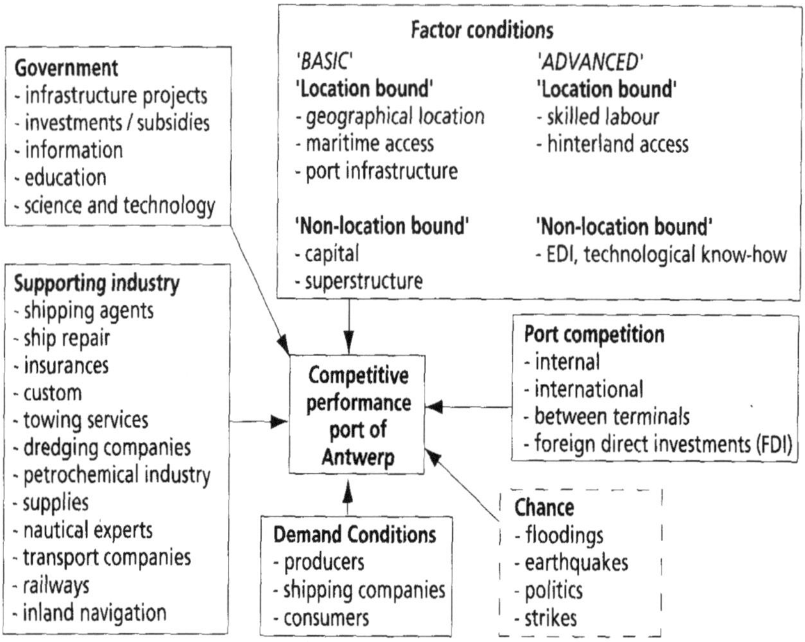

Figure 1: The Extended Port Diamond Applied to Ports

Source: Elvira Haezendonck, *et al.*, "The Competitive Advantage of Seaports," *International Journal of Maritime Economics*, II, No. 2 (2000), 69-82.

[13]Alan M. Rugman and Alain Verbeke, "How to Operationalize Porter's Diamond of International Competitiveness," *International Executive*, XXXV, No. 4 (1993), 283-299, reprinted in Rugman and Verbeke, *Analysis of Multinational Strategic Management: The Selected Scientific Papers of Alan M. Rugman and Alain Verbeke* (Cheltenham, 2005), 206-222.

[14]John H. Dunning, "The Geographical Sources of the Competitiveness of Firms: Some Results of a New Survey," *Transnational Corporations*, V, No. 3 (1996), 1-29, reprinted in Dunning, *The Selected Essays of John H. Dunning* (2 vols., Cheltenham, 2002), II, 315-339.

The six key variables merit elaboration. The first set are factor conditions, which refer to inputs used as key factors of production, such as skilled labour, natural resources, capital and infrastructure. Non-key factors (unskilled labour and raw materials) can be obtained by any firm and hence do not generate sustained competitive advantage, whereas key factors involve large, sustained investments and are more difficult to duplicate. In the case of ports, hinterland connections, maritime access and other means employed for providing port services count as key factor conditions. The second set comprises demand conditions. Porter argues that a sophisticated domestic market is important in producing competitiveness. Firms with a sophisticated domestic market are likely to sell superior products because such a market demands high quality. In the case of ports, the user requirements determine the demand conditions and ultimately the port's competitive position. The third set of factors involves the role of related and supporting industries. Such industries, including feeders, agencies, towing services and ship repairers, are important to the competitiveness of ports. The nature of the strategy, structure and rivalry of firms comprises the fourth set. This refers to the ways operators are organised and managed. Countries with capital markets with a short-run outlook tend to be more competitive in industries where investment is also short term. The fifth factor concerns the role of government. According to Porter, governments ought to encourage companies to raise their aspirations and improve performance. While he considers government to be important, in his model it remains external to the diamond. In the case of ports, however, government is integrated as a fifth corner of the diamond. Finally, chance or risk-related elements, like strikes and earthquakes, may play a role in determining the competitive position of a port.

This model seems a promising place to start, although it is worth noting that some authors have begun to question its applicability. Koi Yu Ng, for example, cites "the specific nature of the port industry, the model's encouragement of supply-led strategies, and overlooking user perception of service quality" as major deficiencies.[15] Such qualitative factors include "subjective influences like flexibility and ease of use, a port's marketing efforts, tradition, personal contacts and the level of cooperation that may be developed between the shipper and the port."[16] Glen D'Este and Steve Meyrick argue that the distinction between quantitative and qualitative factors is blurred because a shipper's perception of the level of port operations may not reflect actual perform-

[15]Ng, "Assessing the Attractiveness of Ports," 249, note 5.

[16]José L. Tongzon, "Port Choice Determinants in a Competitive Environment" (Unpublished paper presented to the International Association of Maritime Economists Conference, 2002).

ance.[17] The perception can sometimes be more decisive than performance in acquiring new trades. Nonetheless, most port research continues to focus upon quantifiable determinants because of the methodological difficulties in estimating qualitative factors. For the perception of service quality, Haezendonk's application of Porter's model obviously falls short of expectations.

A further examination of the model seems appropriate in order to assess its usefulness. Haezendonck and her collaborators consider that each of the determinants in their "extended diamond" is relevant to competitive success. In addition, they argue that "the competitive advantage or disadvantage of a port should be analysed for the various traffic categories separately."[18] They also admit that it is impossible to study all these influences simultaneously and hence that it is necessary to focus on "the critical factors." This approach will be at the centre of the analysis to follow.

Seaborne Cargo Flows of Antwerp and Rotterdam

Figure 2 depicts the expansion of total seaborne throughput in the ports of Antwerp and Rotterdam since 1947. With the exception of the late 1940s, Rotterdam handled more seaborne cargo than Antwerp throughout the entire third quarter of the twentieth century. For a brief period, however, the Belgian port handled more goods because its facilities had not suffered extensive damage during the hostilities.[19] In the meantime, ports like Rotterdam and Hamburg that had been virtually destroyed had the opportunity to rebuild and to consider their needs in a comprehensive manner.[20] Once this process had been completed, the "new" ports soon caught up. Rotterdam first surpassed Antwerp in 1949 (20.7 compared to 19.8 million tons). In the first half of the 1950s, throughput in Antwerp increased by eight percent as opposed to nineteen per-

---

[17]Glen M. D'Este and Steve Meyrick, "Carrier Selection in a Ro/Ro Ferry Trade. Part I: Decision Factors and Attitudes," *Maritime Policy and Management*, XIX, No. 2 (1992), 115-126.

[18]Coeck, *et al.*, "Competitiveness of Seaports."

[19]Oscar Leemans, "Haven van Antwerpen. Oorlogsschade, herstel en toekomstplannen," *Economisch en sociaal tijdschrift* (1948), 102-106.

[20]Paul van de Laar, *Stad van formaat. Geschiedenis van Rotterdam in de negentiende en twintigste eeuw* (Zwolle, 2000), 451-470; Gerard E. van Walsum, *et al.* (eds.), *Rotterdam Europoort 1945-1970* (Rotterdam, 1972), 15-23; Arnold Kludas, Dieter Maass and Susanne Sabisch, *Hafen Hamburg. Die Geschichte des Hamburger Freihafens von den Anfängen bis zur Gegenwart* (Hamburg, 1988), 183-202; and Fernand Suykens, *et al.*, *Antwerp: A Port for All Seasons* (Antwerp, 1986), 457-462 and 481.

cent in Rotterdam. This continued in the second half of the 1950s (nine versus five percent).

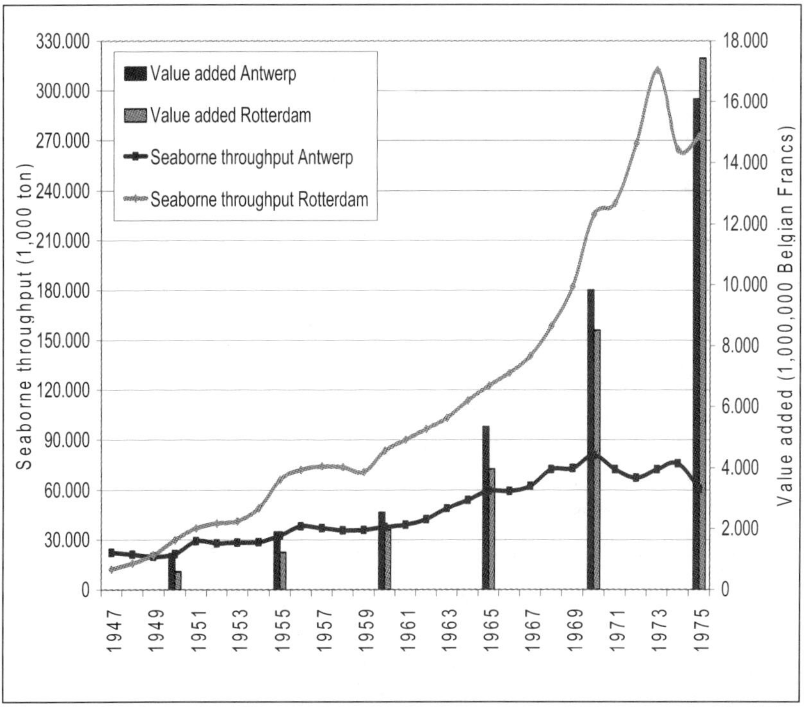

Figure 2: Total Seaborne Throughput and Value Added, Antwerp and Rotterdam, 1947-1975

Sources: Belgium, National Institute of Statistics (NIS), *Jaarstatistieken over de internationale trafiek der havens* (Brussels, 1947-1975); Rotterdamse Kamer van Koophandel en Fabrieken, *Statistiek van handel, nijverheid en verkeer* (Rotterdam, 1947-1975); Reginald Loyen, "From Register Tonnage to Added Value. The Cautious Advent of a New Performance Indicator," in Ferry de Goey (ed.), *Comparative Port History of Rotterdam and Antwerp: Competition, Cargo and Costs* (Amsterdam, 2004), 216-241.

In the first half of the 1950s, throughput reached twenty-nine million tons in Antwerp and thirty-nine million in Rotterdam, and the latter exceeded the sixty-million-ton mark by 1955. The fact that Antwerp would need another decade to attain this level underscores Rotterdam's spectacular growth. Indeed, the Dutch port broke records continuously after the Botlek area opened, and it became the largest port in the world by 1962.[21] In a decade throughput grew from 83.4 to 225 million tons, and Rotterdam opened Europoort to accommodate it. The same type of growth did not occur in Antwerp despite a "Ten Year Plan" for expansion; over the same time span its traffic merely increased from 37.5 to 80.7 million tons. Only in 1960-1964 did Antwerp's throughput expand almost as fast as Rotterdam's. After 1965, Antwerp again grew by just six percent while Rotterdam's traffic expanded on average by ten percent per annum. While the Dutch port stagnated in 1970-1971, this lull was short-lived. Rotterdam peaked in 1973 with 312.5 million tons, while throughput in Antwerp declined to 72.3 million tons. In the first half of the 1970s, Antwerp almost ceased expanding, whereas Rotterdam continued to grow. Antwerp lost great amounts of traffic because of the construction of the Rotterdam-Antwerp Pipeline (RAPL).[22] During the latter half of the 1970s, however, Rotterdam stagnated due to the shocks induced by the oil crises that marred the decade.

An analysis by tonnage clearly shows Rotterdam leading Antwerp. But in terms of value-added created by classical port operations, Antwerp was more important.[23] In 1950 the value-added created in Antwerp was 1189 million Belgian Francs (BEF) versus BEF 593 million in Rotterdam. This is because Antwerp handled much more general cargo, which in turn created many jobs. By 1955, Rotterdam drew closer with BEF 1225 million compared with Antwerp's BEF 1894 million. By 1965, however, despite more than doubling Antwerp's throughput, Rotterdam's value added had reached BEF 3959 million by handling 123 million tons, while Antwerp stood at BEF 5335 million from sixty million tons of throughput. Antwerp maintained its lead in 1970, but by 1975 Rotterdam (BEF 17,432 million) had surpassed Antwerp (BEF 16,082 million) in value-added. Rotterdam surged ahead because the dominant feature of its seaborne throughput changed from liquid bulk to containers as it attracted new high value-added cargoes while Antwerp's general cargo disappeared into containers.

---

[21]A.B.M. van der Plas and B. Westerduin, "Nieuwe wegen naar het achterland. Het achterland van de Rotterdamse haven (1970-1995)," in G.C. Meeuse and Cora Boele (eds.), *Rotterdam een haven* (1970-1995) (Rotterdam, 1996), 21; and van de Laar, *Stad van formaat*, 512.

[22]Suykens, *et al.*, *Antwerp*, 507-510; and Paul Mingret, *La croissance industrielle du port d'Anvers* (Brussels, 1976), 435-464.

[23]Reginald Loyen, "From Register Tonnage to Added Value. The Cautious Advent of a New Performance Indicator," in Ferry de Goey (ed.), *Comparative Port History of Rotterdam and Antwerp: Competition, Cargo and Costs* (Amsterdam, 2004), 216-241.

Composition of Throughput

Compared to Rotterdam, Antwerp attracted a more balanced and diverse slate of cargoes throughout the period. From 1960 onwards more than half of Rotterdam's throughput consisted of crude oil, which expanded on average by more than ten percent per year. In Antwerp, crude oil was also the most significant cargo, but it never comprised more than thirty-nine percent of throughput in a given year. Instead, ores and metals played a major role; together these three goods accounted for sixty to seventy percent of Antwerp's throughput, whereas in Rotterdam crude oil alone accounted for a similar share. As a relatively diverse port, Antwerp was less vulnerable to fluctuations because, at least in theory, other goods could compensate if a particular trade collapsed. Yet the decline caused by the opening of the RAPL indicates the extent to which dependence on one trade can affect a port's performance.

Oil dominated the postwar development of both ports unlike any other commodity. Both contained refineries and petrochemical plants, but Rotterdam soon emerged as virtually the only European port capable of handling the expanding flow of crude oil. The Suez crisis in 1956 accelerated Rotterdam's expansion because a deep-sea oil port was needed for the Ultra Large Crude Carriers (ULCCs) now sailing the oceans. Rotterdam slowly assumed a distribution function for Western Europe.[24] In fact, its sustained reliance on oil in the 1970s resulted from a need to finance the deepening of its maritime access.[25] During the oil crises it became apparent that the port needed the ULCCs to foot the expansion bill. Antwerp, while it relied upon a broader range of cargoes, did not really diversify as much as might have been expected. Of the five trades with a share of ten percent or more in the 1950s, only three remained in the 1970s (crude oil, ores and metals). Agricultural produce had been very important prior to World War II (half of seaborne throughput) but stagnated after the war, at least in part because of the introduction of the European Common Agricultural Policy.[26] Moreover, coal also

---

[24]Several international pipelines were built for that purpose. Ferry de Goey, *Ruimte voor industrie: Rotterdam en de vestiging van industrie in de haven 1945-1975* (Rotterdam, 1990), 82-89; and Willem K. Scholten, "De Rotterdamse haven en het havenbedrijf van 1970 tot 1995," in Meeuse and Boele (eds.), *Rotterdam een haven*, 41.

[25]For the exact financial obligations, see van Walsum, *et al.* (eds.), *Rotterdam*, 78 and 92-94.

[26]Emiel Geeraert, "De graantrafiek in de haven van Antwerpen," *Economisch en sociaal tijdschrift*, XIII, No. 5 (1959), 302-317; Leo van Echelpoel, "Vijfentwintig jaar Europese Economische Gemeenschap: het landbouwbeleid en zijn weerslag op de Belgische havens," in Eddy van de Voorde (ed.), *Haven en vervoer in de hedendaagse*

dropped sharply as the Belgian economy switched to oil, and mines were closed in the hinterland. The advent of nuclear energy and the crumbling steel industry also contributed to the demise of coal.

Table 1
Average Shares of Antwerp and Rotterdam in Total Seaborne Throughput by Standard Goods Classification for Transport (NST) Category, 1950-1974

NST	1950-1954 Antwerp	1950-1954 Rotterdam	1955-1959 Antwerp	1955-1959 Rotterdam	1960-1964 Antwerp	1960-1964 Rotterdam	1965-1969 Antwerp	1965-1969 Rotterdam	1970-1974 Antwerp	1970-1974 Rotterdam
0	51	49	36	64	35	65	32	68	29	71
1	31	69	27	73	26	74	23	77	18	82
2	27	73	23	77	26	74	21	79	23	77
3	22	78	21	79	20	80	24	76	12	88
4	39	61	36	64	36	64	38	62	31	69
5	82	18	80	20	74	26	76	24	72	28
6	71	29	48	52	39	61	30	70	39	61
7	54	46	51	49	47	53	40	60	48	52
8	46	54	42	58	35	65	32	68	33	67
9	65	35	59	41	54	46	55	45	50	50
Total	41	59	33	67	31	69	31	69	22	78

Notes: Calculations by the authors. NST categories: 0: Agricultural produce; 1: Foodstuffs and fodder; 2: Solid mineral fuels; 3: Petroleum and petroleum products; 4: Ores and metal waste; 5: Iron, steel and non-ferrous metals (incl. semi-manufactures); 6: Crude minerals and mineral products and building materials; 7: Fertilisers; 8: Chemical products; 9: Vehicles, machinery and other goods.

Sources: See figure 2.

This brief survey, however, does not reveal which port dominated which cargo flow. Table 1 presents the average market shares of Antwerp and Rotterdam by commodity group and offers a better insight into port competition. We assume that a port dominates a trade if it controls a market share of at least three-quarters (more or less). For Rotterdam this was the case for foodstuffs, coal and petroleum. The Dutch port reverted to foodstuff shipments in the late 1960s when protectionist European legislation hampered the grain

---

economie. Liber amicorum professor Louis Baudez, S.J. (Antwerp, 1982), 133-148; and Suzanne Pirlot, *Evolutie van de graantrafiek, graanopslag en graanoverslag in de haven van Antwerpen tussen 1965 en 1990* (Antwerp, 1991).

trade.[27] Throughout the third quarter of the century Antwerp achieved dominance only in metals: in the 1950s it captured eighty to eighty-two percent of the throughput of metals, a share that shrunk to seventy-two percent by the late 1970s. The collapse of the Belgian steel industry played a major role in this decline.

Neither Rotterdam nor Antwerp achieved dominance in any of the remaining five cargoes. Crude minerals, fertilisers and the "other goods" (NST 9) were among the foci of port competition. In the 1945-1975 period, market shares in minerals fluctuated without either port gaining absolute dominance. There was a similar scenario for fertilisers, where Antwerp had a slight advantage (except for the 1960s). In the case of NST 9, Antwerp initially had a small lead, which diminished from sixty-five percent in the 1950s to fifty-five percent in the 1960s. Thereafter, both ports were well matched. More than anything else, the advent of the container explains this turnaround.[28]

Port Labour

Labour is considered as a separate factor in the port diamond and accounts for an estimated seventy to eighty percent of total cargo-handling costs. According to the model, labour relates to the attributes government and support industry (transport companies). For historians, cargo-handling costs are a difficult subject. Stevedores and their employers' federations often disguised their tariffs so that competitors could not set cheaper rates. On the rare occasions when official tariffs were published, thus enabling systematic comparisons, caution is still required.[29] While we recognise that labour was an important determinant of port competition, our analysis concentrates on the years from the late 1930s to the 1950s because it was in this period that the labour systems in both ports were shaped.

---

[27]Van Walsum, *et al.* (eds.), *Rotterdam*, 87.

[28]Theo Notteboom, "Thirty-five Years of Containerisation in Antwerp and Rotterdam: Structural Changes in the Container Handling Market," in Reginald Loyen, *et al.* (eds), *Struggling for Leadership: A Century and a Half of Antwerp-Rotterdam Port Competition* (Heidelberg, 2003), 117-141.

[29]It is common to award considerable reductions on official cargo-handling rates secretly to important clients. Hugo van Driel, Reginald Loyen and Stéphane Hoste, "Cargo-handling Costs: Competition in the Break-bulk Sector," in de Goey (ed.), *Comparative Port History*, 177-213.

In the interwar period the port of Antwerp found itself in a very favourable position in terms of labour costs.[30] Dockers' wages were considerably lower than in Rotterdam, and Antwerp billed itself as the "quickest and cheapest port of Europe."[31] An additional advantage for Antwerp was that ships could be loaded and unloaded around the clock since its dockers were willing to work overtime as long as employers agreed to pay substantial bonuses, which they were willing to do in peak periods.

From October 1937, however, a sweeping reduction in working hours in Antwerp increased its vulnerability. To end a general strike in June 1936, the Belgian government examined the reduction of working hours in some sectors. Despite strong opposition from the employers' federations in the port, an agreement was agreed to reduce working hours to seven per day and forty per week. The Antwerp Shipping Federation, the organisation of the shipping agents, reacted furiously: "La réduction de la durée des shifts porterait une grave préjudice résultant d'une augmentation sensible du coût des marchandises et d'une diminution sérieuse dans l'efficience du travail portuaire."[32] The Federation argued for a work day of at least 7.5 hours because Rotterdam dockers still worked 8.5 hours per day. If this was not granted, the Federation feared that tramp shipping, which made use of the day shift, would leave for Rotterdam. Despite critical articles in the maritime press, the seven-hour day was nevertheless adopted, thus ending the era when Antwerp labour was less expensive.[33]

---

[30]For an extensive survey of labour relations in the port of Antwerp during the twentieth century, see Stephan Vanfraechem, *Een sfeer om haring te braden: arbeidsverhoudingen in de Antwerpse haven 1880-1972* (Gent, 2005).

[31]Johannes P. Backx, *De haven van Rotterdam: een onderzoek naar de oorzaken van haar economische betekenis in vergelijking met die van Hamburg en Rotterdam* (Rotterdam, 1929), 276; Jos De Keuster, *La concurrence entre trois grands ports nord-européens: Hamburg-Rotterdam-Anvers* (Antwerp, 1930), 231; John Coopman, *De haven van Antwerpen. Haar inrichting, haar bewerktuiging, haar economische beteekenis* (Antwerp, 1930), 230; Marcel van de Velde, *Le port d'Anvers. Aperçu de la situation économique et politique du port national Belge en comparaison avec celle des ports de Rotterdam et Dunkerque* (Antwerpen, 1928), 213; and *Beschouwingen over de haven van Rotterdam: zes lezingen gehouden voor het departement Rotterdam van de Nederlandse maatschappij voor nijverheid en handel* (Rotterdam, 1932), 195.

[32]Antwerp Shipping Federation Archives, Rapports, Assemblées générales, Assemblée générale extraordinaire, 29 December 1936.

[33]*Scandinavian Shipping*, 24 November 1937, refered to the renewal of contracts with shipping lines: "It is precisely the renewal of these contracts which is causing serious misgivings. Rotterdam, Dunkirk and Hamburg have in most cases been asked to quote and if we are to believe information received from authoritative sources,

World War II had a decisive impact on the evolution of the ports. The Belgian port was left relatively intact by the retreating Germans whereas Rotterdam lay in ruins. As a result, the port of Antwerp boomed. More than 20,000 registered dockers worked in the port, more than 5000 more than before the war. This was, however, not the only difference between the competitors. After the Liberation both the Dutch and Belgian governments drew up plans to restrain price and wage growth.[34] Both adopted virtually the same solution when it came to ports: bilateral wage bargaining between trade unions and employers was replaced by a central wage policy controlled by the government. Governments would decide the level of wages in order to control inflation.

But while the medicine was the same, the patients reacted quite differently. In the postwar Netherlands, the Buitengewoon Besluit Arbeidsverhoudingen (BBA), or "Extraordinary Decree Concerning Labour Relations," of 17 July 1944 formed the legal basis for negotiations over wages and working conditions. The BBA was relatively inflexible and limited the freedom of both trade unions and employers considerably. Its main objective was to provide a solid basis for the reconstruction of the national economy, and its impact was enormous. Each collective agreement was to be evaluated by a College van Rijksbemiddelaars (CvR), or "Board of State Mediators," and a Stichting van de Arbeid (SvA), or "Labour Foundation." Each sector had to present the agreement to the SvA which advised the CvR. If the CvR felt that the pact exceeded national levels, the parties were forced to renegotiate. In this way the government maintained effective control over wage rates.

The use of strikes became more difficult under the BBA. Indeed, it limited the ability to strike in several ways. First, the unions agreed that reconstruction was so important that strikes had to be avoided at all costs. Although unions did not agree to give up the ability to strike, it is clear that they accepted that this weapon should not be used during reconstruction. This is why they accepted the edict that strikes were absolutely forbidden during the term of any collective agreement; only during negotiations for a new agreement did

---

Antwerp quotations now would for the first time in history be above those submitted by these competing ports. No doubt this is due to the extra charges resulting from the application of the seven-hour day and it is therefore of the highest importance to recommend new amendments to the new labour charter which is in force in Antwerp, before it is too late as, obviously, once a traffic had found another way, it is exceedingly difficult to regain it."

[34]For Belgium, see Dirk Luyten, *Sociaal-economisch overleg in België sedert 1918* (Brussels, 1995); and Hans Slomp amd Tjeu van Mierlo, *Arbeidsverhoudingen in België* (2 vols., Utrecht, 1984). For the Netherlands, see Slomp and van Mierlo, *Arbeidsverhoudingen in Nederland* (2 vols., Utrecht, 1984). In English, see Slomp, *Labour Relations in Europe: A History of Issues and Development* (New York, 1990).

unions have the right to call a strike. In practice, however, most sectors tried to prevent this by finalising new agreements before the conclusion of the current one. The long-term impact of the BBA was also great, since the Dutch government retained it until 1964, and most aspects of collective bargaining still had to be approved by the CvR and the SvA.

The port of Rotterdam is a perfect example of the way in which wages and working conditions evolved in postwar Holland. Collective bargaining between unions and employers was conducted as usual, but the agreements had to be presented to the CvR and the SvA for final approval. As a result, the negotiating space was quite limited. But strikes could not be completely ruled out. Indeed, tension between the official trade unions (Centrale Bond van Transportarbeiders, or CBT, and the Uniebonden, which was recognized by the government and the employers) and the upstart Eenheids Vak Centrale (EVC) formed the basis of a strike that lasted from 29 June to 3 July 1945. The CBT and Uniebonden had negotiated a twenty-five percent wage increase that was approved by the SvA and the CvR and were discussing its implementation when the EVC condemned the formally-recognized unions for not achieving this more expeditiously. A short strike ensued, with the result that the employers recognized the EVC, which now became a formal participant in future negotiations. Although several smaller strikes followed in the next decade (August 1950 and August 1955), during the immediate postwar period the port was fairly quiet. The main outcome was that wages evolved at a very moderate pace and followed national trends. Thereafter, wage growth, agreed to by the SvA and CvR, was higher than in some other sectors, including the port of Antwerp. The gradual loosening of the central wage policy increased from 1960 until it was formally abandoned by the Dutch government in 1964.

This does not mean, however, that either the employers or the unions were anxious to maintain the *status quo*. Casual employment of dockers, for example, was a subject of discussion and reorganisation. In 1954 the Centrale voor Arbeidsvoorziening, a hiring office which provided casual dockers to the cargo handlers in the port, was established. Most firms went further and engaging former casual workers on contracts, and the majority of dockers in the port of Rotterdam eventually had fixed contracts with one company. The main motivation for doing this from the employers' perspective was that they believed that they could better control the workers under these conditions.

In Belgium the picture was completely different. In September 1944 the government convened a National Labour Conference and invited unions and employers' federations to participate. A series of measures was adopted to prevent uncontrolled wage growth. As a first step, the Conference agreed that wages could increase by no more than sixty percent over the levels of 1940 (a similar agreement in the Netherlands limited this to only one-quarter). Pressure from various sectors – often supported by strikes – led the government to agree in July 1945 to a new twenty-percent wage increase. Before long the

Conference agreements were dead letters: "Dans beaucoup de branches, le blocage des salaires était nominal, les employeurs accordant des 'glissements' pour retenir le personnel. L'action en faveur de la baisse des prix n'eut guère de résultats non plus. En période de conjoncture ascendante aucun des 'blocages' n'était effectif.'"[35]

Where in Rotterdam trade unions supported national reconstruction and tempered their wage demands, labour costs in Antwerp during the period 1944-1948 rose sharply, especially compared to what occurred in the Dutch port. As table 2 shows, the result was that Antwerp became much more expensive than Rotterdam from 1947 onwards.

Table 2
Wages and Indexed Wages in Antwerp and Rotterdam, 1938-1948 (BEF)

Year	Antwerp		Rotterdam	
	Wage (7 hours)	Index	Wage (7 hours)	Index
1938	72	100	81	100
1947	190	263	126	153
1948	195	271	130	159

Note: 1938 = 100

Source: Calculations by the authors.

An important factor in explaining the pattern of wage increases in Antwerp was the presence of a small communist action committee in the port.[36] This committee was quite successful in convincing casual dockers in particular that they were not reaping the benefits of the port's success. After the Liberation more than 20,000 dockers worked in the port, but in the second half of 1945 seaborne traffic stagnated. As a result, unemployment became an important issue. The official trade unions – the socialist Belgian Transport Workers Federation (BTWF) and the Catholic Central of Transport Workers (CCTW) – had many difficulties in controlling the mass of casual labourers. Especially in the immediate postwar period, employers and the formal trade unions often had to deal with wildcat strikes, such as those in August 1945, August 1946, December 1946 and July 1947. Although the evidence is not

[35]B-S. Chlepner, *Cent ans d'histoire sociale en Belgique* (Brussels, 1956; 3rd ed., Brussels, 1972), 248.

[36]On the impact of this communist action committee on collective bargaining and labour relations in the port of Antwerp, see Stephan Vanfraechem, "La peur du rouge: The Impact of Communist Action Committees on Labour Relations in the Port of Antwerp during the 1940s," *The Northern Mariner/Le Marin du Nord*, XIII, No. 2 (2003), 25-42.

great, it appears as though the communist action committee lay behind most of these. Demands for wage increases, greater democracy and better compensation for temporary unemployment among casual dockworkers were recurring themes. Although the action committee had no more than 130 paid members – compared with about 10,000 for the BTWF – it managed to set the agenda for labour negotiations. The BTWF found itself hammered on both sides: the employers claimed that it was acting irresponsibly while the communists claimed that it was doing too little for the workers. The result was that the formal unions kept pushing for wage increases which, for the most part, the employers granted. Antwerp became even more expensive than Rotterdam in terms of labour.

The BTWF tried to find a way to ameliorate the increasingly uncompetitive position of the port of Antwerp by appealing to the international solidarity of its overseas counterparts.[37] For instance, the seven-hour day was a clear disadvantage for Antwerp, especially compared with the situation in Rotterdam, where the working day was still 8.5 hours. The Belgians wanted the foreign unions to fight for equal wages and working conditions. While the Dutch (along with the French and British) unions supported the introduction of the seven-hour day and a forty-hour week in their home ports, they rejected the calls for equal wage rates in 1948:

> as far as wages were concerned, owing to the existence of a government control of wages and prices, a policy backed by the labour and trade-union movement, coupled with the fact that dockers today ranked amongst the highest paid skilled occupations, it was not practicable to press for further increases on a general scale.[38]

International solidarity proved difficult to attain. From the mid-1950s the BTWF became stronger and was able to pursue a more realistic course:

> In a common market competition will become more and more dominant. The expansion and the modernisation of the port is simply a necessity...In a new Europe without frontiers our port will have to face the competition of other ports. Our

[37]ITF Archives (London), Report on Activities and Financial Report, Congress held in Zürich, 6-12 May 1946, "Inter-port Competition and Working Conditions," 91.

[38]*Ibid.*, 251.

> main target should be not to maintain our traffic but to expand it.[39]

This new vision was put into effect during the wage negotiations of May 1955. Even before the negotiations began, expectations were tempered. When the dockers asked for a raise of thirty to fifty BEF, the secretary of the BTWF responded that even twenty-five BEF was too much in light of government initiatives to lower the prices of Belgian manufacturers. A pay increase of twelve BEF was agreed and presented to the dockers as non-negotiable. The union backed this by arguing that high wages were making it increasingly difficult for Antwerp to compete with Rotterdam. In the following years the unions actively tempered the expectations of their members. Demands for the introduction of a five-day week in 1956 and a significant pay increase in 1959 was rejected by the unions. In 1961 the secretary of the BTWF even stated that a return to the eight-hour day was inevitable if the five-day week was introduced. In the end, the five-day week was approved on the condition that daily working hours were increased to 7.5 hours.

The gap between Antwerp and Rotterdam in labour costs would, however, diminish only gradually. In fact, it was only after the Netherlands completely abandoned its central wage policy in 1964 that wage growth in the two ports began to be synchronised (see table 3). This brief survey of labour relations in both ports indicates that labour indeed played a major role in port competition.

Table 3
Wages and Indexed Wages in Antwerp and Rotterdam, 1956-1961 (BEF)

Year	Antwerp		Rotterdam	
	Wage (7 hours)	Index	Wage (7 hours)	Index
1956	257	100	155	100
1957	269	105	176	114
1958	281	109	183	118
1959	281	109	189	122
1960/61	298	116	212	137

Note: 1956 = 100

Source: See table 2.

Ship-handling Costs

The port diamond model also considers ship-handling costs as important determinants of port competition. According to the model ship-handling costs

[39]Archief BTB, Verslagboeken: Uitvoerend comité, Algemene vergadering der dokwerkers, 18 March 1958.

relate to the attributes "government" and "supporting industry" (towage services and nautical experts). Unlike cargo-handling charges, however, ship-handling costs represent only a small part of total port costs.[40] In fact, despite the attention often paid to them, the dues payable to port authorities are generally much less significant than cargo-handling costs and the opportunity costs of a ship's time in port.[41] In other words, the shipowner will rarely consider them heavy financial burdens or strategic problems. Yet it is important to remember that a dollar can only be spent once and that every shipowner will bargain for the best rate possible. But from the perspective of port authorities, port dues remain the most important generator of revenue for future investments in infrastructure.

Apart from port dues, ship-handling costs also include pilotage, towage and berthage.[42] These three activities are obviously interconnected. Towage costs are divided into charges for towing while still at sea, on the river and in the port. They are calculated according to the draught of a vessel and increase proportionally with distance and duration. Pilotage dues are calculated in much the same way. The dues can be divided into two parts: pilotage during access to the port and pilotage while in the port. The mooring and unmooring of vessels are done by boatmen. It is usual that charges are levied based upon the time required; since bigger vessels require a longer mooring time, ship length is generally used to set the rates.

As early as 1914, Antwerp implemented a reasonably balanced system of port dues. It comprised an extensive range of frequency reductions that constituted an important advantage for liners. Rotterdam, on the other hand, was only in 1933 able to develop a dues structure in relation to the needs of the port when it was freed from government control. The statute of 1933 in fact reconsidered the custom of Rotterdam to give a tariff advantage to liner shipping. Partly due to the fact that the Rotterdam port authority was well informed about the abolition of the privileged Antwerp tariff for liners moored

---

[40]Jansson and Shneerson, *Port Economics*, 89; and Martin Stopford, *Maritime Economics* (London, 1988; 3rd ed., London, 2000), 160 and 170-171.

[41]Richard O. Goss, "Economic Policies and Seaports: The Economic Functions of Seaports," *Maritime Policy and Management*, XVII, No. 3 (1990), 212; and Jean-Georges Baudelaire, *Administration et exploitation portuaires* (Paris, 1979), 257.

[42]In Rotterdam an additional fee, called "quay dues," was charged for ship handling. These dues varied by ship type (sea-going or inland) and calculated according to the vessel's length. In the port of Antwerp no comparable system existed. After 1945 the Antwerp port authorities rented the mooring places directly to the shipowners and their agents, but the cost was not converted into an extra charge. See Stéphane Hoste and Reginald Loyen, "Ship Handling Costs: Competition over Port Dues," in de Goey (ed.), *Comparative Port History*, 149-150.

along the quays on the Scheldt, a large reduction in dues was introduced depending on the amount of cargo handled. The Rotterdam authority argued that while gross tonnage was indeed related to costs, it was an unjust standard when a ship was only partly loaded. This is why Rotterdam devised a formula that corrected for the load factor (a similar revision of the Antwerp port dues only came about in 1980). On the eve of World War II the two ports clearly had different priorities in assessing port dues.

Pilotage dues, predominantly those covering maritime access, also generated competition between Antwerp and Rotterdam in the interwar period. The problem with these dues was that they were linked with one another in terms of decision-making and pricing systems. This difficulty was partially solved in 1936 when both ports reduced the initial tariffs to no less than fourteen percent.[43] But the principle of free pilotage choice for navigation on the Scheldt fed a rivalry between Belgian and Dutch pilotage services active on the river.[44] This competition eventually came to an end in July 1950 when the two countries signed a treaty to divide the profits from pilotage dues.[45] But the level of the dues remained an issue because of exchange rate issues and the interpretation of key clauses in the Belgian-Dutch Separation Treaty of April 1839.[46]

Shortly after World War II a new conflict led to a situation where sea pilotage dues were 5.5 times higher in Rotterdam. The Dutch representatives on the Permanent Committee that supervised navigation on the Scheldt proposed to recalculate pilotage dues based upon the gold standard. Existing

---

[43]D. Roos, "Maas- en Scheldemond; loodsgeldtarief gebonden," *De Nederlandse Loods*, XXVIII, No. 3 (1986), 8; and J. Verseput, *Gedenkboek Kamer van Koophandel en Fabrieken voor Rotterdam 1928-1953* (Rotterdam, 1955), 99-101.

[44]"When a ship was in the sight, then the sloops with rowers of both services got into action, after which one service raced the other to bring his pilot on board of the ship first. The most confusing situations occurred. The captain of the ship, not always familiar with the local situation, was confronted with two pilots offering both their services. It was not unusual that, if he did not make up his mind rapidly, the pilots flew at each other." Cited in D. Roos "De concurrentiestrijd tussen de Nederlandse en Belgische loodsdiensten op de Westerschelde en haar mondingen (1839-1939)," *Zeeuws Tijdschrift*, IV (1983), 126.

[45]*Ibid.*, 132-134.

[46]This passage gave rise to conflicts because the length (and interpretation) of Dutch and Belgian nautical miles differed. Moreover, at the settlement of the Scheldt and Maas tariff, only the distance proportions were taken into account as far as the "inland tariff" was concerned. The "sea tariff," on the other hand, for the Scheldt estuary was as much as for the Maas estuary although the distance was three to four times longer; Roos, "Maas- en Scheldemond," 8-10.

charges would be multiplied by a factor of twenty. On legal grounds, however, this could not be realised. A solution materialised after 1947 when both the Belgian and Dutch governments agreed on a multiplication factor of 5.7. The equalization of Dutch and Belgian pilotage dues was finally realized in 1958 when the differences arising from the 1839 treaty were resolved. Because the pilotage dues decreased in the totality of ship-handling costs in the 1950s (from sixteen to six percent for a typical cargo liner), the conflict, although protracted, had only a limited impact on port choice.[47] The complete equalization of Dutch and Belgian pilotage dues nevertheless closed a long-standing element of competition. While it would thus be tempting to exclude them as explanatory variables in the context of Antwerp-Rotterdam competition, it should be noted that the share of pilotage dues as a component of ship-handling costs increased sharply in the second half of the 1960s to thirty-five percent for a typical cargo liner.

Rotterdam started offering a full liner service tariff - in the sense that liners paid a lower maximum than tramps - in April 1948. Moreover, a supplementary reduction of twenty percent was granted to liners that visited the port at least once a week, although even this was insufficient compared to the discounts that Antwerp offered liners. On the other hand, bulk shipping had a major advantage in Rotterdam. Taking advantage of the increases in scale, port dues were revised so that the bigger the ship, the bigger the difference compared with the Antwerp tariffs. During the period that Rotterdam rose to become the biggest port of the world (1948-1964), port dues were not increased, while in Antwerp port dues were increased by twenty-six percent in 1958. As a consequence, bulk ships paid thirty to forty percent less in ship-handling costs in Rotterdam. For liners the difference amounted to twenty percent. This, however, was levelled out by additional frequency reductions in Antwerp for ships making more than twenty passages per year.[48]

Because investments in infrastructure and maritime access started to weigh heavily on the municipal budget, the Rotterdam port authority increased its port dues in 1965 by one-quarter. The difference in ship-handling costs between the two ports by then had almost vanished. Although for bulk carriers and liners the difference amounted to ten to fifteen percent in favour of Rotterdam, the lack of any fixed port dues for container ships meant that total ship-handling costs for a second-generation container vessel were almost identical in both ports. What shifted, however, was the charge levied for unloading oil tankers in Rotterdam in 1969. The result was that while in the 1960s a typical oil tanker paid thirty percent less in ship-handling charges in Rotterdam, in the 1970s they paid sixteen percent more than in Antwerp. The reason for this was

[47]Hoste and Loyen, "Ship Handling Costs," 161.

[48]*Ibid.*, 163.

the need to deepen the New Waterway, a cost that the government declined to share.[49]

Yet because Rotterdam enjoyed a near monopoly position in distributing crude petroleum to Western Europe, this more expensive tariff did not lead to a shift away from the Dutch port. Indeed, something rather different occurred. While the Antwerp port authority lost a major part of its revenues from port dues and other ship-handling costs, Rotterdam used its dominance in petroleum as a "cash cow" to finance new infrastructure. In other words, the port of Rotterdam made good use of its position by adapting its port dues for oil tankers. For the first time a tariff was introduced for a specific type of ship (oil tanker) with a specific load (crude oil). This triggered a gradual diversification of the port dues in Rotterdam and Antwerp during the last quarter of the twentieth century. Both port authorities, often simultaneously, opted for further differentiations of the tariffs according to sector and ship type. In Antwerp this was manifested in 1971, the year that the RAPL opened, by the introduction of considerable additional reductions for ships over 6500 gross tons. Antwerp therefore promoted, by means of its tariffs, the calls of larger ships.

Until the 1980s Antwerp abandoned a simple and clear system for charging port dues. But compared to the port of Rotterdam the system was less flexible and more expensive. Indeed, Rotterdam adhered to the principle of charging lower port dues than Antwerp until it became the world's biggest port. Reductions for a second call on a single voyage had no parallels in Antwerp, whereas in Rotterdam ships had already profited from this advantage for several decades. Conversely, the reductions for liner shipping were considerable in Antwerp: they could rise from thirty-nine to seventy-one percent compared with maximum reductions of one-third in Rotterdam.[50] It is important to note that the spectacular traffic increases in Rotterdam in the 1950s and 1960s and Antwerp in the 1980s were accompanied by offers of cheaper port dues.[51] In 1980 Antwerp revised its port dues, just as Rotterdam had done fifty-seven years earlier, to a tariff based upon cargo handled. The objectives of both port

---

[49]The state, however, took into account all maintenance costs; see *Zeehavenbeleid van Rotterdam 1967-1975. De jongste geschiedenis van de ontwikkelingen rond Europoort, Maasvlakte en de Gouden Delta. Deel 1: jaaroverzichten* (Rotterdam, 1977), 21; and B. Wiebinga, "De Rotterdamse haven van 1965 t/m 1970," in van Walsum, *et al.* (eds.), *Rotterdam*, 91-94.

[50]Gemeentelijk Havenbedrijf Antwerpen, *Overzicht van de in de zeehavens gebruikte stelsels voor de berekening van havenrechten en kadegeld* (Antwerp, 1968), 48.

[51]Hoste and Loyen, "Ship Handling Costs," 164; and Loyen, "Port Competition and the Inertia of Long-established Custom: An Analysis of Post-war Seaborne Throughput," in de Goey (ed.), *Comparative Port History*, 99-105.

authorities were at this time also met by comparable port dues, and as such the comparability of the different ship-handling costs between both ports became the more central principle.

Maritime Access

In the diamond model maritime access is considered as a basic location-bound factor. It also relates to the attributes "government" and "supporting industry" (dredging companies). Antwerp is still served by its original and natural access, the Scheldt, whereas Rotterdam constructed an artificial access route, the New Waterway, during the last quarter of the nineteenth century.[52] Before World War II the maximum draught for incoming ships to the two ports was comparable, but competitive disadvantages were in the making for Antwerp. The increasing size of shipping added a new dimension to the old problem of access to Antwerp, a route which for the greater part of the journey is situated in the Netherlands. By 1905 Antwerp demanded dredging on Dutch territory, and by 1927 the Belgians were conducting more dredging in the Netherlands than in Belgium.[53] Immediately after World War II the maritime access to Antwerp and Rotterdam did not need to be thoroughly adapted as the lack of ships and shipbuilding capacity led to a further specialisation of ship types. According to a leading port administrator at the time, it was the unprecedented increase of ship sizes in the 1950s and 1960s that placed maritime access at the heart of Antwerp-Rotterdam port competition.[54] Indeed, it was only after the closure of the Suez Canal in 1956 that the growth in ship dimensions became a global trend. The revival of world trade in the early 1960s and the second closure of the Suez Canal in 1967 exacerbated this. The growth of ship sizes was most apparent in the oil tanker market, but the oil crises of the 1970s ended this.[55] With its river port situated far inland, the arrival of larger bulk ships slowly caused a new problem with accessibility in Antwerp in spite of dredg-

---

[52]Van de Laar, *Stad van formaat*, 65-70; Henrik A. van IJsselsteijn, *De haven van Rotterdam* (Rotterdam, 1908), 18-20; and Backx, *De haven van Rotterdam*, 132-136.

[53]H. Belmans, "Verdiepings- en onderhoudsbaggerwerken in Wester- en Zeeschelde," *Water*, XXXXIII (1988), 186-187; and Technical Scheldt Commission-Subcommission Western Scheldt, *Deepening Westerscheldt 48/43'* (Antwerp, 1984), 13-20.

[54]Suykens, *et al.*, *Antwerp*, 471.

[55]The first Very Large Crude Carrier (VLCC) was built in 1966 and the first Ultra Large Crude Carrier (ULCC) was launched two years later. Stopford, *Maritime Economics*, 56-63.

ing. Rotterdam, on the other hand, almost doubled the capacity of the New Waterway through its large-scale port expansions of 1950-1975, making the port accessible to ships with draughts up to nineteen metres.[56]

The dredging of the Scheldt was an recurring point of dispute between the fundamentally opposed interests of the two states and their most important ports. For Belgium, the Scheldt was the only maritime access to the ports of Antwerp and Ghent. But the Netherlands, as supervisor of the navigable channel, experienced difficulties related to the conservation of the waterway. Due to the economic importance of this maritime access, Belgium was forced to be flexible in the ongoing negotiations with the Netherlands. The result eventually was that Belgium paid the greater part of all works and maintenance on the Scheldt.

Table 4
Arrival of Ships in the Antwerp, 1955-1975
(draught in feet)

Draught	1955	1960	1965	1970	1975
30'-33'	292	415	510	450	336
34'-37'	8	111	498	431	174
38'-40'	0	0	105	438	140
41'-43'	0	0	0	52	80
Total	300	526	1113	1371	730

Source: Port of Antwerp, *Annual Bulletin of Statistics* (Antwerp, 1950-1975).

From the second half of the 1950s fierce debates raged in Antwerp over maritime access to the port.[57] In a survey published in 1958 the former Inspector General of the Antwerp Maritime Services, Leon Bonnet, noted the changes in the river required to enable ships with draughts of twelve and fourteen metres to reach Antwerp.[58] While in Rotterdam the New Waterway was deepened to handle larger ships, Antwerp was only beginning to make plans to get vessels with draughts of up to fourteen metres to the port. Because the Bonnet plan was not immediately realised, Antwerp suffered. Indeed, experts calculated that only sixty percent of oil tankers would be able to reach the port

---

[56]Jan W. Schraver (ed.), *Rotterdam. De poort van Europa. De geschiedenis van haven en handel van Rotterdam* (Rotterdam, 1946), 148-149; Cornelius Wiskerke, *De scheepvaartwegen van Rotterdam naar zee* (Rotterdam, 1948); and Wiebinga, "De Rotterdamse haven," 90-99.

[57]Suykens, *et al.*, *Antwerp*, 472-480.

[58]Leon Bonnet, *De bevaarbaarheid der Schelde voor zeeschepen met grote diepgang* (Antwerp, 1958).

by 1968.[59] As table 4 indicates, maritime access to Antwerp could not keep up with the larger vessels, not even in the dry bulk sector.[60]

In spite of the dredging of ninety-five million cubic metres between 1950 and 1965, maximum draught was only extended by one metre.[61] Table 5 shows that only in the 1970s were dredging operations on the Scheldt intensified significantly. This means that the expansion of the infrastructure in the port of Antwerp that began with the Ten-Year Plan (1956-1965) was not supported by improved maritime access. This hampered the growth of the transhipment of raw materials and fuel (coal, grain, ore and crude oil) in the port to the benefit of Rotterdam. In 1968, for example, the Antwerp oil refineries began to suggest that a steady flow to their facilities could only be secured by means of a pipeline from Rotterdam. Although various alternatives were considered, the government decided to approve the construction of the RAPL. Clearly, the port of Rotterdam benefited greatly from its superior maritime access, and by 1972 almost twenty million tons of crude oil were transported by pipeline from Rotterdam to Antwerp. Maritime access, and by extension geographical location, are therefore persuasive determinants in explaining the shift of certain kinds of cargo. That Antwerp became a hinterland of Rotterdam when it came to oil explains the eagerness in Antwerp to deepen the Scheldt in order not to lose other cargo flows.

Table 5
Dredging Operations on the Scheldt in Dutch Territory, 1951-1980
(million cubic metres)

	1951-1960	1961-1970	1971-1980
Estuary	N.A.	15.1	93.6
River	41.9	65	129.4
Total	41.9	80.1	223

Note: Includes Zandvliet

Source: Technical Scheldt Commission-Subcommission Western Scheldt, *Deepening Westerscheldt 48/43'* (Antwerp, 1984).

Conclusion

Port competition is determined by the interaction between a host of economic, political, financial, geophysical, technological, organisational, social and cul-

[59]Mingret, *La croissance industrielle*, 193-197.

[60]Patrick M. Alderton, *Port Management and Operations* (London, 1999; 2nd ed., London, 2005), 46-47.

[61]AGHA, Beleidsnota 1993, 42.

tural determinants. An increasing number of authors have attempted to model these variables. Although a theoretical or methodological consensus has not been reached, the literature increasingly features an application of the well-known Porter model to the port sector. The present article contributes to this discussion by examining the validity of this model through an examination of Rotterdam and Antwerp. The central question is whether it provides helpful new insights to explain developments. To do this we test three key determinants in the period 1945-1975.

This period presents an interesting case study. In terms of seaborne throughput Rotterdam expanded much faster in the 1950s and 1960s than did Antwerp. Rotterdam, at the time the largest port in the world, peaked in 1973 when it handled four times Antwerp's seaborne throughput. In terms of value-added, however, the view that Antwerp was much smaller needs to be reassessed. By this criterion Antwerp led Rotterdam because it handled more general cargo.

In the article the model has been tested by examining port labour, ship-handling costs and maritime access. Labour costs are essential to port users, and Rotterdam benefited from being much less expensive in the postwar years. In the 1950s port labour in Antwerp on average was 1.5 times more expensive. Antwerp also had less flexible working conditions, although much could be done on an informal basis. From the mid-1960s the gap between the two slowly diminished. The importance of ship-handling costs was also highlighted. Differences regarding these costs clearly weakened from the 1960s, but the spectacular postwar traffic increases did correlate with tariff politics. Finally, maritime access was, particularly after 1960, the most convincing determinant to explain large shifts in cargo from Antwerp to Rotterdam.

In investigating these determinants, we also uncovered some shortcomings in the model. The different determinants are often more interrelated than has been suggested. For instance, the Rotterdam example shows that monopolistic conditions regarding maritime access can be exploited by port authorities through port dues and other ship-handling costs to gain revenue to improve infrastructure. In Antwerp, by contrast, more money needed to be spent on dredging in order to keep maritime access competitive.

Another shortcoming is the inclusion of "strikes" in the category "chance." Strikes should be seen as one aspect of labour relations. Research on dockside conditions has shown that many labour stoppages are related to structural matters and problems such as temporary unemployment and poor hiring facilities. Strikes on the docks should not be treated as isolated phenomena but should be seen in close relation to other aspects of labour relations. For this reason we suggest that strikes not be part of the category "chance" but rather should be studied as part of labour relations.

Another weak point is service quality. Although we believe that the model can be applied to ports, we subscribe to the observation that it overlooks user perceptions of service quality. Flexibility, tradition, personal contacts and the shipper's perception of the level of port performance are undeniably key issues in port competition.

Still, the present analysis of the various determinants of the model remains incomplete. In part, this is because of some obvious lacunae in our historical knowledge of port competition. The impact of hinterland transport (infrastructure, costs, policy issues), competition on the port operator level and the influence of port authorities remain promising fields for future research. Since port operators generate cargo flows, it would perhaps also be appropriate to focus future research on the decision-making process of multinational maritime companies. How these firms evaluate the competitive advantages and disadvantages of particular ports and allocate cargoes will yield further insights into the conditions determining the evolution of ports.

The Environmental Impact of Ports: An Australian Case Study[1]

Malcolm Tull

Introduction

It is widely recognised that an efficient transport system which allows the economical movement of goods, resources and people is vital for economic growth and globalisation.[2] During the nineteenth century improvements in transport and communications were major factors in this expansion. In the twentieth century the communications revolution continued with innovations such as the motor car, aeroplane, large bulk carriers, container ships and pipelines for oil and gas. Improvements to road transport and the introduction of railways caused land transport costs to fall by about ninety percent between 1800 and 1910. The real cost of ocean shipping fell by over eighty percent between 1750 and 1990, and by 1980 the real cost of airfreight had declined by about seventy-five percent from its level in the late 1930s.[3] According to the United Nations Conference on Trade and Development (UNCTAD), the increased participation of developing countries in world trade "would not be possible without global shipping networks, port reforms and investments in transport infrastructure as well as trade and transport facilitation." Moreover, there exists "a virtuous cycle where better transport services lead to more trade, and more trade in turn helps to encourage improved transport services."[4] By the beginning of the twenty-first century the "tyranny of distance," while perhaps not completely tamed, was greatly diminished.

---

[1]I would like to thank Gino Valenti, General Manager, Business Sustainability, Fremantle Port Authority, and Amy Lomas, Western Australian State Treasury, for their comments. I am, of course, responsible for any errors or omissions that remain.

[2]See, for example, Wilfred Owen, *Transportation and World Development* (London, 1987).

[3]N.F.R. Crafts and Anthony J. Venables, "Globalization in History. A Geographical Perspective," in Michael D. Bordo, Alan M. Taylor and Jeffrey G. Williamson (eds.), *Globalization in Historical Perspective* (Chicago, 2003), 329.

[4]UNCTAD, *Transport Newsletter,* No. 25 (2004), 14-16.

In the late twentieth century growing public concern over the environment sparked interest in the long-run impact of humans on the environment and the emergence of the new field of environmental history. A greener generation of historians recognised that "transport systems, although critical to the rise of civilizations, have carried significant environmental costs for global ecosystems for many millennia."[5] As transport activity has increased, so have its side effects, including air and noise pollution, CO_2 emissions and congestion.[6] The expansion of transport infrastructures like ports, roads, railways and airports can potentially cause serious environmental damage.

Australia's large area and limited population has meant that transport has been vital in overcoming the "tyranny of distance."[7] The cost of ocean transport is especially significant as it affects the competitiveness of the country's exports and effectively provides a tariff wall for manufacturing. Because Australia in an island nation its ports are vital gateways and interfaces in the transport network. The volume of traffic through its ports increased from about 30.3 million tonnes in 1949-1950 to 157.4 million tonnes in 1969-1970 and 518.8 million tonnes in 1999-2000. In the last half of the century the scale of port activity increased seventeen-fold, leading to substantially increased pressure on the environment. At the same time, there were major changes in the composition, technology and location of port activity, so it cannot be assumed that there was a linear relationship between the scale of port activity and environmental degradation. The mineral boom of the 1960s led to the development of specialised bulk-handling ports in remote places and spread the impact of port activity over a larger area. By the late 1970s Port Hedland, for example, was transformed from a sleepy backwater to a port handling forty million tonnes of cargo per year, about forty times the level of the mid-1960s.

For many years Australian ports had a reputation for inefficiency, industrial militancy and restrictive practices, but in the 1980s deregulation of transport systems, labour market reforms and the corporatisation and privatisation of port authorities led to major improvements in port efficiency.[8]

---

[5]Shepard Krech III, J.R. McNeill and Carolyn Merchant (eds.), *Encyclopedia of World Environmental History* (3 vols., New York, 2004), III, 1224.

[6]John Ballingall, Doug Steel and Phil Briggs, "Decoupling Economic Activity and Transport: The State of Play in New Zealand," New Zealand Institute of Economic Research Working Paper, 2003, 2 (http://www.nzier.org.nz/SITE/Default/SITE/Publications/reports/2003/Reports.asp, accessed 16 June 2005).

[7]For a general survey of Australia's maritime history, see Frank Broeze, *Island Nation: A History of Australians and the Sea* (St. Leonards, NSW, 1998).

[8]For general surveys, see Malcolm Tull, "Australian Ports since 1945," in Lewis R. Fischer and Adrian Jarvis (eds.), *Harbours and Havens: Essays in Port His-*

In view of their potential impact on the environment ports, unlike other transport sectors, have received surprisingly little attention from environmental historians. Indeed, Elisabetta Tonizzi has called attention to the dearth of historical research on the environmental impact of ports.[9] Remarkably, while the recent *Encyclopedia of World Environmental History* includes an entry on transport, there is no discussion of transport infrastructure such as ports.[10] The standard works on Australia's environmental history by Geoffrey Bolton, Stephen Dovers and Donald Garden pay relatively little attention to the impact of transport.[11]

According to Dovers, environmental history can inform policy-making in three ways: by providing historical context (how did we get here?); by compiling "ecological and human baselines" (what was the environment like in the past?); and by learning lessons from experience, although he warns against expecting "too much from history."[12] While an historical perspective will not provide all the answers, it can help us understand port/environment interactions and inform the development of environmentally sustainable port policies.

The aim of this essay is to present a case study of the port of Fremantle as a first step in gauging the long-run impact of Australian ports on the environment. It considers the general relationship between ports and the environment; briefly outlines the history of the port of Fremantle; examines the port's environmental impact; and finally draws some preliminary conclusions.

---

tory in Honour of Gordon Jackson (St. John's, 1999), 111-138; and Tull and James Reveley "The Merits of Public Versus Private Ownership: A Comparative Study of Australian and New Zealand Seaports," *Economic Papers,* XX, No. 3 (2001), 75-99. For detailed data on port performance, see Australia, Bureau of Transport and Regional Economics, *Waterline* (http://www.btre.gov.au/docs/waterline/wline.aspx).

[9]M. Elisabetta Tonizzi, "Environmental Impact of Ports: The Case of Genoa, 1815-2004" (Unpublished paper presented to the Fourth International Congress of Maritime History, Corfu, 22-27 June 2004).

[10]Krech, McNeill and Merchant (eds.), *Encyclopedia of World Environmental History*.

[11]Geoffrey C. Bolton, *Spoils and Spoilers: Australians Make Their Environment* (Sydney, 1981; 2nd ed., North Sydney, 1992); Stephen Dovers (ed.), *Australian Environmental History: Essays and Cases* (Melbourne, 1994); Dovers (ed.), *Environmental History and Policy: Still Settling Australia* (South Melbourne, 2000); and Donald S. Garden, *Australia, New Zealand, and the Pacific: An Environmental History* (Santa Barbara, CA, 2005).

[12]Stephen Dovers, "Still Settling Australia: Environment, History and Policy," in Dovers (ed.), *Environmental History and Policy*, 5-7.

Figure 1: Major Railways and Seaports

Source: Australia, Bureau of Transport and Regional Economics, *Australian Transport Statistics 2005* (Canberra, 2005) (http://www.btre.gov.au/statistics/general/trnstats05/ATS05.pdf).

Ports and the Environment

It is generally agreed that as the total volume of transport activity has increased, so have negative externalities like pollution and congestion. In effect, transport growth is "coupled" with environmental damage.[13] As a result, "transport costs" do not necessarily include all the real costs that transport imposes on the economy.[14] There are, of course, positive externalities associated with transport growth, such as increased regional growth and improved communications for isolated communities. It is unrealistic to expect transport to be completely "green," and the environmental costs of transport operations and industries such as ports have to be weighed against their considerable eco-

---

[13]See Ballingall, Steel and Briggs, "Decoupling Economic Activity."

[14]Great Britain, Department of the Environment, Standing Advisory Committee on Trunk Road Assessment (SACTRA), *Transport and the Economy: Full Report*, 1999, 8 (http://www.dft.gov.uk/stellent/groups/dft_econappr/documents/page/dft_econappr_022512.hcsp, accessed 30 May 2005).

nomic benefits.[15] Some environmental damage may be acceptable if transport activity generates positive net benefits to society.

Transport industries generate significant environmental impacts, such as pollution, noise and traffic congestion. Transport is a major user of energy and therefore generates emissions. Australia produces more than four and a half times the world per capita average of transport-related emissions. The US (over 6.5 times) Canada (5.5 times) and New Zealand (four times) also have high levels of transport-related emissions.[16] In Australia, transport accounted for fourteen percent, or seventy-seven kilotonnes, of national greenhouse gas emissions in 2001, an increase of twenty-five percent from the level in 1990, although almost ninety percent of this was accounted for by road transport.[17]

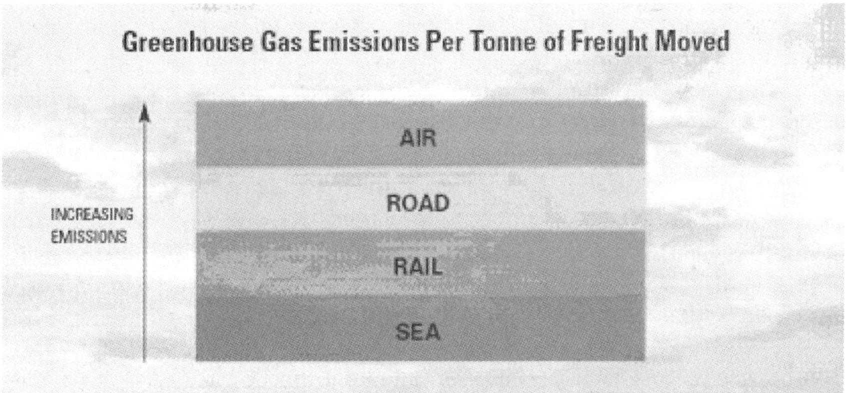

Figure 2: Greenhouse Gas Emissions per Tonne of Freight Moved

Source: South Australian Freight Council, "South Australia's Freight Transport Infrastructure," April 2005 (http://www.infrastructure.gov.au/submissions/SAFreightCouncil/Submission.pdf, accessed 7 June 2005).

While it is difficult to disentangle sources of pollution, figure 2 suggests that sea transport generates the lowest level of greenhouse gas emissions per tonne of freight handled. A report on the North Sea found that of the six activities with the highest impact on the ecosystem, shipping made up only one

[15]A.C. Burdall and H.J. Williamson, "A Green Port: An Engineer's View," in C.R. Ford (ed.), *Ports into the Next Century* (London, 1991), 247-248.

[16]Australian, "Special Article - Environmental Impacts of Australia's Transport System," *Year Book Australia* (Canberra, 2003).

[17]Australia, Bureau of Transport and Regional Economics, *Australian Transport Statistics 2004* (Canberra, 2004).

(anti-fouling substances), fisheries accounted for three (removal of target species, seabed disturbances and mortality of discards and by-catch) and inputs from the land (organics and nutrients) accounted for two.[18] Thus, shipping transport appears to be relatively "green."

Specific impacts associated with shipping include oil spills and the discharge of ballast water and other wastes and toxic chemicals from anti-fouling paints. *Torrey Canyon*, a supertanker wrecked off the southern English coast in 1967 with a cargo of 120,000 tonnes of oil, showed the devastating impact that oil spills can have on the local environment. The spillage of 20,000 tonnes of oil from *Erika* onto the French coast in 1999 led to tighter EU environmental regulations and accelerated the phasing-out of single-hulled tankers.[19]

Fortunately, Australia has not experienced major pollution disasters, although between 1982 and 1998 there were twenty-seven oil spills greater than ten tonnes in Australian waters.[20] For example, in July 1991 the Greek tanker *Kirki* lost its bow off the coast of Western Australia, spilling about 17,280 tonnes of oil. Where oil spills have occurred in ports, such as the accident that led to the loss of 250 tonnes of oil from *Laura D'Amato* in Sydney harbour in 1999, the port emergency procedures have usually ensured that they have been contained rapidly. It has been estimated that about fifty-five species of fish and invertebrates and some seaweeds have been introduced to Australia by discharged ballast water.[21]

Over half a century ago it was claimed that "port and harbour works, being protective and local in effect, have a rare distinction among man's activities in changing the face of the earth; they are almost universally beneficial, and it is seldom possible for their effect to be harmful."[22] Environmentalists,

---

[18]OSPAR Commission for the Protection of the Marine Environment of the North-East Atlantic, *Quality Status Report 2000, Region II Greater North Sea* (London, 2000), cited in Dan Laffoley and Mark L. Tasker, "Marine Environment" (Unpublished paper produced to support the report *Net Benefits – A Sustainable and Profitable Future for UK Fishing*), 30 (http://www.strategy.gov.uk/downloads/files/marine2.pdf, accessed 9 June 2005).

[19]Evangelia Selkou and Michael Roe, *Globalisation, Policy and Shipping. Fordism, Post-Fordism and the European Union Maritime Sector* (Cheltenham, 2004), 81-86.

[20]Fremantle Port Authority, *Protecting Our Marine Environment* (Fremantle, 2002).

[21]Australia, "Special Article."

[22]Lester E. Klimm, "Man's Ports and Channels," in William L. Thomas (ed.), *Man's Role in Changing the Face of the Earth* (Chicago, 1956), 539.

who sometimes consider ports to be "hot spots" of pollution, would not accept this sanguine view.[23] Specific impacts associated with ports include dredging and land reclamation, pollution, noise, smells, traffic congestion and hazards from the handling of dangerous goods.[24] In 2003, the top three environmental concerns of European port managers were garbage/port waste, dredging disposal and dredging.[25]

Dredging operations and the disposal of dredging wastes are one of the major sources of port-induced environmental damage. Dredging can destroy the habitats of marine species. Mud, silt and sediment dredged from channels or harbour bottoms are often highly polluted by hydrocarbons and heavy metals, although this may not be the result of port operations but a legacy of land-based agricultural, industrial and urban activities.[26] Many ports are located in or close to major cities, which are themselves major sources of pollution. The development of specialised container and bulk-handling facilities with their twenty-four-hour operations has increased noise and other pressures on the environment.

The proximity of ports and cities raises the possibility that accidents handling flammable or toxic cargoes could cause major loss of life and serious disruption to shipping and trade. In a horrific accident at the Canadian port of Halifax in December 1917, a ship carrying a full cargo of explosives collided with another vessel and exploded. The massive explosion instantly killed 1600 people, injured more than 9000 and left 25,000 homeless. It was reputedly the largest man-made explosion in history until the detonation of the first atomic bomb.[27] In April 1947 two ships loaded with ammonium nitrate exploded in Texas City, a port on the Gulf of Mexico. The explosions left 568 dead, over 3500 injured and caused enormous damage to the port and surrounding city.[28]

---

[23]Jean-Pierre Dobler, "Are Ports the Hot Spots of Marine Pollution or Its Best Checking Points?" in *Ports and Environmental Issues* (Yokohama, 1998).

[24]See C. Trozzi and R. Vaccaro, "Environmental Impact of Port Activities," in C.A. Brebbia and J. Olivella (eds.), *Maritime Engineering and Ports II* (Southampton, 2000), 151-161.

[25]R.M. Darbra, *et al.*, "The Self Diagnosis Method: A New Methodology to Assess Environmental Management in Sea Ports," *Marine Pollution Bulletin*, XLVIII, Nos. 5-6 (2004), 421.

[26]Dobler, "Ports," 198.

[27]Janet F. Kitz, *Shattered City: The Halifax Explosion and the Road to Recovery* (Halifax, 1989).

[28]Michael Richardson, *A Time Bomb for Global Trade: Maritime-related Terrorism in an Age of Weapons of Mass Destruction* (Singapore, 2004), 47-48.

Of course, there has been over half a century of learning since these events, and safety standards have been improved to reduce this risk.

Serious damage has been inflicted on port cities during wartime. Aware of community concerns about the environment, navies, including the Royal Australian Navy, today emphasise environmental compliance and the development of environmentally "sustainable" warships.[29] Since 2001 there has been concern about the potential damage that terrorists might cause if a ship was deliberately blown-up in a port located close to a densely populated city. In 2002 the International Maritime Organisation introduced an International Ship and Port Facility Security Code to attempt to improve security.

Another problem both for the environment and ports is that the expansion of industrial, commercial and residential development has led to increased "competition" between ports and cities for land use. In many port cities the relative importance of maritime activity fell over time as other industrial and service activities grew. By the late nineteenth century Hamburg, while still a major port, had become "the hub of commercial enterprise throughout Germany," and its expansion was increasingly driven by service enterprises which competed with the port for scarce urban land.[30] After the Second World War, ports were required to provide adequate depths, space for large bulk carriers and tankers and extensive land areas for container terminals – requirements not easily met in cramped metropolitan ports.

Many ports were eventually forced to break out of their metropolitan straitjackets and develop new port areas, sometimes with mixed success.[31] In Sydney, for example, in the 1970s a second port was developed at Botany Bay, only about ten kilometres south of the city centre. The port's policy was to spread the impact of port activity across the urban area so that "each affected community suffers a little but not to such a degree as to be totally intolerant of port and related activity."[32] Yet according to one assessment, port planning was poorly integrated with city development, and environmental impact inquiries, held only "as last ditch confrontations with affected city populations," were "totally inadequate."[33] In 2004, a Commission of Inquiry was set up into

---

[29]Glenn Kerr and Barry Snushall (eds.), *Future Environmental Policy Trends to 2020: Impact on Ship Design and Operation* (Canberra, 2005).

[30]Richard Lawton and Robert Lee (eds.), *Population and Society in Western European Port Cities, c. 1650-1939* (Liverpool, 2002), 275.

[31]Tull, "Australian Ports," 123-124.

[32]J. Hayes, "Port Development and Management in a City Environment – Sydney's Experience," in *Ports and Environmental Issues*, 286.

[33]Noel G. Butlin (ed.), *The Impact of Port Botany* (Canberra, 1976), 93.

controversial proposals to more than double Port Botany's capacity. There was strong opposition from local councils, community groups and residents who stressed that port expansion, airport operations, traffic growth and management of the Bay "are inextricably linked and that this demands a holistic approach to planning."[34] The Commission concluded that the desired container throughput capacity of 3.2 million TEUs per year could be achieved with a smaller expansion than proposed by the Sydney Ports Corporation. This would minimise adverse impacts on the five key values that captured the Bay's essential characteristics: "people and lifestyles, biodiversity and natural systems, economic importance, place in history and Bay-side character." [35]

Globalisation has increased pressure to lower transport costs and improve service levels. One outcome has been a move away from a mode-specific world to intermodalism, which is "the use of at least two different modes of transport in an integrated manner in a door-to-door transport chain."[36] Thus ports are viewed not in isolation but as key interfaces in global and domestic logistics chains. But the implementation of intermodalism is both complex (especially with fragmented government and private ownership of transport infrastructure and equipment) and costly, with the benefits widely dispersed across a large number of users and existing pricing systems that do not adequately allow for cost recovery.[37] The "Cost 340" project on the history of trans-European connections and internodal transport has attempted to cast light on why intermodal connections take so long to develop.[38]

In 2000 the British government released a sustainable distribution policy which reduced the emphasis on privatisation, competition and deregulation in favour of sustainability, intermodal integration, environmental protection and better regional and local planning. One effect is to favour maritime transport and especially ports with good land transport connections. An important

---

[34] Australia, Commission of Inquiry, *Proposed Construction and Operation of a New Container Terminal at Port Botany, Botany Bay City. Volume One: The Report, 2005*, 28 (http://www.coi.nsw.gov.au/inquiry/view.php?InqId=93, accessed 10 February 2006).

[35]The values were identified in Australia, Department of Infrastructure, Planning and Natural Resources, *Towards a Strategy for Botany Bay* (Canberra, 2004), cited in Commission of Inquiry, *Proposed Construction,* 31.

[36]Organisation for Economic Co-operation and Development (OECD), *Intermodal Freight Transport: Institutional Aspects* (Paris, 2001), 12.

[37]*Ibid.*, 42.

[38]Technical and Scientific Cooperation Action (COST 340), "Towards a European Intermodal Transport Network: Lessons from History," was established in 2000. See http://www.cordis.lu/cost-transport/src/cost-340.htm.

strategy is to increase the proportion of cargo carried overland by rail in order to reduce congestion on metropolitan roads.[39] Rail, however, is best suited to carrying cargo over long distances rather than short hauls, so this may limit its use at some ports. A high proportion of container movements at Australian capital city ports, for example, are over relatively short distances; they do not use two-to-three-kilometre-long trains double stacked with containers like those that travel daily between Los Angeles and the American Midwest.[40]

All these issues have increased the complexity of port management, which now has to balance port and broader community interests. The main aim of port managers was to provide a high quality service to users – primarily shipping companies, stevedores and importers – rather than to manage the environment. Their approach to port development traditionally focussed on technological optimisation and treated the port as a "stand-alone" structure rather than as part of a larger interdependent coastal ecosystem.[41] Until the 1970s concern for the environment was often limited to environmental impact assessments taken after development plans were formulated, a process that did not necessarily result in sustainable development policies.[42] Since then, under pressure from governments and local communities, ports in developed economies have gradually ensured that environmental considerations are better integrated into the planning cycle. Since the 1990s there has been an increasing emphasis on triple bottom-line approaches to economic, environmental and social issues.[43] In 1999 a set of guidelines on environmental management was developed for British ports.[44] The EU's Ecoports project, completed in 2005, has provided a unified approach to the environmental management of ports through training programmes and by encouraging cooperative efforts to deal

---

[39]Sidney Gilman, "Sustainability and National Policy in UK Port Development" (Unpublished paper presented to the IAME conference, Panama, July 2002).

[40]Sea Freight Council of Western Australia, *Annual Report* (Fremantle, 2003-2004), 18.

[41]J.H. Vandermeulen, "Environmental Trends of Ports and Harbours: Implications for Planning and Management," *Maritime Policy and Management*, XXIII, No. 1 (1996), 55-66.

[42]Alastair D. Couper, "Environmental Port Management," *Maritime Policy and Management*, XIX, No. 2 (1992), 168-169.

[43]See, for example, Environment Australia, *Triple Bottom Line Reporting in Australia: A Guide to Reporting against Environmental Indicators* (Canberra, 2003).

[44]E. Paipai, A. Brigden and C. Wooldridge, "Guidelines for Port Environmental Management," in Brebbia and Olivella (eds.), *Maritime Engineering and Ports II*, 197-206.

with environmental problems.[45] One outcome is a self-diagnosis tool to help managers evaluate the status of a port's environmental management.[46]

Because of more stringent environmental regulations, ports have faced increased costs in a variety of areas, including planning and design, operating expenses, intergovernmental and community negotiation and opportunity costs of lost revenues from planning delays.[47] In economic terms, ports increasingly have been required to internalise the external costs of development.

Port planning is complicated by the fact that the powers of port authorities are usually limited to the immediate port areas; they have no control over metropolitan development. The provision of land transport links, for example, depends on the joint efforts of different public and private agencies, each with differing and possibly conflicting interests and responsibilities. Due to the complexity of modern port management, it is not hard to sympathise with the Los Angeles Harbour Commissioners who in 1973 complained that their port "must serve a worldwide manufacturing and shipping boom, an energy crisis [and] an ecological renaissance...all in the same decade."[48]

History of the Port of Fremantle

The port of Fremantle, located on the eastern edge of the Indian Ocean, was established in 1829 to provide the British with a gateway to the western part of the vast Australian continent.[49] In its early years Fremantle was far from an ideal location because a rock bar blocked the mouth of the Swan River, and ships had to use a few exposed wooden jetties. The colony struggled in its early years, which was reflected in the low level of port activity: the average number of vessels rarely exceeded seventy per year until the 1890s. The provision of an adequate harbour had to wait until the 1890s when the gold rushes transformed the economy and provided revenues for large public infrastructure projects. By 1897 the rock bar had been removed; two moles built at the

---

[45]See www.econports.com.

[46]Darbra, *et al.*, "Self-Diagnosis Method," 420-428.

[47]Herman L. Boschken, "The Demands of Conflicting Change on Public Enterprise: West Coast Seaport Development and Environmental Regulation," *Public Administration Review*, XLII, No. 3 (May 1982), 223.

[48]Port of Los Angeles, *Annual Report* (1973), 12, cited in Boschken, "Demands," 223.

[49]This section provides only a brief outline of the port's history. For more details see Malcolm Tull, *A Community Enterprise: The History of the Port of Fremantle, 1897 to 1997* (St. John's, 1997).

mouth; the harbour dredged to thirty feet (nine metres); and about 7000 feet (2100 metres) of timber wharves built with cargo sheds. The first ocean-going vessel to enter the new harbour, the Blue Funnel Line's *Sultan* in May 1897, symbolized Western Australia's economic take-off and integration into the British Empire. In 1903 the Fremantle Harbour Trust, later renamed the Fremantle Port Authority (FPA), was established to manage and develop the port.

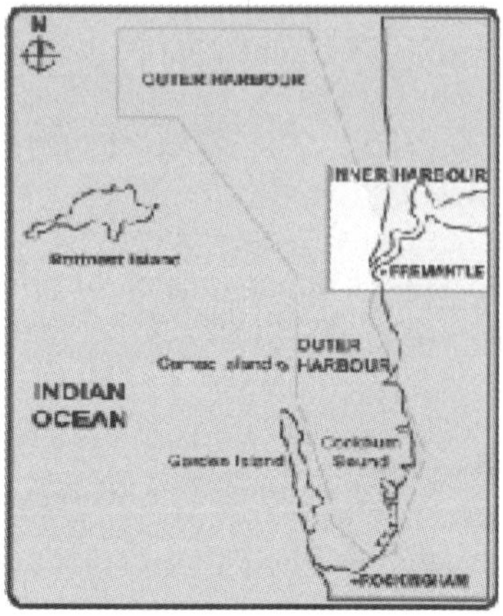

Figure 3: Map of the Port of Fremantle

Source: Fremantle Port Authority website.

The completion of North Quay in 1916 brought the total length of wharfage to almost 10,000 feet (3000 metres), a level at which it remained for many years. Although there have been many changes in the Inner Harbour, including dredging to increase the depth and the mechanisation of cargo-handling technology, its basic physical layout remains unchanged to this day.

Western Australia's population grew from 184,000 in 1901 to about half a million in the 1940s. By the 1990s the state's population had reached 1.5 million, with over seventy percent living in the metropolitan area. As the city developed, competition between port and metropolitan land-use activities increased, but this was less serious than in older port cities such as Sydney.[50]

[50]See John A. Roberts, "Planning Sydney's Transport 1875-1900," in Max Kelly (ed.), *Nineteenth-Century Sydney: Essays in Urban History* (Sydney, 1978), 24-36; Malcolm Tull, "The Development of Port Administration at Sydney, 1901 to 1936," *The Great Circle*, IV (1982), 92-104; Garry Wotherspoon (ed.), *Sydney's Transport: Studies in Urban History* (Sydney, 1983); and Peter R. Proudfoot, *Seaport Sydney: The Making of the City Landscape* (Sydney, 1996).

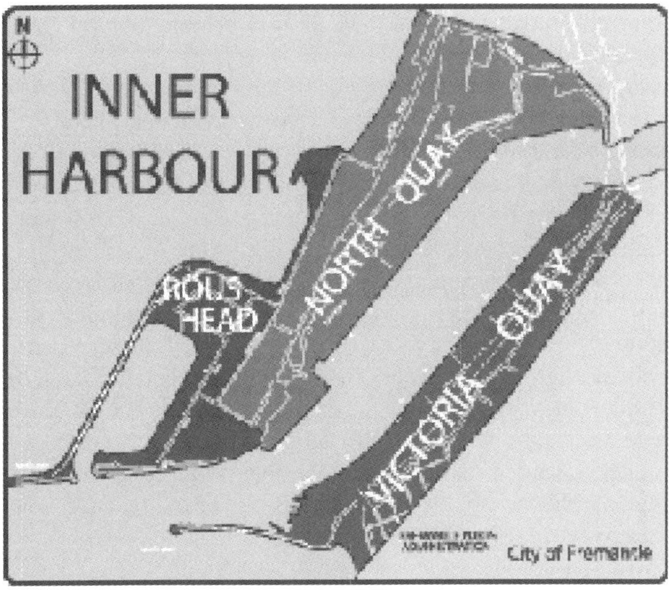

Figure 4: Map of the Inner Harbour

Source: See figure 3.

A breakout from the confines of the Inner Harbour did not occur until the mid-1950s, when to accelerate industrialisation the state government funded the dredging of channels to provide access to a new deep-water port at Cockburn Sound, about twenty kilometres south of Fremantle. Anglo-Iranian Petroleum (later BP) was offered incentives to establish a refinery at Kwinana on the shores of the Sound; this was completed in 1954 and led to large increases in imports of crude oil and exports of refined petroleum products. An iron and steel works (1954), alumina refinery (1964), fertiliser plant (1969) and nickel refinery (1970) helped establish Kwinana as an industrial hub. Planning for the port was well integrated with overall metropolitan development, and adequate access for land transport and space for industry was provided.

While the locus of port activity began to shift away from the Inner Harbour, it still retained the lion's share of high-value general cargoes. In the late 1960s container-handling facilities were constructed on the northern side of the Inner Harbour. A second container terminal was opened in 1983. Containerisation made the wharf cranes and cargo sheds on Victoria Quay obsolete, and it – and to some extent the city of Fremantle – acquired a "decaying" image. When in 1983 Alan Bond, one of Western Australia's most colourful and controversial entrepreneurs, succeeded in temporarily snatching the America's Cup from the clutches of the New York Yacht Club, the city was rejuvenated in preparation for its defence in 1987. Many facilities on Victoria Quay were adapted for leisure activities and a museum.

In 1998-1999 the total economic impact of the port was estimated at $728 million. The Inner Harbour accounted for sixty-seven percent, although it handled only eighteen percent of cargo tonnage; this was because it specialised in relatively high-value container and general cargoes. The total employment impact of the Inner and Outer Harbours was estimated at 3896 and 1896 jobs, respectively, highlighting their economic importance to the local economy.[51]

There has been some debate about the long-term viability of the Inner Harbour as a commercial port. Martyn Webb, for example, has suggested that rather than develop overflow container facilities in the Outer Harbour all container operations should be transferred there and the existing container area be redeveloped as a residential, tourist and visitor complex linked to the city by a light railway system; he claims this would revitalise the city of Fremantle.[52] The FPA has, however, declared that the Inner Harbour "will continue in the longer term, throughout the twenty first century, as a major, dynamic container and general cargo port facility."[53]

Environmental Impact of the Port of Fremantle

By world standards Fremantle is not a large port, and this limits the scale of the pressure on the environment. In 1903-1904 it handled only 706,000 tonnes of cargo; in 1949-1950, 2.7 million tonnes; in 1969-1970, 12.8 million tonnes; and by 1999-2000, 23.4 million tonnes. Therefore, in the latter half of the twentieth century the scale of port activity and the implied pressure on the environment increased nine-fold, compared to seventeen-fold for Australia as a whole, although it should be noted that changes in trade composition and technology limit the accuracy of such comparisons. Until the mid-1950s all cargo passed through the Inner Harbour; by 1999-2000, due to the diversion of bulk cargoes to the Outer Harbour, only about twenty percent did so. The gradual shift of bulk cargoes to the Outer Harbour spread the impact of port activity

---

[51]Australia, Bureau of Transport Economics and Australian Association of Ports and Marine Authorities, *Fremantle Port: Its Economic Impact* (Canberra, 2000) (http://www.fremantleports.com.au/Educaton/Economic/index.aspx?section=3, accessed 16 June 2005.

[52]Martyn Webb, "Reinforcing Conservation through Redevelopment: Incorporating a Revitalised Port within the City of Fremantle" (Unpublished paper presented to the ICOMOS National Conference, Fremantle, 9-11 November 2006).

[53]Fremantle Port Authority, *Inner Harbour Port Development Plan* (Perth, 2000).

over a larger geographical area. Cargo handled in the Inner Harbour per linear metre of wharf increased from 876 tonnes in 1949-1950 to 1441 tonnes in 1999-2000, an implied productivity increase of about sixty-four percent. This was mainly due to the mechanisation of general cargo handling (unitisation and later containerisation) and major waterfront reforms in the 1980s.

Table 1 provides an approximate summary of environmental pressures in the Swan River and Cockburn Sound since the 1850s. It is clear that the majority of pressure on the environment comes from sources other than the port. As we have seen, however, key impacts associated with ports include dredging, traffic congestion, pollution (including noise and smells) and the risks and hazards from the handling of dangerous ships and goods. Each will be considered in turn.

Table 1
Changes in Environmental Pressures in the Swan River and Cockburn Sound since the 1850s

1850s	**1900s**	**1950s**	**2000s**
Sewage Shipping and trade at exposed ocean Jetties	Sewage Shipping and trade Inner Harbour (1897 onwards)	Sewage Shipping and trade Inner and Outer Harbours (1955 onwards)	Sewage Shipping and trade Inner and Outer Harbours
Fishing	Fishing	Fishing	Fishing and aquaculture
Forestry Agricultural runoff	Forestry Agricultural runoff Industrial effluents Urbanisation and urban runoff	Forestry Agricultural runoff Industrial effluents Urbanisation and urban runoff Petroleum Metals Synthetic organics	Agricultural runoff Industrial effluents Urbanisation and urban runoff Petroleum Metals Synthetic organics Naval Base
		Recreational activities	Recreational ativities

Source: Adapted from a table in J.H. Vandermeulen, "Environmental Trends of Ports and Harbours: Implications for Planning and Management," *Maritime Policy and Management*, XXIII, No. 1 (1996), 59.

Dredging

Since the removal of the rock bar in the 1890s only minimal maintenance dredging has been required to maintain depths in the Inner Harbour; this has helped limit pollution from this source. In 1916 dredging to increase the depth from thirty (nine metres) to thirty-six feet (eleven metres) started, but due to limited finances it was not completed until the mid-1920s. By the 1950s this depth was limiting access by oil tankers and was one reason for the development of the Outer Harbour, which was provided with twelve-metre access channels. The Inner Harbour remained at eleven metres until 1989 when the FPA increased the depth in most of the harbour to thirteen metres. The dredged material was used to create reclaimed land for a new commercial boat harbour, known as Rous Head, on the northern side of the North Mole. In 1994 the FPA introduced the use of the Dynamic under Keel Clearance System, which enables the clearance between the hull and the ocean floor to be predicted so accurately that ships can safely use the port with fuller loads. Although originally developed for use in the Outer Harbour, it now allows larger and deeper-draft (post-Panamax) container vessels to use the river port.

Road and Rail Access

It is clear that the provision of adequate road and rail access is vital to the smooth functioning of the port. There is little point in making improvements to port facilities if land transport cannot cope with the increased cargo flows.

Until the development of containerisation, the majority of the port's road traffic went via Victoria Quay because North Quay specialised in bulk cargo that was normally transported by rail. When the Fremantle Harbour Trust (renamed the Fremantle Port Authority in 1964) was formed in 1903 it found Cliff Street, the main approach to Victoria Quay, a congested and "highly dangerous thoroughfare." It was used by all types of city traffic and was criss-crossed by railway lines; every week between 4000 and 5000 vehicles travelled along the road to and from the port, and about 600 lines of railway trucks were shunted backwards and forwards across the street. By 1905 it had been transformed into "a fine, straight, well-built roadway" with adequate lighting and a broad footpath for pedestrians. The relocation of the railway station in 1907 also improved access to Victoria Quay.[54]

Fremantle was provided with railway connections to the old sea jetty in 1891. The railway system, which was narrow gauge (three feet six inches), developed in two directions: northwards, via Perth, which was the major route, and southwards, via Robbs Jetty. The northward route crossed the Swan

---

[54]This and the following paragraph draw on Tull, *Community Enterprise,* chapter 5.

River immediately upstream of the port, connected with the Midland Railway at Midland Junction and after 1917 provided a connection to the eastern states via the Trans-Continental Railway. But rail access between Victoria Quay and the North Quay was via the mainline only, and both the mainline and port system operated in a restricted land area behind the wharves: the system grew "up over half a century into a cramped lay-out, barely adequate to meet the trade of the moment, not capable of overload, and inefficient in operation."[55] At the beginning of the 1970s the mainline marshalling yards were transferred to South Fremantle, thus releasing land for port uses on Victoria Quay.

In 2001-2002 about ninety-seven percent of containers were handled by road and only three percent by rail. Since one train can carry the equivalent of seventy-ninety trucks, greater use of rail has the potential to reduce pressure on the road system. Unfortunately, the bulk of Fremantle's containers travel less than fifty kilometres, and road transport has a comparative advantage over rail for short distances.[56] Nevertheless, the FPA aims to increase the proportion of containers handled by rail to thirty percent by 2010. To help achieve this, a new dual-gauge rail loop line and terminal on North Quay was completed in March 2006.[57] The FPA estimates that land transport links will be adequate to cater for trade growth until at least 2020.

Pollution

Prior to World War II, pollution was probably less of a concern in Western Australia than in the more developed eastern states, but problems did arise from time to time. In 1912 there was opposition to further upriver expansion:

> The city does not want it; the country, as much interested as the port or capital, would refuse assent to a scheme that would turn the waters of the banks into a wilderness of dingy wharves and factories, with perpetual volumes of smoke from shipping driving over the city.[58]

---

[55]F.W.E. Tydeman, *Report on the Port of Fremantle* (3 vols., Perth, 1948-1949), II, 130.

[56]N. Matthews, "Shifting to Rail – Issues for Fremantle's 30% Strategy" (Unpublished paper presented to the Planning and Transport Research Centre [PATREC] Industry Conference on Maritime Logistics, Landside Issues and Opportunities, Fremantle, 25-26 November 2004).

[57]K. Sanderson, "Land-side Port Logistics: Planning for Fremantle's Future" (Unpublished paper presented to the PATREC Conference, 2004).

[58]*West Australian*, 15 October 1912.

In 1928 the Minister for Public Works opposed development south of the river mouth on the grounds that it would spoil Fremantle as a seaside resort, turning it into "a mere mass of wharves and boats."[59] In the early 1950s there was renewed opposition from local councils to upriver port development due to fears of pollution. It was, however, claimed that the port had a negligible impact on the overall pollution of the river.[60] The river has regularly suffered from algae blooms and other pollution problems caused by land clearing and fertiliser runoff in the catchment area. In the mid-1920s algae blooms in the marshy foreshore near the Causeway were used to justify dredging the river.[61] The Swan River Trust, set up in 1989 to protect the environments of the Swan and Canning rivers, in 2005 considered dredging as a solution to algae problems, but there were concerns about the environmental side effects.

The Outer Harbour has also had an impact on the environment. An agreement in 1971 between the government and Cockburn Cement Pty Ltd. to remove sand from the Parmelia and Success sandbanks for use in the manufacture of cement and lime proved controversial due to damage to sea grasses. In 1968 the Cockburn Sound Conservation Committee was established to advise on problems caused by pollution. In 1979, a controversial study by Dr. Graham Chittleborough identified serious water quality problems in the Sound, but these had little to with port operations.

The noise and smells associated with some port operations have also generated community concerns. Live sheep shipments, for example, have attracted criticism regarding the care of the animals and the smells emanating from the sheep carriers, although improvements in carrying and feeding operations have led to high survival rates for the livestock, and specialised vessels now service the trade. The FPA has considered moving the live sheep trade to the Outer Harbour, but at present there are no suitable facilities available.

In 1999 the state government passed the Port Authorities Act which attempted to create a common approach to port authority management in Western Australia. Section 30 (1)(f) included among the functions of port authorities the duty "to protect the environment of the port and minimise the impact of port activities on that environment." This appears to have spurred the FPA into action, as the same year it launched an environmental policy statement and established an Environmental Awareness Team; by 2001 it had gained ISO 14001 certification (the international standard for environmental management) for its environmental system. The FPA is undertaking extensive community

---

[59]A. McCallum, *Fremantle Harbour: Proposals for Extension. Schemes Outlined and Compared* (Perth, 1928), 9.

[60]Tydeman, *Report*, II, 39.

[61]J.S.H. Le Page, *Building a State. The Story of the Public Works Department of Western Australia 1829-1985* (Leederville, WA, 1986), 415.

consultation regarding the development of new container and general cargo facilities in the Outer Harbour. Figure 5 summarises the planning process.

Despite the detailed planning, in 2006 the Environmental Protection Authority raised concerns about the impact of the proposed new container port in Cockburn Sound, claiming it could damage marine life and pollute water used to supply a nearby desalination plant.[62] The FPA, on the other hand, sees the environmental risk as minimal and stresses that this is the only viable option once the Inner harbour reaches full capacity. The scene is thus set for another classic debate over "growth versus the environment."

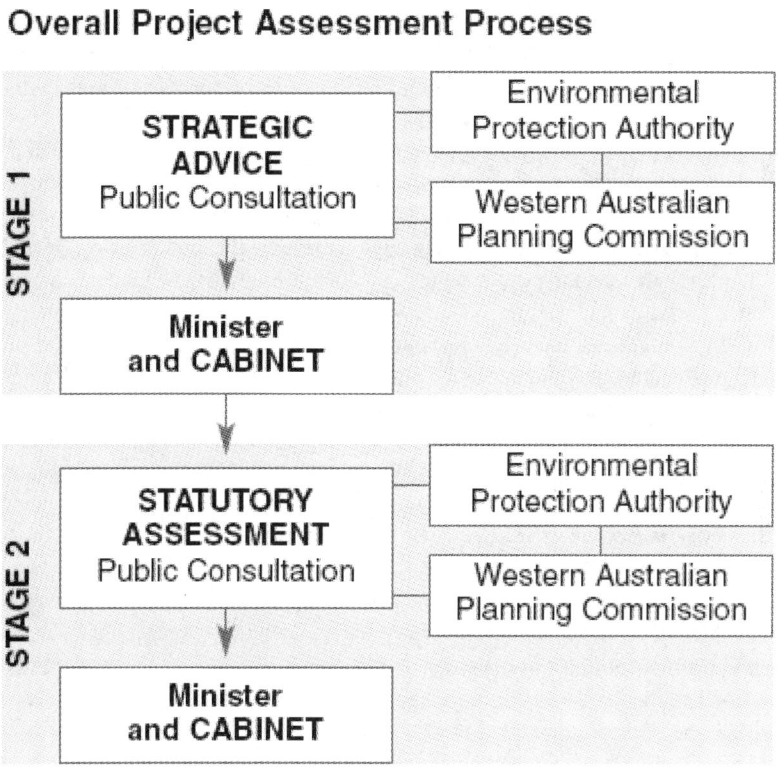

Figure 5: Planning Process for the Outer Harbour

Source: Western Australian Planning Commission, *Fremantle Ports Outer Harbour Project Information Brochure* (Perth, 2004).

[62] *West Australian*, 26 September 2006.

Environmental Risks and Hazards

There have, of course, always been risks with locating ports close to metropolitan areas. The advent of oil bunkering and bulk oil handling in the early 1920s led to concerns about the dangers of fire and water pollution. At that time there were no regulations or appliances to guard against oil spills. In 1918 SS *Polgowan*, reputedly carrying sufficient TNT to blow up Fremantle, caught fire at the North Wharf, but fortunately the ships' crew and the local fire brigade brought the blaze under control. A serious fire on *Panamanian* during the Second World War also highlighted the potentially hazardous nature of port operations. Wharf labourers were sometimes at risk from dangerous cargoes, such as blue asbestos, which as late as the 1960s were handled with woefully inadequate procedures.[63] The Dangerous Goods (Transport) (Dangerous Goods in Ports) Regulations 2001 set out detailed procedures for safety management systems and emergency response plans for dangerous cargo operations.

The opening of a naval base (Fleet Base West) on Garden Island in 1978 led to increased naval activity in the Outer Harbour. Fremantle receives regular visits from foreign naval vessels, some of them nuclear-powered, which poses risks to the environment and increases the potential for terrorist attacks, although nuclear-powered vessels do not enter the Inner Harbour. On the other hand, expenditure by crews from visiting US naval vessels in 1998/1999 created additional economic output of twenty-two million dollars and 193 full-time-equivalent jobs.[64] The Australian Maritime Transport Security Act 2003 now requires ports to have security plans approved by the Office of Transport Security, and this has led to increased restrictions on access to their working areas.

In recognition of the need to provide adequate separation between the working port and other urban uses, the FPA commissioned a Buffer Definition Study (2001).[65] This led to the development of a three-level buffer scheme to provide appropriate separation between port and non-port activities depending on the level of individual and societal risk; its main recommendations have been incorporated into town planning schemes.

Conclusions

There is a broad consensus that transport growth is "coupled" with environmental damage and that the development of infrastructure such as ports has the

---

[63]Tull, *Community Enterprise,* 207-208.

[64]Bureau of Transport Economics, *Fremantle Port*.

[65]Halpern Glick Maunsell Pty Ltd., *Fremantle Inner Harbour Buffer Definition Study* (Leederville, WA, 2001).

potential to degrade the environment. Key impacts associated with ports include dredging, traffic congestion, pollution and the risks and hazards from the handling of dangerous ships and goods. Ports located in river estuaries may appear to be environmental "hot spots," but a large part of the pollution is often generated by upstream activities. Pressure on the environment comes from many sources, and it may be more appropriate to view ports as pollution "check points" rather than "hot spots."[66] After the Second World War, due to urban encroachment and the pressure to provide deep water, many ports developed new port areas, a spatial shift which reduced environmental pressure at existing locations. It is hard, however, to imagine a truly "green port," and clearly the environmental costs of port operations have to be weighed against the considerable economic benefits. All these trends and pressures were apparent at the port of Fremantle.

Until the Second World War the relatively small scale of port activity at Fremantle limited pressure on the environment, and there is no clear evidence of serious port-related environmental degradation. A breakout from the confines of the Inner Harbour was not necessary until the mid-1950s, when the port began to exploit the deep water and extensive land areas of Cockburn Sound. Increased economic and port activity led to negative environmental impacts, especially in the Kwinana industrial zone, but in the last two decades the FPA has endeavoured to be a good corporate citizen and to develop sound environmental management strategies. In 2005, it was awarded the Lloyds DCN Corporate Citizen Award. One simple measure of the success of its environmental management is the fact that dolphins can regularly be seen swimming in both the Inner and Outer Harbours. The port is an important transport hub serving the needs of both industry and the community, and it is the only place in Western Australia where rail, sea and land transport modes closely interlink. The Inner Harbour facilitates community enjoyment of the local environment and coastline, with ferry access to the offshore tourist island of Rottnest and ocean access for yachts and other vessels from further upriver. Yet, as in many capital city ports, there are tensions over the allocation of scarce waterfront land between port and city uses and the environmental impact of port activities. In 2006 Lindsay Fox, a transport magnate, claimed that a planned expansion of the port of Melbourne would compound the already pressing problem of congestion: "cities around the world today do not have an intermodal activity plum in the centre of the city...If you look at Melbourne and use it as a keyhole, you block up the whole centre. How can you move when the whole centre is blocked?"[67] He advocated a more decentralised strategy of port development using regional ports. The issues of congestion and

[66]Dobler, "Ports."

[67]*The Age* (Melbourne), 21 August 2006.

land values are less pressing in Fremantle but may eventually seal the fate of the Inner Harbour.

It is clear that to be successful, port managers need to be responsive to community demands and to educate the public on the value of working ports. It took the Sydney Ports Corporation about four years (2001-2005) to get all the necessary planning approvals for the expansion of container facilities at Botany Bay, leading one staff member to comment that "the environmental and social aspects of port expansion can be more challenging to deal with than the economics."[68] Another port manager has observed that "a history-conscious community will see the value in preserving a working waterfront and will be unlikely to press for every metre of shoreline to be dedicated for urban waterfront projects.[69]

This lesson has not been lost on the FPA, which has helped to sponsor a major historical project called "Voices from the West End." This project aims to record and publicise the history of the West End of Fremantle, which until the latter part of the twentieth century was the heart of the working port.[70] While the focus of the West End of Victoria Quay is increasingly shifting to urban activities, the FPA is keen that it also remains part of a working port well into the twenty-first century.

---

[68]M. Calfas, "The Greening of Ports," *Ports and Harbors*, LI, No. 2 (March 2006), 12.

[69]Hayes, "Port Development," 291.

[70]For details, see http://www.scase.murdoch.edu.au/voices.

A Survey of the Operations of the Port of Kaohsiung, 1949-1957: The Policies for Survival?

Chih-lung Lin

This brief paper investigates the performance of Kaohsiung, the biggest port in Taiwan, from 1949 to 1957, an era that should be thought of as the pre-takeoff period. The literature on port history in Taiwan is heavily concentrated on the years before 1945. Moreover, most research has been conducted from the perspective of economic geography.[1] This paper will shed some new light on the subject, not only by looking at a later period but also by treating the Kaohsiung Port Authority (KPA) as a business corporation. I will use the archives from the Academia Historica in Taiwan to discuss the operation of the KPA from the assets revaluation in 1949 until 1957, when a Twelve-Year Development Plan for port development, a large Keynesian-inspired macroeconomic policy, was put into place. I will show that the authorities adopted a policy of "survival" during this period due to on-going, and largely economic, difficulties.

The port of Kaohsiung is located in the south-western part of Taiwan, a sub-tropical zone, 224 miles north of Keelung, 165 miles west of Amoy and 341 miles south of Hong Kong. Due to the nature of its sandy coast, dredging is always necessary to keep the port open. Kaohsiung was not developed under Chinese rule until it began to trade with Hong Kong in 1858. Taiwan was opened to foreign trade by the Tianjin Treaty between China and the United Kingdom. The British asked for trading rights at Kaohsiung in 1863, and a British consulate was opened in 1865. The British set out a plan to expand the port but never acted on it. Later, when the Chinese government began to build infrastructure it did so for defence against a possible French invasion rather than for commercial reasons.

Japan took over Taiwan after the Shimonoseki Treaty of 1895 and began to investigate Kaohsiung's potential in 1900. There were three development plans approved between 1906 and 1944. During this time Kaohsiung overtook Anping to become the biggest port in Taiwan despite the fact that the Japanese did not implement any of their plans fully.[2]

---

[1]An example of the geographic approach is Lin Yuru, *The Spatial Structure of Ports in Ch'ing Taiwan* (Taipei, 1996).

[2]Shao-ceng Zhang, "Taiwan zhi gong ye gang," *Taiwan yin hang ji kan*, XII, No.2 (1961), 134-137.

During the Second World War, half the transport facilities in Taiwan were destroyed. Kaohsiung suffered heavy damage, and the Japanese even sank their own vessels to prevent an American invasion before they surrendered. By August 1945, the port had lost half of its pontoons and all of its buoys and cranes. Only two warehouses were left standing, compared to fifteen at the outbreak of hostilities.

The Japanese overhauled the port's administration in 1943, and these emergency wartime measures continued in place even after the Nationalist government took over Taiwan following its expulsion from mainland China. Meanwhile, the military continued to have an influence over port operations, as it had done during the Japanese occupation. In February 1949 the provincial government nationalised the various port authorities, transforming them into public corporations.[3]

Conditions in Taiwan became unstable following the spread of civil war in mainland China. In August 1949, a vessel exploded at Wharf No. 10, causing severe damage to the port.[4] The military authorities seized this opportunity to establish a new division in the Harbour Bureau to manage military traffic. The shipping companies, and especially the foreign merchants, were unhappy about this and request a more unified system. According to evidence in British archives, the UK government suspected that the Americans had forced the Bureau to bow to its wishes.[5] This might well have been true, since the United States was influential in East Asia during this period as the tensions stemming from the Cold War escalated. Meanwhile, other evidence confirms that the US suggested that the Nationalist government adjust the transport tariffs as a condition for the extension of American aid to Taiwan. As a result, the Nationalists launched an evaluation of the transport facilities on the island as part of a re-organisation of the domestic fiscal regime.[6]

---

[3]The government took over the Japanese transport companies in August 1945 and established a provincial corporation. There was also one private company in the business. In the port of Kaohsiung, the transport market became an oligopoly when in November 1946 two companies reached an agreement, and the government corporation engrossed three-quarters of the market. But this agreement was suspended in May 1947, and five more private companies were established. Another agreement was reached in August 1949, and the provincial government forced some modifications in September 1954. See the Academia Historica Archives (AHA), 275-4/0066; *Kaohsiung gang san shi nian* (Kaoshiung, 1975), 167-169.

[4]Robert L. Jarman (ed.), *Taiwan Political and Economic Reports, 1861-1960* (10 vols., Slough, 1997), VIII, 470-471 and 482.

[5]*Independent Evening News* (Taipei), 8 October 1950; and Jarman (ed.) *Taiwan*, IX, 313-314.

[6]Bao Yi-rong, *Zi zhan chong gu jiashi wu* (Taipei, 1961), 43.

Table 1
HCD and the Distribution of Proceeds, 1950-1957
(New Taiwan Dollars)

	1950	**1951**	**1952**	**1953**
All HCD(a)	—	41,315,183	54,952,854	67,786,085
Kaohsiung HCD(b)	12,591,947.24	16,282,226.39	23,601,559.44	32,162,338.44
(b)/(a)	—	39.41%	42.95%	47.45%
Construction budgets to Kaohsiung(c)	11,590,183.78	12,225,437.94	15,154,986.75	17,180,659.98
(c)/(b)	92.04%	75.08%	64.21%	53.42%

	1954	**1955**	**1956**	**1957**
All HCD(a)	84,726,000	104,488,000	126,509,000	155,330,000
Kaohsiung HCD(b)	34,139,477.18	51,112,502.84	73,711,686.15	72,926,453.35
(b)/(a)	40.29%	48.92%	58.27%	46.95%
Construction budgets to Kaohsiung(c)	25,216,745.82	18,067,002.61	16,540,470.08	25,311,446.74
(c)/(b)	73.86%	35.35%	22.44%	34.71%

Source: AHA, 471-001, *Kaohsiung gang san shi nian* (*Annual Report Tax Statistics of Taiwan*), 1966.

As a result of this exercise, Taiwan's provincial government introduced Harbour Construction Dues (HCD, *gang gong juan*), placing a levy of 1.5 percent of total value on all goods; the revenue went to the Harbour Bureau. The local city councils were anxious to share in the substantial proceeds, and they were permitted to use part of the dues after July 1949. Moreover, it was decided in January 1950 that the dues would go up to two percent and that the city councils would receive one-quarter of the total. The Department of Customs in the Ministry of Finance also laid a charge of 0.1 percent as an administrative fee. Finally, in January 1951, the government took charge of the fee distribution, with the result that not all of the dues were used for improvements in the port.[7] The entire system represented a kind of tax on trade that was not always reasonable either to the traders or the port. For starters, the dues were charged on value rather than quantity, unlike in other ports around the world. Moreover, Kaohsiung did not receive its fair share of the proceeds. Although the port generated more than forty percent of the revenues from the HCD, it received only between twenty and thirty percent of the proceeds (see

[7]Dong Da jiang "Gang gong juan cang sang," *United Daily* (Taipei) 22-23 August 1955.

table 1). Finally, the military, which was a heavy user of the port, paid no dues. These conditions illustrate well the problems faced by the KPA.

The American government resumed its aid to the Nationalist government after the outbreak of the Korean War.[8] Nonetheless, some contemporary evidence suggests that the amount was insufficient for the port's needs. As a result, the government tried to get more financial assistance from the US for port construction.[9] As Taiwan struggled to recover after the wartime damages, Kaohsiung had become the most important port in the country, but it still had a great need for improvements.[10] Despite this, up to January 1954 only 0.3 percent of US aid went for harbour construction in Taiwan.[11] But since the US was offering some non-repayable funds, the KPA was able to re-construct Wharf No. 10 in March 1952 after it received funding of $7,334,391 New Taiwan dollars (NT).[12] After 1954, more of the aid was spent on the port construction and the KPA was able to repay the Provincial Government, with allowances for depreciation and reserves. Yet it appears that the Bureau was not able to cover its operating costs except by raising the military service charge by ten percent.

US aid helped the Bureau to solve its financial difficulties. The Bureau had to undertake construction once it entered into contracts after receiving this assistance. But the process of letting out contracts was difficult because the staff lacked experience in port construction.[13] Meanwhile, repaying that part of the aid which was granted in the form of loans was a burden. Yet the work needed to be done, since as table 2 shows, the port of Kaohsiung handled over seventy percent of exports and over half of imports in Taiwan. In addition to

---

[8]Robert Accinelli, *Crisis and Commitment* (Chapel Hill, NC, 1996), 67-68.

[9]AHA, 078-114.

[10]*Kaohsiung gang* (Kaohsiung, 1952), 33. In 1952, over half of the salt and more than ninety percent of sugar exports left through Kaohsiung. *Ibid.*, 223-2410.

[11]The US government had agreements with the Nationalists Government which required the latter to deposit matching funds in a special account called "counterpart funds" to stabilise prices and facilitate further economic planning. According to the Industrial Committee minutes of 1 April 1954, only 5.76 percent of these funds were expended on harbour construction in Taiwan between 1950 and 1954. See US State Department Central File: Formosa, 1950-1954.

[12]*Independent Evening News*, 7 October 1950; *United Daily*, 22 September 1951; *Kaohsiung gang san shi nian*, 55-70; and*Taiwan Kaohsiung gan wu ju yun yong mei yuan cheng guo jian tao* (Taipei, 1967), 8-11.

[13]*Taiwan gongye fu shing shi* (Taipei, 1960), 603.

US aid and funds from the government, revenues, especially from charges for loading and discharging vessels, was used to improve the infrastructure.

Table 2
Throughput in the Port of Kaohsiung, 1950-1957
(metric tonnes)

	1950	**1951**	**1952**	**1953**
Kaohsiung imports (a)	582,647	672,727	758,552.2	723,693.3
All imports in Taiwan (b)	—	—	1,282,761	1,507,115
(a) / (b)	—	—	59.13%	48.02%
Kaohsiung exports (c)	765,039	598,087	688,973.6	1,167,350
All exports in Taiwan (d)	—	—	975,313	1,680,044
(c) / (d)	—	—	70.645%	69.48%
Kaohsiung throughput (e)	1,347,686	1,270,814	1,447,525.8	1,891,043.3
Taiwan throughput (f)	—	—	2,258,074	3,187,159
(e) / (f)	—		64.10%	59.33%

	1954	**1955**	**1956**	**1957**
Kaohsiung imports (a)	1,053,706.8	1,238,538	1,435,019	1,669,143
All imports in Taiwan (b)	1,865,606	2,072,298	2,334,594	2,604,856
(a) / (b)	56.48%	59.77%	61.47%	64.08%
Kaohsiung exports (c)	882,030	1,067,237	1,095,835	1,218,452
All exports in Taiwan (d)	1,223,630	1,518,272	1,500,716	1,688,878
(c) / (d)	72.08%	70.29%	73.02%	72.15%
Kaohsiung throughput (e)	1,935,736.8	2,305,775	2,530,854	2,887,595
Taiwan throughput (f)	3,089,236	3,590,570	3,834,770	4,293,754
(e) / (f)	62.66%	64.28%	66.00%	67.25%

Sources: *Transportation Information*, I (1978), 86-87; *Kaohsiung shi zhi gai shu pian* (Kaohsiung, 1956), 124-150; and *Statistical Abstracts of Taiwan, 1946-1967* (Taipei, 1971), 622-623.

The problems were exacerbated by the effects of the Second World War. About three-quarters of Taiwan's industrial capacity had been destroyed during the conflict. While 30,000 Japanese staff returned home after the armistice, the country's population continued to grow as over 1,000,000 people fled to Taiwan from China between 1945 and 1949, increasing the total population by about twenty percent by 1950. Although some of these new migrants had experience working in ports, many of them lacked knowledge about local conditions. The same was true in the industrial sector, which made it difficult to meet growing demands. The export sector also suffered dislocations. Before the war Japan had been Taiwan's most important export market, but it ceased to have the same capacity after its defeat. Moreover, trade with China ended during the civil war on the mainland, and it was impossible to resume it after the victory of the Communists. After 1949, of course, Taiwan was placed under military rule due to the threats from the mainland. As part of this, the ports were nationalised. All of this placed new strains on port administrations, but their financial positions remained weak. All the ports, including Kaohsiung, were forced to rely on the government budget, supplemented by borrowings, limited aid from the US and a special tax system to maintain operations. Because of its growth, the problems were greatest in Kaohsiung. Although its operating income represented over half of total port revenues in Taiwan, the government took some of it for other needs.

Nonetheless, by 1955 the port began to make profits, albeit largely by depreciating its assets at a very rapid rate. This was a stark contract to conditions in 1951 and 1952 when the KPA was close to insolvency and possessed few liquid assets. During those years the port relied on bank overdrafts and short-term loans to overcome its difficulties.[14] One economist has suggested that the first economic plan in Taiwan, which covered the period 1953-1957, was insufficient, especially for ports. Indeed, the KPA in those years had little idea of what resources it could expect and was forced to operate in an exceedingly uncertain economic climate.[15]

In short, the history of the port of Kaohsiung between 1949 and 1957 reflected all the problems that were inherent in Taiwan as a whole. Since the Nationalist government did not understand the role of Taiwan in the tears immediately after 1949, it was in no position to develop a long-term port policy. But even had it wanted to do so, it lacked sufficient assets to upgrade the port facilities. As a result, any improvements in the ports capacities were initially made to facilitate short-term transport rather than to make profits which would have provided funds for long-term improvements. Ports like Kaohsiung in this period were more about survival than about development.

---

[14]AHA, 471-001; and *Kaohsiung gang san shi nian*, 385-387.

[15]Lin Weishing (Lin Jongshong), "Taiwan jing ji jian she ji hua yu zi jin," *Taiwan yin hang ji kan*, XXI, No. 1 (December 1970), 84-88.

The Northwest Portuguese Seaport System in the Early Modern Period[1]

Amélia Polónia

Analytical Framework

This essay examines the Portuguese seaport system in the early modern period. The analysis focuses on the evolving network in the northwest and its connections with Lisbon, the country's main port. Ports historically have been the foci of local, regional, national and international economic development and social change. These linkages with both hinterland and foreland make ports a fertile ground for understanding the historical transformation of economic, commercial, transport and technological networks, as well as industrial development and social and urban change. Historians increasingly view ports not simply as infrastructure but rather as complex systems shaped by economic, political, social and cultural forces. They are also increasingly seen as active agents in the processes of modernisation, technological innovation and urbanisation. As a result, port history in recent decades has undergone a renaissance, although the focus has mainly been on economic and technological issues.

Although port historians have concentrated on the modern period, the significant role of ports in the sixteenth, seventeenth and eighteenth centuries is undeniable. Ports structured political and economic spaces and were essential junctions in supra-regional interactions. New nautical techniques, new trade networks and the increasing tonnage of seagoing vessels all served to increase the prominence of maritime communication routes from the coastal to the trans-oceanic. In the early modern period, economic hegemony was contested between city-ports such as Lisbon, Seville, Antwerp, Amsterdam and London. Connections between Europe and other continents were maintained through ports at the same time that the internal implications of those dynamics were projected onto maritime centres. In fact, the strategic centrality of seaports in the early modern age has given rise to specific historical phenomena and dynamics that need to be studied. The creation of a world economic system and

---

[1]Some of the data in this paper derive from a research project entitled "HIS-PORTOS: A Contribution to the History of Northwest Portuguese Seaports in the Early Modern Age" (POCTI/HAR/36417/2000).

the concentration of population generated demographic, social and mental phenomena that set port zones apart from inland regions.[2]

The growing role of "sea power," both naval and commercial, enhanced the role of ports.[3] The growth of international fleets and lucrative trades based in key ports motivated pirates and led to the construction of military fortifications. The exposure of port cities to both land and sea made them more vulnerable to epidemics and disease; improvements in health protection were also features of the internal dynamics of such places. Moreover, advances in engineering, especially in the eighteenth century, awakened authorities to the need to invest in a variety of infrastructure, such as bridges, fortifications and ports. Seaport cities began to play new roles. In turn, the new functions led to intervention by various states, as demands outstripped the ability of local authorities to cope.

Although historians throughout Europe have studied these and other issues, Portuguese scholars have not produced enough detailed studies to make useful comparisons. And while port historians elsewhere have increasingly looked at port systems and hierarchies, this approach has been absent in Portugal. In short, there is a need to fill a number of gaps in order to enable an international dialogue. This is where the Hisportos project comes in. This collaborative research programme aims not only to examine the kinds of macroeconomic issues that have been the focus elsewhere but also to comprehend the internal dynamics and specific profiles of each seaport in northwest Portugal in their local and regional contexts. We believe it is sensible to study ports in all their human, social, urban, technical, administrative and economic complexity.

To be fair, some studies already exist on the seaports of northwest Portugal. Indeed, Viana, Vila do Conde, Porto and Aveiro have been the subjects of scholarly studies.[4] But in general, authors have been concerned with

---

[2]On the concept of the seaport town, see Fernando Monge and Margarita del Olmo, "Un contexto de análisis para el concepto de ciudada portuaria: las cidades americanas en el Atlántico," in *Puertos y Sistemas Portuarios (Siglos XVI-XX)* (Madrid, 1996), 215-233.

[3]See Jacob M. Price, "Competition between Ports in British Long Distance Trade c. 1660-1800," in Agustin Guimerá and Dolores Romero (eds.), *Puertos y sistemas portuários (siglos XVI-XX): Actas del Coloquio Internacional el Sistema Portuaria Español* (Madrid, 1996), 19-36; and Philippe Contamine (ed.), *Guerre et concurrence entre les États européens du XIVe au XVIIIe siècle* (Paris, 1998).

[4]On Viana, see Manuel António Fernandes Moreira, "O porto de Viana do Castelo e as navegações para o Noroeste Atântico" in *Viana – o mar e o porto* (Viana do Castelo, 1987); Fernandes Moreira, *O Porto de Viana do castelo na época dos descobrimentos* (Viana do Castelo, 1984); Fernandes Moreira, *Os mareantes de Viana e a construção da Atlantidade* (Viana do Castelo, 1995); and Fernandes Moreira, *Os mercadores de Viana e o comércio do açúcar brasileiro no século XVII* (Viana do Cas-

economic, demographic and urban issues and have ignored some key topics that Hisportos aims to examine. In what ways did geo-morphological conditions affect the potential of each port? How did various governmental bodies and politics affect the construction and function of ports and coastal towns? How were ports linked into larger regional, national, continental and intercontinental systems? Based upon these and related questions the Hisportos team, which includes historians, archaeologists, cartographers, engineers and architects, developed a research plan.[5]

Answers to the questions we raised were not found in the extant literature, which contained considerable gaps prior to the nineteenth and twenty centuries.[6] We discovered that there were three main kinds of works. First, there were the mostly descriptive studies written by local researchers. Second, some works concentrated on a particular plan drafted by a specific engineer, generally without checking the geo-morphological conditions and historical dynamics that motivated them. Finally, there were scholarly studies which aimed to tackle economic and social issues, although often without the contexts in which we were interested.

Because the available secondary literature is so spotty, the first phase of the project entailed the construction of a database of documentary and cartographic material.[7] It is an impressive resource, but it should be viewed merely as the first part of a larger programme to amass evidence on key sectors of the various ports. This essay contributes to the long-term goal by setting out some of the issues to be pursued in the future.

---

telo, 1990). On Vila do Conde, see Amélia Polónia, "Vila do Conde. Um porto nortenho na expansão ultramarina quinhentista" (Unpublished PhD thesis, 2 vols., University of Porto, 1999); and Polónia, *Expansão e Descobrimentos numa perspectiva local. O porto de Vila do Conde no século XVI* (2 vols., Lisbon, 2007). For Porto, see Amândio Barros, "Porto: a construção de um espaço marítimo nos alvores da Época Moderna" (Unpublished PhD thesis, University of Porto, 2004); and António Barros Cardoso, *Baco and Hermes. O Porto e o comércio interno e externo dos vinhos do Douro (1700-1756)* (2 vols., Porto, 2003). For Aveiro, see Inês Amorim, *Aveiro e sua Provedoria no séc. XVIII (1690-1814) - estudo económico de um espaço histórico* (Coimbra, 1997).

[5]Amélia Polónia, "HISPORTOS - A Research Project on Portuguese Seaports in the Early Modern Age," in *European Seaport Systems in the Early Modern Age: A Comparative Approach* (Porto, 2007), 28-39.

[6]Even for this period there are few studies. See Eduardo Frutuoso, Paulo Guinote and António Lopes, *O movimento do porto de Lisboa e o comércio luso-brasileiro (1769-1836)* (Lisbon, 2001); and Jorge Fernandes Alves and Fernando de Sousa, *Leixões. Uma história portuária* (Porto, 2002).

[7]See http://www.hisportos.com.

Northwest Portuguese Ports in the Early Modern Age: New Approaches

This essay builds upon some of the theoretical assumptions that guided the Hisportos project. It combines new data for each port with some major themes in Portuguese history, such as overseas expansion, the country's declining military and economic strength and the political enlightenment centred on the activities of the Marquis of Pombal to shed light on some issues related to the evolving port system. We will combine local dynamics with central politics and international and overseas economic and maritime contexts to articulate a comprehensive analysis of the northwest Portuguese seaport system and to identify the variables that shaped it.

The theoretical premise behind this research is that a micro-analysis is an excellent way to facilitate the search for answers that cannot be found from a macro-historical perspective.[8] The early modern period was marked by the consolidation of transport networks between the coast and the interior, some of which used waterways. The study of the hinterland is therefore crucial to understand the economic dynamics of more extensive regions.[9] It is important to study local and regional interactions to better comprehend both local situations and intercontinental connections.

Because it is important to study ports in all their complexity, we have adopted the concept of a seaport system, as suggested by Augustin Guimerá and others.[10] Ports are difficult to analyse because they embody a series of multifaceted economic, cultural, social, political and spatial relations. These factors are often interrelated. The character of a port may be determined by a single commodity or many goods, regardless of value: by long-haul merchant vessels or coastal traffic; by fishermen or passengers; by shipbuilding or transport logistics. Some ports may be comprehensible by examining the most im-

---

[8]Amélia Polónia and Inês Amorim, "Hisportos - Contribuição para o estudo dos portos do Noroeste português. Apresentação de um projecto de investigação" (Unpublished paper presented to the Thirteenth Congress of European Historians of Latin America, Ponta Delgada, 3-8 September 2002).

[9]Gordon Jackson, "The Maritime Experience of a Region without Ports: Argyll, Scotland, c. 1740-1840," *International Journal of Maritime History*, XVII, No. 2 (2005), 261-284.

[10]Guimerá and Romero (eds.), *Puertos y sistemas portuários*.

portant elements that comprise the port system, but others can be understood only by studying the relationship between several variables.[11]

Our goal is not to focus solely on the larger ports but to include the smaller ones as well. This perspective does not, however, obviate the need to define a seaport hierarchy. Unequivocal hierarchies, though, do not exist: the parameters on which we base our definition determine the relative position of a port in relation to the others. For instance, a large commercial port may not be a large transport and shipbuilding port and *vice versa*. Moreover, the relative rank of a port may shift over time depending upon geo-economic, political or even logistical changes.

Our second premise concerns the existence of networks of complementary ports. The linkage may be economic or financial, tied together by the pattern of merchant networks, sustained by capital transfers, nurtured by the placement of agents in trading markets or bolstered by logistical factors. A large commercial port may depend upon several smaller ports, especially if its mercantile fleet is insufficient to sustain its trade routes. The same may be said about nautical complementarities on which the large fleets depend to recruit their crews. Ports such as Vila do Conde, Peniche, Setubal and Sesimbra historically have been important suppliers of seamen, and their role has changed distinctly over time depending upon their relations with larger seaports.

These networks of complementary ports may also be established around shipbuilding. Small ports had a specialised labour force that sustained shipbuilding in ports with large shipyards. This was the case with Ribeira das Naus in Lisbon, which was staffed by both voluntary and compulsory recruitment that forced shipyard workers from all over the kingdom to move to Lisbon. It was also the case with Ribeira do Ouro in Porto, where a 1656 document shows that seventy-six percent of the shipbuilders were originally from the Entre-Douro-e-Minho, the area running from north of the Douro to the border with Galicia covering several municipalities in Porto's hinterland.

Thus, it is important to examine all types of networks and not simply those that tied together the major international ports. The historical position of these great maritime centres often relied upon local inter-port networks. In fact, from the perspective of logistics, shipbuilding, transport capacity and the availability of seamen, a cosmopolitan port almost always relied on other ports and on areas where agriculture and crafts were the predominant occupations. Indeed, this was so for Lisbon during the period of overseas expansion.

Yet even if we restrict our study to the commercial dynamics of a port over time, the networks we identify will seldom be unambiguous. For example, a certain port simultaneously might be part of a local network in which it

---

[11]Helena Osswald and Inês Amorim, "The Hisportos Case. Scientific Options and Research Programme: A Possible Approach to Northwest Portuguese Seaport Studies," in *European Seaport Systems*, 56-63.

functioned as a kind of a hub; a regional network encompassing a much broader area; or a continental (or even intercontinental) network. In the case of early modern Portugal, the latter could be a colonial or even a metropolitan-hinterland network. These latter two networks were often two sides of the same coin, since a port might be a re-export hub for colonial merchandise destined for European markets. Access to these latter two types of port systems is of fundamental importance for this study because it determined the international centrality of each port, shaped its evolving dynamics, impacted its position within the Portuguese economy and affected its internal social structure.

With these points in mind, this essay will demonstrate two things. The first is that the early modern period was characterised by some significant developments in the ranking of several northwest Portuguese ports within the port-system hierarchy. The second is that the relative rank of each port, and the differential access they enjoyed to various trade circuits, was related to some distinct factors, including geo-morphological advantages or restrictions, global mercantile and financial dynamics and evolving economic strategies, many of which were shaped by an increasingly interventionist state. Of particular importance to this last point in the eighteenth century was the role of the Marquis of Pombal, whose centralist policies restricted the access of individual entrepreneurs to the colonial economy (especially Brazil) while promoting the rise of large, well-capitalised trading companies based in Lisbon.

Diachronic Evolution of the Northwest Portuguese Seaport Hierarchy

The choice of northwest Portugal (see figures 1 and 2) was based upon geographical - the characteristics of the coastline and port accessibility - and historical criteria. The coast and rivers provided incentives to create ports of various sizes. These ports played important roles in the trading networks of the early modern period, interacting closely with harbours in Spain, Northern Europe, Africa and South America. The commercial dynamics had implications not only for infrastructure development but also for the exercise of leadership and economic opportunity.

We can begin with an analysis of the relative importance of each port in northwest Portugal. It is important, however, to understand that the political and administrative status of these ports was different than those of Lisbon, which was both the capital and from the sixteenth century the hub of a vast overseas empire. Lisbon was not only a port city but also a political and administrative centre. Moreover, in the sixteenth and seventeenth century it was one of the largest port cities in Europe, home to about 165,000 inhabitants by 1620.[12]

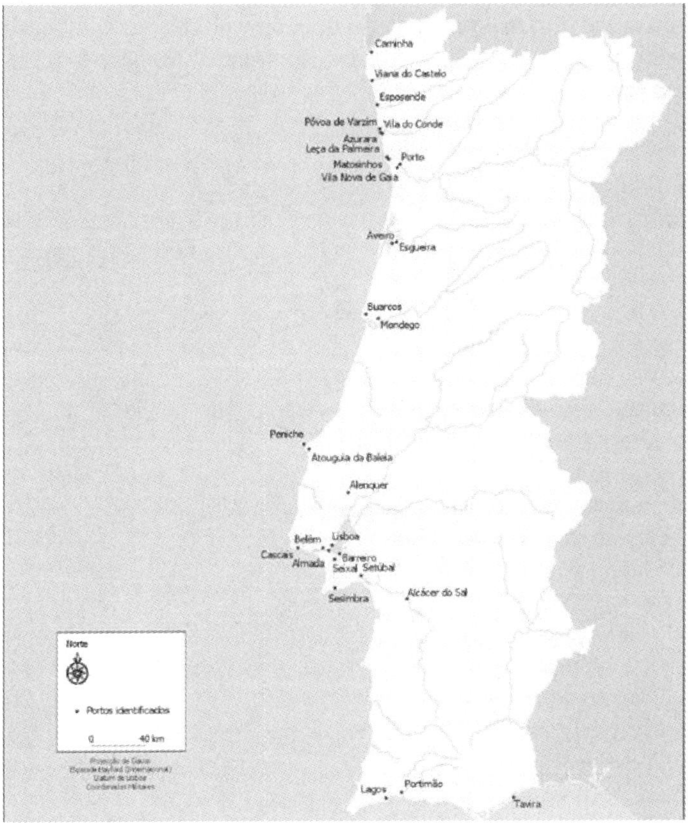

Figure 1: Main Portuguese Seaports

Source: Courtesy of the author.

Porto, the kingdom's second city, was a district capital and highly important in the domestic economy. Its population in 1620, however, was less than 20,000 (see figure 3).[13] As the nucleus of the northwest, it had traditional

[12]Teresa Rodrigues, "Um espaço económico em expansão. Da Lisboa de Quinhentos a Lisboa do século XX," *Penélope. Fazer e desfazer a história*, No. 13 (1994), 95-117.

[13]Helena Osswald, "A evolução da população na diocese do porto na época moderna," in *Actas do 1 Congresso sobre a diocese do porto. Tempos e lugares da memória* (Porto, 2002), 73-95.

links to the Mediterranean and northern Europe. A commercially and financially vibrant centre since medieval times, it lost some of its significance in the sixteenth century due largely to a monopolistic overseas trading policy. Still, its shipyards, renowned for their quality, built many of the vessels which sailed to India and, as other ports in the region, contributed to the crews that sailed around the Cape.[14]

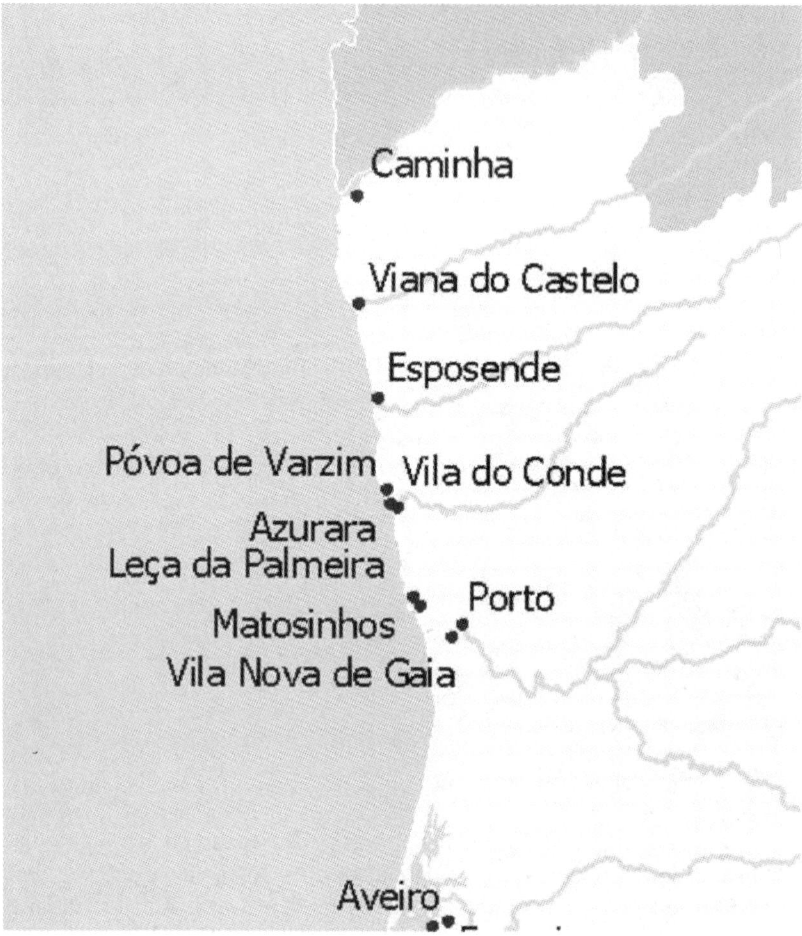

Figure 2: Northwest Portuguese Seaports

Source: See figure 1.

[14]Barros, "Porto."

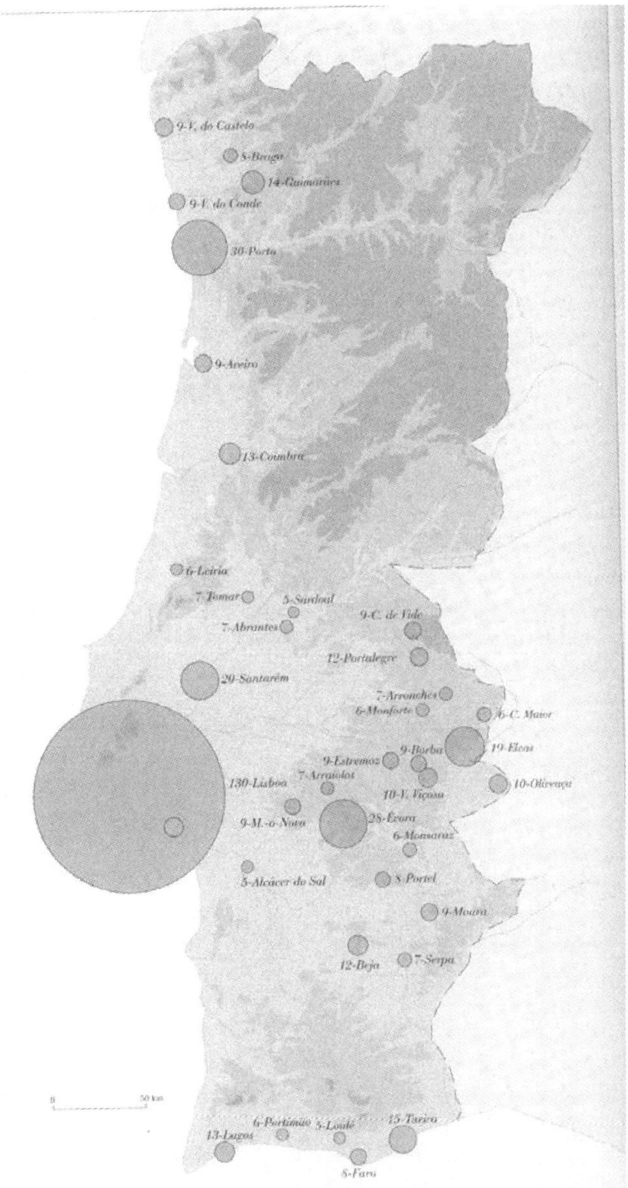

Figure 3: Population Distribution in the Seaports, 1527-1532

Source: José Mattoso (ed.), *História de Portugal* (8 vols., Lisbon, 1993), III, 232.

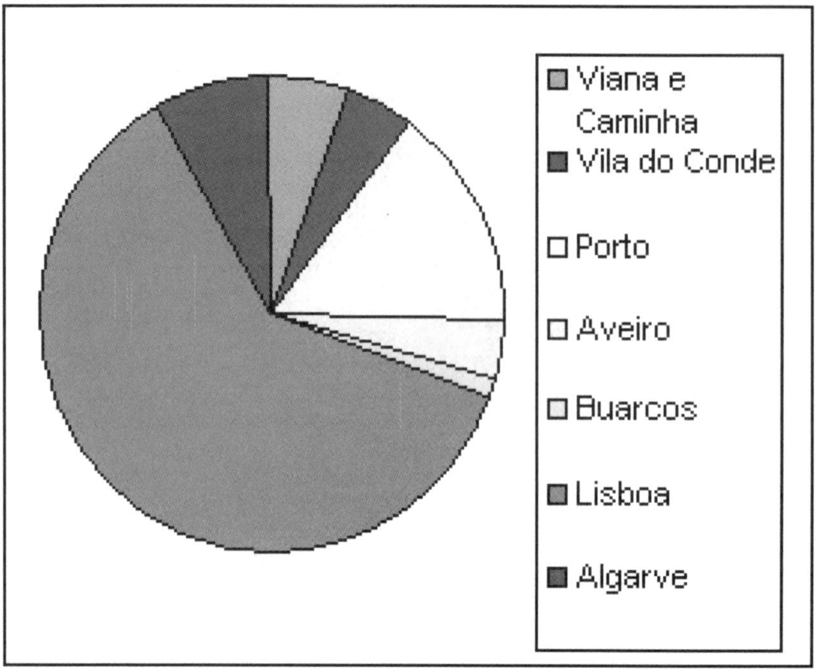

Figure 4: Customs Revenue, 1526 (Budget)

Source: General Archives of the Lisbon Customs House (AGAL), Lv. Reg. Geral Alf. V. Conde, fls. 194-195; and João Cordeiro Pereira, "A receita do estado português no ano de 1526. Um orçamento desconhecido," in *Estudos de História de Portugal, Vol. II* (Lisbon, 1983), 15-55.

In the seventeenth century Porto, along with Viana do Castelo, became increasingly prominent in relation to Lisbon, particularly in Brazilian trade, which the government saw as an alternative to commerce with the East from the 1560s. The Brazilian trade lacked the administrative controls that existed in Indian commerce, which reduced the advantages possessed by Lisbon in the latter. This allowed more ports to become involved. The main colonial product was sugar, which Portuguese ports redistributed throughout Europe and the Mediterranean. The role of the various ports can be seen in reports on customs revenues, which we will use as an initial approach to identify a seaport hierarchy.

Unfortunately, systematic customs records do not exist for all ports for all periods. For this reason, our analysis of their relative commercial prominence is based on three sets of documentation: state budgets from 1526 and 1557 and the revenue of some maritime customs houses in the period

1602-1607; the values of customs rents in the northwest ports for 1525 and 1554- 1557; and the value of extraordinary taxes imposed by the Portuguese crown on the various districts in 1612 and 1631.

The data show an exponential increase in customs revenue, which grew from about fifteen *contos* in 1526 to about sixty-two *contos* in 1557 and 178 *contos* in the period 1602/1607 owing largely to high rates of inflation (see figures 4-6).[15] They also show the dominance of Lisbon, which accounted for more than sixty percent of maritime customs revenues, peaking at eighty-four percent in the period 1602-1607. The evidence also underscores the position of Porto as the second most important post, generating fifteen percent of revenues in 1526 and ten percent eighty years later. But in 1557 Porto contributed only about five percent, a share lower than that of Viana do Castelo, a finding that we are still seeking to explain. Nevertheless, in the tax revenues for 1601 and 1622, Porto accounted for ten and fourteen percent, respectively.[16]

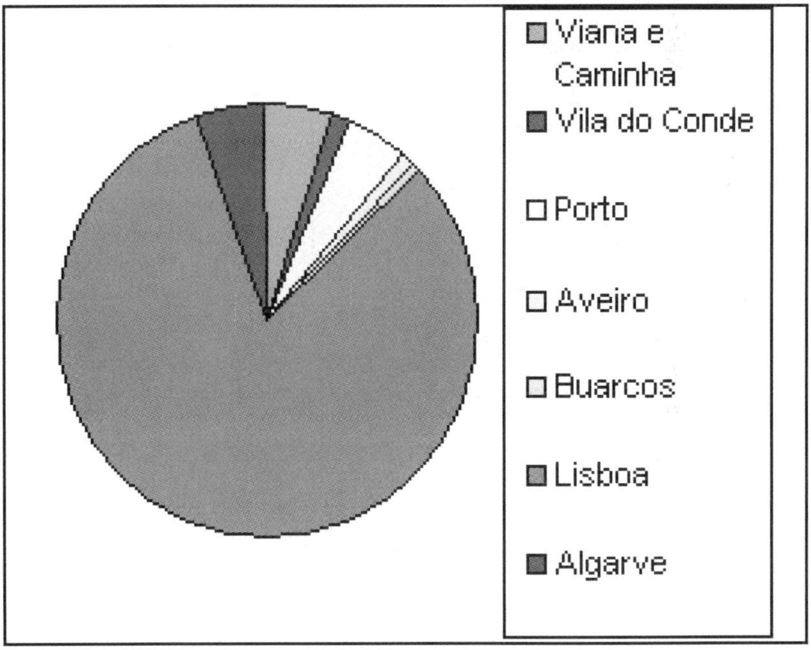

Figure 5: Customs Revenue, 1557 (Budget)

Source: Porto District Archive (ADP), Contadoria da Comarca do Porto, lv. 20, fl. 341-348v.

[15]The *conto* was the major Portuguese monetary unit until the twentieth century.

[16]Cf. Freire Costa, "O transporte," 94.

Taxes for the customs houses of the northwest, including Aveiro, varied from thirty percent in 1526, twelve percent in 1557 and about fourteen percent in 1602/1607 (see figures 7 and 8). In the period 1554-1557, Viana do Castelo vied with Porto; its rise from 14.3 percent of the total revenue from northwest ports in 1526 to forty-one percent in 1557 shows the port's increasing importance. The Brazilian sugar trade was a major reason why tax revenues rose so rapidly in both Porto and Viana. But the smaller regional ports suffered a dramatic relative decline. This was true especially for Vila do Conde, Aveiro and the Algarve ports, which fell from 8.1 percent in 1526 to 1.5 percent by 1602-1607.

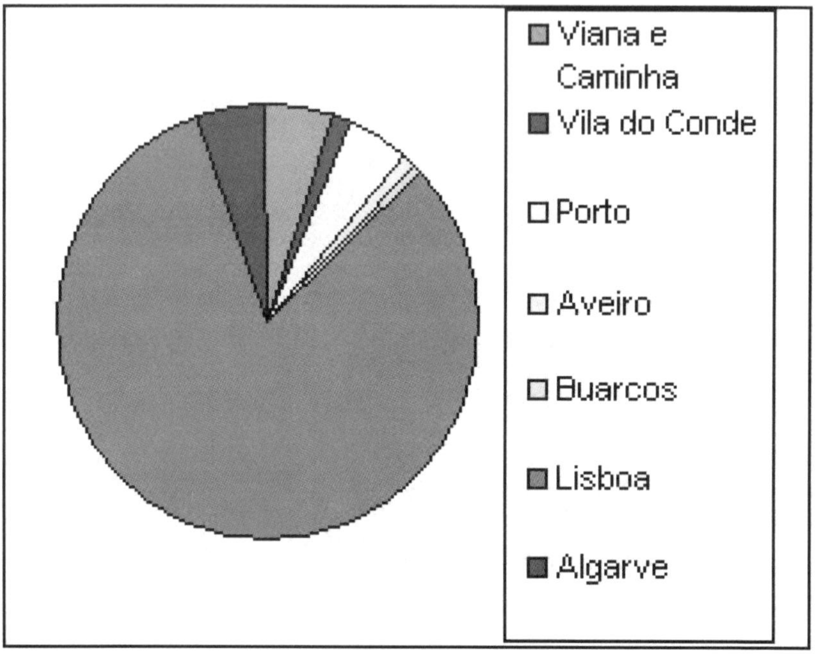

Figure 6: Customs Revenue Rents, 1602/1607

Source: *Livro primeiro do Governo do Brasil (1607-1633)* (Rio de Janeiro, 1958), 178; and Leonor Freire Costa, "O transporte do Atlântico. As frotas do açúcar (1580-1663)" (Unpublished PhD thesis, Technical University of Lisbon, 2000), 92.

An examination of the values of the extraordinary taxes demanded by the monarchy is more complex because these do not reflect the real position of the ports but rather the view of the central authorities about the ability of various places to pay. Nonetheless, it is noteworthy that the share demanded from

Porto and Viana do Castelo rose from 15.4 percent in 1612 to 20.5 percent in 1631, while the expected contribution from Lisbon fell in these years by about five percent, and the southern districts, including the Algarve, declined from 16.4 to 8.7 percent (see figures 9 and 10).

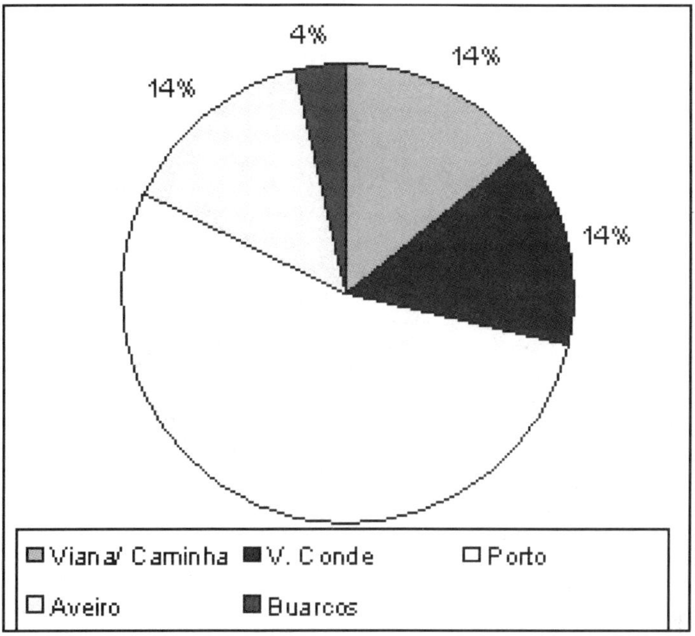

Figure 7: Customs Revenue of the Entre-Douro-e-Minho, Aveiro and Buarcos Ports, 1525

Note: Rent values.

Source: Portugal, National Archive, Torre do Tombo (IAN/TT), NA 590.

While it is easy to criticise this source, it is important to note that even the sources which might appear more "reliable" have their problems. For example, customs revenues do not necessarily reflect the intrinsic commercial vitality of the several seaports. This is especially apparent in the case of Vila do Conde, where the existence of a private customs house, outside of royal control, distorted reality due to the practice of discounts and subsidies which led to the clearing of merchandise destined in fact for other coastal locations from Caminha to Porto. This port, operating as a maritime trading post for the vast hinterland of Entre-Douro-e-Minho, also attracted significant cargoes from merchants in Braga, Guimarães, Chaves and Barcelos. Indeed, the commercial and financial capacity of the Vila do Conde merchant community was considerably lower than suggested by the customs revenues in 1526. The distortion was less important in 1557, however, when the private customs house was closed.[17] Such data problems make the construction of an accurate seaport hierarchy in northwest Portugal more difficult.

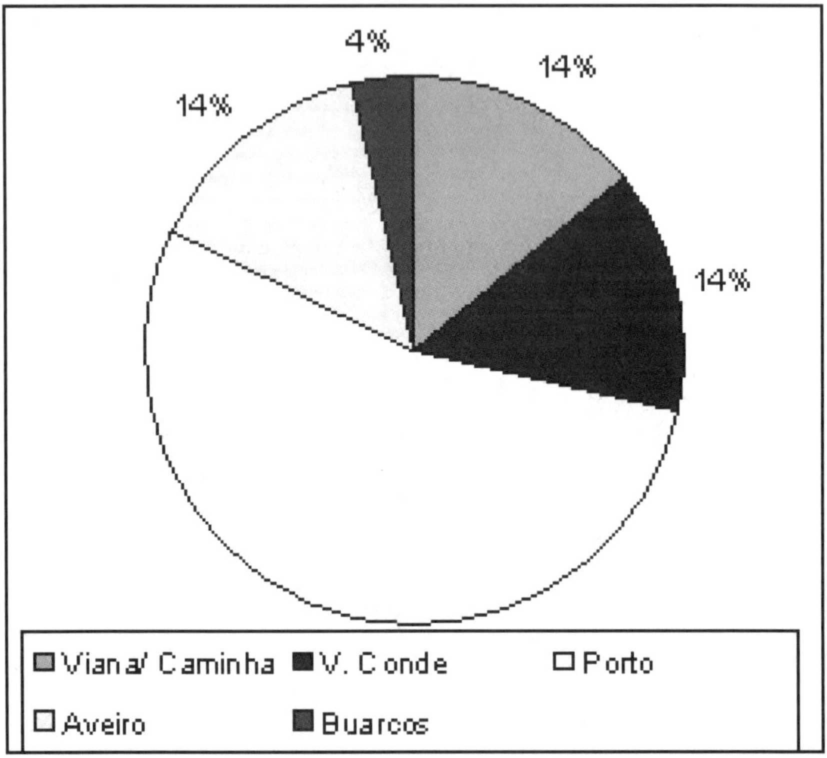

Figure 8: Customs Revenue of the Entre-Douro-e-Minho, Aveiro and Buarcos Ports, 1554/1557

Note: Annual rent values.

Source: ADP, Contadoria da Comarca do Porto, lv. 20, fl. 341-348v.

Furthermore, some of the kingdom's ports were revitalised by commercial capital from other ports. We can document this for Vila do Conde in

[17]Cf. Polónia, "Vila do Conde," I, 557-574.

the first decades of the seventeenth century, the New Christian merchant community of Porto, which was responsible for an increasing mercantile movement,[18] and the port of Viana do Castelo, where the import of Brazilian sugar was sustained by commercial partnerships involving merchants and capital from Lisbon who wanted to take advantage of a customs tax system which was clearly beneficial to them. It was also easier to evade the embargoes the monarchy imposed on ships and economic agents from the United Provinces, a traditional trading partner of Portugal. Such a strategy implies the internal migration of commercial agents, the transfer of capital and the existence of merchant networks, all of which would have diluted a pyramidal seaport hierarchy, the traditional model used to analyse port dynamics. On the other hand, it is clear that such shifts are normal. That is, regardless of the mechanisms that drive the mercantile prominence of certain ports, they are prone to change them over time. Indeed, in Portugal some of the factors that affected the port hierarchy were introduced by those dynamics.

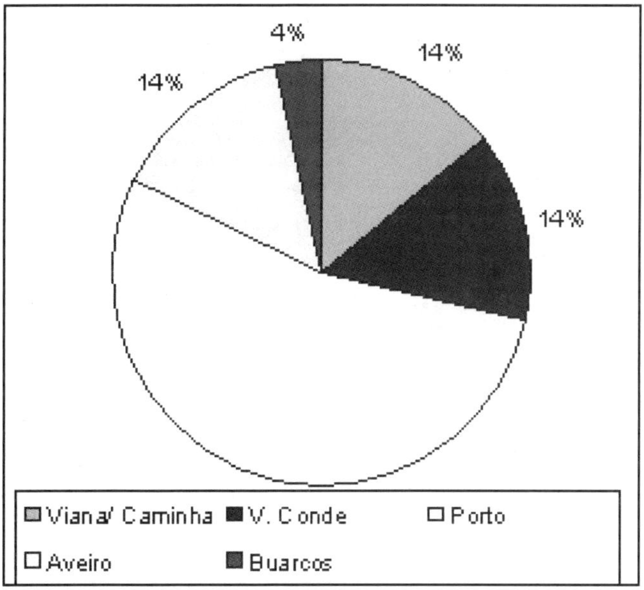

Figure 9: Distribution of Extraordinary Taxes by Maritime District, 1612

Note: *Comarca* is an administrative district.

Source: E. Freire de Oliveira, *Elementos para a história do município de* Lisboa (2 vols., Lisbon, 1882-1891), II, 289-290; and Freire Costa, "O transporte," 90.

[18]*Ibid.*, I, 586-595.

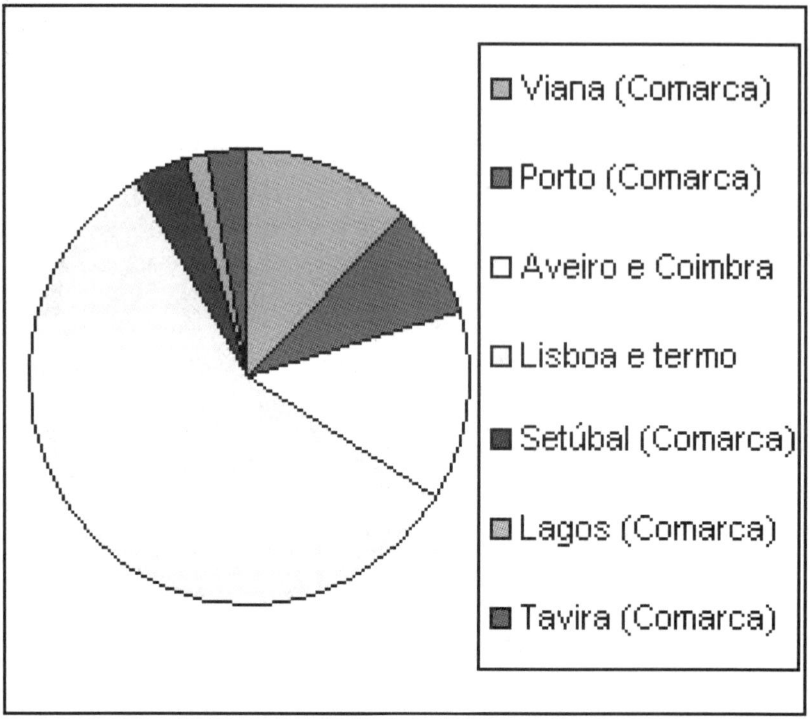

Figure 10: Distribution of Extraordinary Taxes by Maritime District, 1631

Note: See figure 9.

Source: See figure 9.

Despite the difficulties with sources, an analysis of notarial records in Porto and Lisbon prove the existence of strong inter-port complementarity at the regional level. It is possible, for example, to distinguish between shipbuilding, shipowning and commercial ports. While Lisbon, Porto and Viana dominated the Brazilian trade, they were surrounded by smaller ports which made important contributions by providing vessels, seamen or other factors necessary for the continuation of commerce. The distribution of seafaring communities buttresses this conclusion. Figures 11 and 12 depict the distribution of seamen in Portuguese seaports in the late sixteenth and early seventeenth centuries and indicate their relative importance in supplying seamen.[19] The distri-

[19]On the general supply of European seamen, see John Armstrong and Andreas Kunz (eds.), *Coastal Shipping and the European Economy 1750-1980* (Mainz,

bution confirms the service function of small- and medium-size ports. In fact, unlike the data on customs revenues and taxes, the seafaring communities were dispersed all along the coast, and the ranking of each port is clearly different.

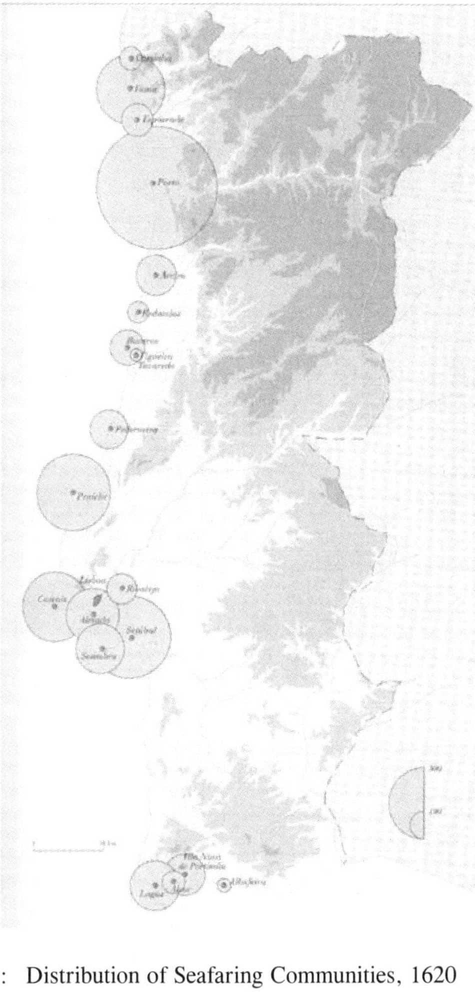

Figure 11: Distribution of Seafaring Communities, 1620

Source: Mattoso (ed.), *História de Portugal*, III, 239.

2002); Paul C. van Royen, Jaap R. Brujin and Jan Lucassen (eds.), *"Those Emblems of Hell?" European Sailors and the Maritime Labour Market, 1570-1870* (St. John's, 1997); and Ina Baghdiantz McCabe, Gelina Harlaftis and Ioanna Pepelasis Minoglou (eds.), *Diaspora Entrepreneurial Networks: Four Centuries of History* (Geneva, 2005).

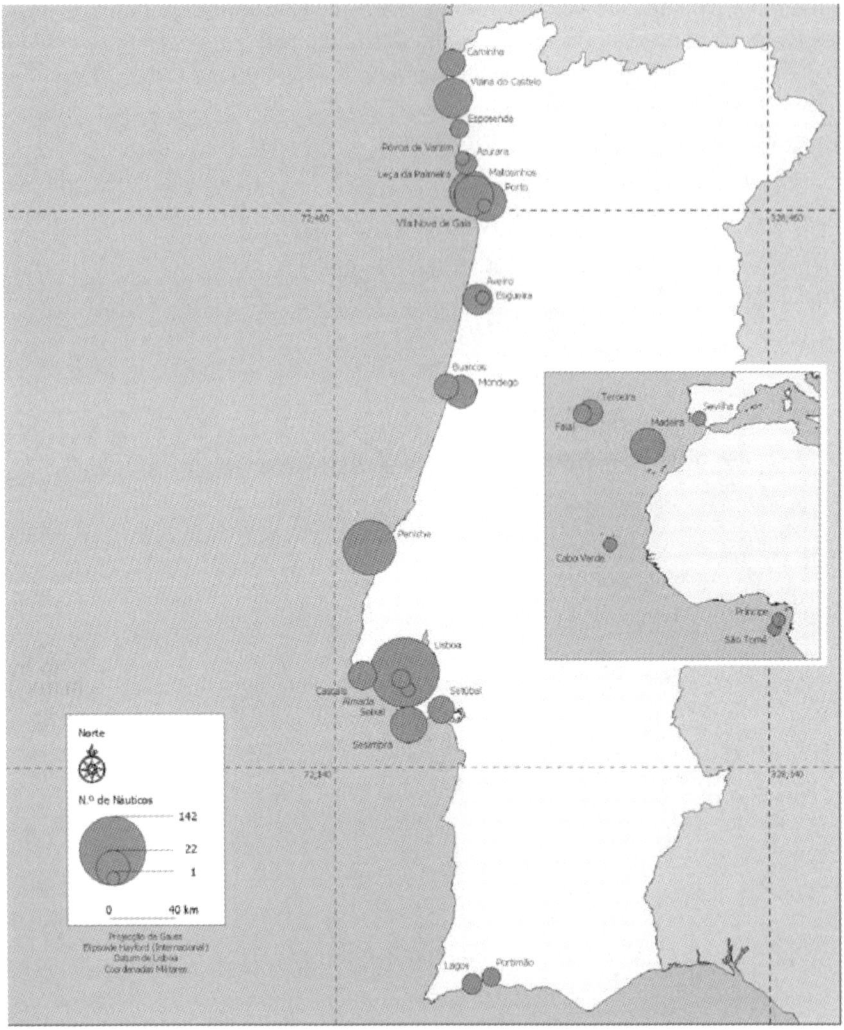

Figure 12: Seamen Examined, 1596-1649

Source: See figure 11.

The minor ports were clearly subsidiaries of the larger harbours; they were interested in shipping but did not necessarily provide finance or engage in colonial trade. Setúbal, Sesimbra and Peniche revolved around Lisbon, while Matosinhos, Leça, Azurara and Vila do Conde provided men and ships for

Porto.[20] There clearly were networks and complementarities. Consortia among shipowners of diverse geographic and professional origin were common.[21] The trade cycles of a port thus affected not only its own internal socio-economic dynamics but also those of the other members of its network. For example, the decline of Lisbon's role in the Brazilian trade and the corresponding rise of Porto created shock waves in the economies and societies of port towns throughout northwest Portugal.

Another consequence of the changing roles of Porto and Lisbon in the Brazilian trade concerned the redistribution of sugar and other colonial products to Northern Europe. The Portuguese merchant fleet, drained in the seventeenth century by privateers, its participation in the defeat of the Spanish Armada and the War of Independence, was unable to meet the increasing demand for transport, leading to a clear predominance of foreign vessels in trade between Portugal and Europe. This was increased by the Westminster Treaty of 1654 which opened Portuguese trade to British merchants. This reduction in the availability of domestic shipping and the dominance of foreign vessels in Portuguese trade was also increased by foreign restrictions on maritime transport, such as the British Navigation Acts, and was reflected in the increasing precariousness of the small ports of the northwest which had traditionally provided these services to the commercial ports.

This situation was exacerbated during the eighteenth century. Porto by this time was specialising in the export of port wine; even though it remained involved in foreign and colonial trade, port movements were restricted somewhat by the geo-morphological condition of its bar at the mouth of the river, and European connections were mostly conducted by foreign fleets, especially the British.[22] Lisbon reasserted its dominance over colonial trade with the as-

---

[20]According to data provided by Leonor Freire Costa, "Redes interportuárias nos circuitos do açúcar brasileiro. O trajecto de Gaspar Pacheco, um banqueiro de D. João IV," in Mafalda Soares da Cunha (ed.), *Do Brasil à metrópole. Efeitos sociais* (Évora, 2001), 36-37, in the period 1580-1601 only 44.5 percent of the vessels in the Brazilian trade registered in Lisbon notarial records were from that port. The remainder were provided by other ports, including Setúbal, Alcácer, Sesimbra, Sines, Cascais, Peniche, Atouguia, Buarcos and Mondego; 16.6 percent came from the northwest ports of Porto and Viana. The Brazilian trade from Porto was similarly dependent upon vessels from elsewhere: only 67.4 percent were provided by local owners. The other northwest seaports (Matosinhos, Leça, Caminha, Esposende, Azurara and Aveiro) provided an additional 26.5 percent.

[21]Polónia, "Vila do Conde," I.

[22]The Porto case is, in this dominion, paradigmatic. According to Barros Cardoso, *Baco and Hermes*, II, 78, of the vessels entering the Douro between 1704 and 1747, 8.3 percent were Portuguese according to the nationality of their shipping agents.

sistance of the central government, especially through the creation of monopolies granted to companies sustained by state capital.

The policies of the Marquis of Pombal were designed to promote favoured economic groups through the creation of the Chambers of Commerce and to restrict the freedom of trade. Among the more important monopolies created by Pombal were the Asia Trade Company (1753), the Grão Pará e Maranhão Company (1755), the Alto Douro Wine Company (1756) and the Pernambuco and Paraíba Company (1759). He also renewed the monopolistic tobacco and soap contracts. At the same time, access to capital was constrained through restrictions on loans and interest, while a law was passed in 1755 to ban "travelling commissaries," small merchants linked to the Brazilian trade. This was an attempt by the state to restrict trade to a select minority, mostly located near the centre of power in Lisbon. This commercial legislation concentrated profits from colonial and international trade, thus preventing domestic competition.[23] By contrast, international traders were left alone, if only because Portuguese authorities were less able to control them.

These policies profoundly affected the small- and medium-size ports in the northwest, changing their ranking and status within the regional and national port systems. At the same time, they also disrupted the inter-port complementarity networks, woven as they were around maritime logistics. Shipbuilding and transport suffered due to the diminished role of the Portuguese fleet in colonial and European trade. Seaports like Caminha, Vila do Conde, Azurara and even Viana do Castelo, which had been active and had grown steadily during the sixteenth and seventeenth centuries in close connection with Porto or Lisbon, now lost a large part of their importance.

The reality of these changes in the status of northwest ports may be seen through fluctuations in wealth, demography and investments in harbour

---

The remainder were English (seventy-six percent), Dutch (7.2 percent); Hamburgers (6.7 percent); and French (7.5 percent).

[23]On this issue, see Jorge Borges de Macedo, *A situação económica no tempo de Pombal* (Lisbon, 1989); Borges de Macedo, *Elementos para a história bancária de Portugal (1797-1820)* (Lisbon, 1982); Borges de Macedo, *O Marquês de Pombal, 1699-1782* (Lisbon, 1982); David Justino, *A formação do espaço económico português* (2 vols., Lisbon, 1988-1989); H.E.S. Fischer, *The Portugal Trade: A Study of Anglo-Portuguese Commerce, 1700-1770* (London, 1971); and Jorge M. Pedreira, *Os homens de negócio da praça de Lisboa. De Pombal ao Vintismo (1755-1822). Diferenciação, reprodução e identificação de um grupo social* (Lisbon, 1995).

[25]Since these databases are still being refined, the numbers presented should be treated as preliminary. But we have a good deal of confidence that future revisions will not alter the conclusions.

works. The latter in particular is an excellent indicator of the survival, growth or decline of the ports within a broader seaport system.

Evolution of the Northwest Seaports: Evidence of Harbour Construction

Some of the evidence most relevant to a discussion of seaport networks comes from information on harbour works. It is important to learn whether the historical context discussed above was decisive in determining investment in infrastructure. Information from the Hisportos databases should help us to uncover the answer.[25] Figures 13 and 14 present some of these data.

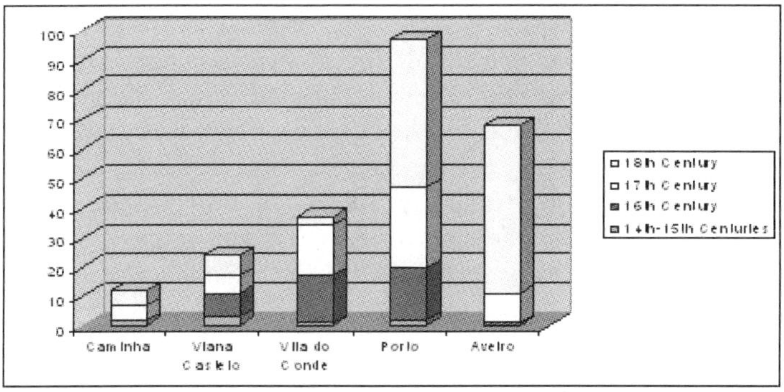

Figure 13: Number of Harbour Works in Northwest Ports, 14th-18th Century

Source: Hisportos databases.

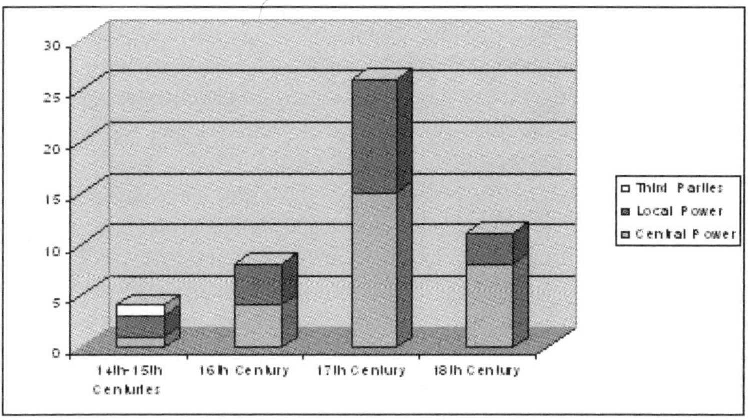

Figure 14: Funding and Financing Approvals, 14th-18th Century

Source: See figure 13.

Taken together, the two figures suggest that the number and complexity of harbour improvements rose in the seventeenth and eighteenth century. The precise level of increase, however, is less certain, since the lack of documentary sources prior to sixteenth century may lead us to underestimate work carried out in that period. Moreover, the number of these works funded by the central government increased compared to those paid for locally. Against the backdrop of warfare throughout the seventeenth century, however, both sources of funding were significant.[26] Eighteenth-century investments by the crown were overwhelmingly concentrated in the larger ports of the northwest, Porto and Aveiro.

Some additional context may be useful to interpret these findings. Construction in seaports and harbours obviously reflected political, military and economic interests. Most construction in the sixteenth century, especially in Vila do Conde and Porto, were designed to improve harbour entrances and to construct quays and docks to facilitate overseas trade. Those that took place in the seventeenth century, however, were for the most part directed at the building and maintenance of fortifications and defensive structures due to the lengthy periods of warfare. The harbour works undertaken in the eighteenth century were largely the result of the policies of the central government in Lisbon discussed above.

The number of interventions reflects the decline in the seventeenth and especially the eighteenth century of small ports, such as Vila do Conde, Caminha and even Viana do Castelo. This reality was related not only to their internal situation but also to an economic policy which favoured the major seaports. This tendency reached its apex in the third quarter of the eighteenth century under Pombal. Since harbour works depended increasingly on funding from the centre, improvements were not made, and maintenance was neglected. This led to significant changes in the inter-regional port system in the northwest, disrupting the complementarity networks and weakening the ties between the ports and their hinterlands. Ports which had been relatively important, even on a small or medium scale, became "unimportant ports," in the sense proposed by Gordon Jackson:

> Those with a poor or backward hinterland and few external connections; with a small or no share of national imports and exports and, contrary to expectations, a small share of coastal trade, which was also dominated by major ports; with exceptions they owned and built few ships; they had inadequate facilities for larger ships; few warehouses; no comprehensive mercantile community or direct foreign link-

---

[26]The significant number of local authority interventions in Vila do Conde can only be explained because of its manorial jurisdiction.

> ages; few industries and small populations; in sum, they had no opportunity for self generated trade.[27]

The lack of investment in infrastructure led to an irreversible loss of status and economic capability in the smaller ports of the northwest.

If the infrastructural investments in Porto can be understood in the context of economic growth, the case of Aveiro is quite distinct and illustrates another dimension of seaport construction. Porto dominated the national and international trade in port wine in the eighteenth century. The Douro River and the entrance to the harbour were pivotal factors at a regional and international level to facilitate connections with regional and international markets. From this perspective, investments were both understandable and justified. But at the same time Aveiro suffered from the decline of the salt trade, its traditional staple, and it had no other product to export. The need to rebuild the port was argued persistently by the local authorities and merchants. Between 1759 and 1808 a long list of Portuguese, German, French and Italian engineers passed through Aveiro. Even though actual investments only began in 1802 with the construction of a dike, there were numerous technical improvements paid for by the crown during the eighteenth century, a period when the customs and other trade and economic revenues could not support the cost of maintaining the open harbour. Nevertheless, the works and the planning continued in association with other proposals to promote Aveiro, despite all the geomorphological and economic restrictions.[28] In short, what happened in Aveiro was based on political and economic theories rather than anything promising in the local or regional context. During the eighteenth and nineteenth centuries Aveiro's port improvements were based on theoretical assumptions and technical experiences rather than on its national or international relevance or its local or regional dynamism.

This seems to comprise one of the three models of seaport construction and port growth in northwest Portugal during the early modern age. The second was to be found in the small ports of Caminha, Vila do Conde and Viana do Castelo, all of which were destined to become "unimportant ports" despite their internal and hinterland importance in the sixteenth century (Vila do Conde and Caminha, associated with overseas trade) and the seventeenth century (Viana do Castelo, associated with the Brazilian sugar trade in

---

[27]Gordon Jackson, "The Significance of Unimportant Ports," *International Journal of Maritime History*, XIII, No. 2 (December 2001), 1-17.

[28]Inês Amorim, "Portuguese "Free" Ports at the Turn of the Eighteenth Century - A Strategy to Promote "Unimportant" Ports," in *Proceedings of the 4th International Congress of Maritime History* (Corfu, 2005) [CD-Rom].

connection with Lisbon's merchant community).[29] The third was to be found in Porto, where sustainable economic growth based on wine and the Brazilian trades led to improvements in the Douro and significant investments in the harbour even though the geo-morphological constraints of the harbour entrance seemed to argue against significant construction. Indeed, in the nineteenth century most of the trade and investment was transferred to Leixões. What was at stake was the centrality of the town which was dependent in the long term on the condition of its harbour and the navigability of the Douro.

Conclusions

This study demonstrates that northwest Portuguese ports in the early modern age functioned as a network based upon complementarities. The small- and medium-size places were service ports, subsidiaries either to Porto or Lisbon, neither of which were self-sufficient shipping and seafaring communities. The dark side of this relationship, however, was that when one of the major ports ran into difficulties, their satellite ports also suffered. Moreover, the policies of the central government interfered with the development of some ports (Lisbon in the sixteenth and eighteenth centuries; Porto in the eighteenth century), and was responsible for some of the northwest harbours during the seventeenth and eighteenth century becoming "unimportant ports." Indeed, interference from the centre seems to have been more constrictive in the eighteenth than in the sixteenth and seventeenth centuries, when colonial trade in particular opened new opportunities for small- and medium-size ports.

National and international economic trends, as well as transformations in the international hierarchy of ports, were quite influential in the evolution of all the northwest seaports. Indeed, Portuguese overseas expansion was a more important factor in explaining which port grew or declined than were their roles as nodal axes between the hinterland and foreland. Finally, the growing complexity and cost of harbour works during the eighteenth century made ports even more dependant on central funding and placed them at the mercy of priorities determined in Lisbon.

These conclusions, based on the analysis of a variety of data, remind us that there are other historical indicators, whether demographic or urban, which require analysis before we can comprehend fully the development of Portuguese ports. This is one of the main goals of Hisportos II.[30]

---

[29]Freire Costa, "O transporte," 94.

[30]This project has been submitted for funding to the FST (Portuguese Foundation for Science and Technology).

Discourse and the Container Revolution in Finland in the 1960s and 1970s

Kari Teräs

The fact that the standardised container has revolutionised transport is somewhat astonshing. Compared to many other technological innovations, the container is a rather simple device. Indeed, its real importance is revealed only when we think of it as comprising an all-embracing "socio-technological system" and pay attention to its more wide-ranging economic, cultural and social impacts.[1] Frank Broeze has noted that the broad meaning of the container was only shaped gradually and that this involved several actors:

> Containerization provides an almost perfect model of what may be termed complex innovation. Its first stage was extremely simple in theory and execution. But once the first steps had been taken and the true revolutionary power of the system could be imagined, it swept before it every aspect of liner in a process of rapid transformation at sea, ashore on the wharf and in office, and deep inland.[2]

Marc Levinson aptly notes that "the value of this utilitarian object lies not in what it is, but in how it is used." The container became both the core and symbol of economic change in transport because it facilitated the development of highly automated, door-to-door transport. In effect, the "box" enabled the creation of a sophisticated system of intermodal transport. Containers radically changed world trade, shipping and ports as they seamlessly linked various modes of transport. As they lowered transport costs, containers began to

---

[1]See Thomas P. Hughes, *Networks of Power: Electrification in Western Society, 1880-1930* (Baltimore, 1983); and Hughes, "Evolution of Large Systems," in Wiebe E. Bijker, Thomas P. Hughes and Trevor J. Pinch (eds.), *The Social Construction of Large Technological Systems: New Directions in the Sociology and History of Technology* (Cambridge, MA), 1987.

[2]Frank Broeze, *The Globalisation of the Oceans: Containerisation from the 1950s to the Present* (St. John's, 2002), 25.

change not only transportation but also production, trade and consumption, thus providing a strong impetus to economic globalisation.[3]

Despite their great significance, until recently the history of containers has been the subject of surprisingly little research. Nonetheless, a general picture of their introduction and spread is starting to emerge. The latest research, however, makes the container revolution seem much more complex than we previously thought, and the subject has by no means been exhausted.[4] Future studies of the development of container transport in various countries which allow for international comparisons should help to clarify our understanding of this great logistic transition.

From the beginning containerisation has generated an enormous amount of talk, inspired a good deal of writing and led to many seminars and training sessions. In Finland, this was described as "container enthusiasm" or "container fever." At the outset, when containers were still relatively marginal in maritime transport, the volume of hype considerably oustripped the rate of adoption, and even when it became apparent that containers were not a passing fad, there was still a great deal of dithering. In this essay, I will discuss the first phase of the container revolution in Finland during the 1960s and early 1970s by examining contemporary debates. My basic assumption is that the discourse that occurred influenced the way containers were received, the meanings placed upon them and the way they were used within the Finnish transport system. I will focus on the expectations that contemporaries had for containers and on whether they considered their adoption inevitable. I will argue that the fact that everyone in the close-knit maritime community talked about them had an impact on their relatively rapid and fairly smooth adoption. The container revolution had significant social effects on transport because it brought together all the players. This can be shown by examining the kinds of discussion, plans and visions that containers produced in the early phase of the logistic revolution in Finland. Technical thinking changed rapidly as a result of the increase in container traffic. Central to this new way of thinking was a broadening of the context in which transport was considered and an acceptance that there were going to be social consequences as a result of this shift.

Even though I will primarily concentrate on discourses, I will also examine the progress of the first phase of the container revolution in Finland. The focal point of my examination is ports, where the various transport

---

[3]Marc Levinson, *The Box: How the Shipping Container Made the World Smaller and the World Economy Bigger* (Princeton, 2006), 1-15; and Broeze, *Globalisation*, 9-25.

[4]See Broeze, *Globalisation;* Levinson, *The Box*; Brian J. Cudahy, *Box Boats: How Container Ships Changed the World* (New York, 2006); and Arthur Donovan, *The Box That Changed the World: Fifty Years of Container Shipping – An Illustrated History* (East Windsor, NJ, 2006).

technologies intersected. Ports offer an ideal perspective from which to view the larger revolution, since they had to adjust constantly to changes in production, fleets, cargoes and cargo-handling techniques, as well as shifts in other modes of transport.[5] At the time of the container revolution, passive adaptation was no longer sufficient.

This article is mainly based on two types of material. First, I will rely on Finnish technical magazines that focus on the transport and shipping industries; these featured many articles on the technical properties of containers and on container transport in international shipping. In other words, I am primarily looking at the problems faced by engineers, the technical experts of the transport sector, in the 1960s and 1970s. The other group of sources comprises research implemented or funded by the state. From the mid-1960s several committees, consisting of a wide range of representatives from public author-ities and various transport modes, were established to discuss the role of ports in this on-going revolution. These committees strove to find solutions to enable Finland, which relied heavily on maritime transport, to cope with the rapid changes in the sector. Although containers also attracted a great deal of interest from the non-specialist Finnish media, these will not be examined in detail here.

The Finnish debate was hampered intially because people did not know what to call this novelty. Since there was no word for it in Finnish, it became customary to use the English word, container, or its Finnish spelling, *kontaineri*. Those attempting a Finnish translation simply called it *kuljetussäiliö*, or "transport container." From the late 1960s the word *kontti* gradually became established. The term was apt, as it originally referred to a traditional type of a rucksack.[6] Its pronunciation also connected it to the English term. And so it was that this "international revolution" succeeded in taking on a national and even colloquial flavour in Finland.

The Industry as Metaphor

During the early phase of the introduction of containers, Finland was rapidly changing from an agrarian to a modern industrial nation. Industrialisation, urbanisation, commercialisation and mechanisation of the society all progressed in tandem. As Tapio Bergholm has written, after the Second World War Finland developed from a relatively poor state that exported primarily raw materials into a wealthy industrial country which increasingly shipped pro-

[5]Malcolm Tull, *A Community Enterprise: The History of the Port of Fremantle, 1897 to 1997* (St. John's, 1997), 2-3; and Broeze, *Globalisation*, 4 and 167.

[6]Kari Teräs, "Modernisoituvat satamat: Teknologia, työ ja satamien kehittäminen," in Ali Pylkkänen, Tapio Bergholm and Kari Teräs, *Satamillaan maa hengittää. Suomen Satamaliiton historia 1923-2000* (Helsinki, 2002), 136.

cessed goods abroad.[7] Industrial output became a common measure of well-being, and as job opportunities in the rural areas decreased, industrialisation was associated with hopes for a better future.

Systematic attention had been focused in Finland on manufacturing since the Second World War. Mechanisation, increased efficiency and the drive to increase the value-added component of production were regarded as national goals, even during the period of reconstruction. Once foreign trade was freed from regulation in the late 1950s, the Finnish economy increasingly was integrated into the international economy. Finnish companies had to meet the challenges of international competition by becoming more efficient and by examining the ways in which goods eventually reached consumers through transport and trade. Since large amounts of capital were invested in industry, the distribution system became increasingly important to economic efficiency.

It was easy for experts to point out the worst transport bottlenecks. Their rhetorical device frequently was to compare a highly automated industrial facility with a backward-looking port which handled valuable cargo in more-or-less the same way it had done a hundred years earlier. Irregular work, unstable employment relationships, susceptibility to weather and the labour-intensive methods of shifting cargoes stood in sharp contrast to the modern industrial facilities. In magazines specialising in transport technology in the mid-1960s it was customary to exaggerate the differences between these two worlds and to ask why loading and discharging cargoes in ports could not be as efficient as work in the production phase.[8] If production was well organised, why were several intermediate processes needed in ports? If the mass-produced goods flowing from the factories were standardised, why were the ports handling cargoes in a myriad of different shapes and sizes? When factories worked around the clock, why was there only a single shift in ports?

To demonstrate this stagnation, technical magazines in the 1960s provided rough estimates of the lengthy turnaround times in ports. As much as thirty or forty percent of total operating times of vessels carrying break-bulk cargoes were spent in ports. It was generally claimed that cargo-handling in ports represented a third of total transport costs.[9] Similarly, shipowners com-

---

[7]Tapio Bergholm, "Satamaliikenne ja yhteiskunta," in *ibid.*, 35-38.

[8]J. Rissanen, "Uusista suuntauksista kappaletavaran käsittelyn alalla," *Kuljetus*, No. 5 (1965), 4-10.

[9]*Ibid.*; Matti Vainio, "Lift-on-Lift-off"- järjestelmän mukaisen kontaineriliikenteen aiheuttamat kustannukset," *Kuljetus*, No. 3 (1966), 27-30; and Kaarle J. Tuurna, "Laivanvarustuksen rationalisoinnin näkökulmia," *Ahtaajat*, No. 2 (1966), 11-12. Johan Woxenius, *Containertransportens historia* (Göteborg, 1992), 23 and 61, estimated that at the beginning of the 1960s traditional cargo ships spent roughly one-half of their operating time in ports.

plained that cargo vessels spent more than half their service lives in harbour and that "the ports only work at half capacity."[10] Engineers took an even dimmer view of port efficiency. Although a large-scale, state-sponsored study published in 1965 by the Dutch consultants NEDECO reported that the average cargo-handling rate in Finnish ports was good and that the productivity of dock workers was higher than that in many European ports, they recommended the introduction of two shifts to increase efficiency.[11]

Specialists in transport technology immediately discovered the possibilities offered by containers to narrow the difference in efficiency between factories and ports. Cargo unitisation already had a long tradition, and the container offered similar potential rationalisations.[12] Handling costs, as one 1965 article enthused, could be lowered to "a fraction of their current levels."[13] The language and objectives of modern harbour planning were borrowed from manufacturing; ports had to become industrial facilities based on mass production. In practise, this meant that the industrial revolution, which in Finland began in the mid-nineteenth century, was now being extended to the economy's last pre-industrial outpost.

Finnish ports in the 1960s were still a long way from matching the vision of industrial efficiency, even if they had been modernised and mechanised to a degree after the Second World War. The number of forklifts and cranes increased during the 1950s, but the machinery was inefficient for handling large units. An important milestone in cargo unitisation was reached in 1957 when the first experiments were made loading sawn wood in packages. The results were positive, and it was soon possible to eliminate the manual handling of bulk goods. Two years later, the first roll-on roll-off (ro-ro) car ferry in Finland started to operate in coastal traffic, and in 1961 a regular car ferry connection began on the Turku-Stockholm route. Progress in the decasualisation of labout soon brought Finland to the same point as large European ports, such as London, Amsterdam and Hamburg. The need to develop container traffic contributed to the achievement of permanent employment in stevedoring in 1972, finally putting port labour on the same level as manu-

---

[10]T. Westerberg, "Suuryksikkökuljetukset käytännön kuljetustoiminnassa," *Kuljetus*, No. 10 (1966), 51-52.

[11]NEDECO, *A Survey on Transportation in Finland* (The Hague, 1965).

[12]Anders Björklund, *Slaget om hamnarna. Om ny teknik och fackliga gränser i fem svenska hamnar* (Lund, 1988), 34-37; Broeze, *Globalisation*, 30-31; Levinson, *The Box*, 29-35; and Teräs, "Modernisoituvat satamat," 134-136.

[13]Harald Lindahl, "Kontainerikulketusten taloudellisuus," *Suomen Merenkulku Finlands Sjöfart*, No. 11 (1965), 395.

facturing. The internal preconditions for radical change in Finland were now in place, even if the impetus came from outside the country.[14]

In the Vanguard or Rearguard of the Revolution?

New international trends in shipping were followed with interest in Finnish technical magazines. Although American experiences were examined carefully, experts initially paid attention mainly to the technical properties of containers, ignoring to a great extent the all-embracing transport possibilities that they represented. For example, the 1962 book *Meri ja me* (*The Sea and Us*) barely mentioned the logistic revolution.[15] Once the trade magazines began to write about the practical applications of the new technology for Finland, however, the push for containerisation reached new levels. In 1963, regular traffic began between Helsinki and Central Europe using so-called "auto-containers" developed for international road transport; these were plywood boxes with supporting legs that could be moved using the truck's interchangeable platform system.[16] Even if the volume of traffic initially was modest, it stimulated a good deal of interest in container transport. Through practical experiments, container-related discourse became more concrete; the revolution was now knocking on the door.

From the beginning it was possible to formulate clearly the benefits of this new form of transport. Significant savings could be achieved when goods were transported from the sender to the recipient with no intermediate handling: packaging could be made economical; the risk of damage in transit was lower; the probability of theft was lessened; and the need for storage *en route* was eliminated. Because of the containers, cargoes - except for hazardous goods - became more anonymous. Virtually the only technical drawback was

---

[14]Kari Teräs, "Hampuuseista ahtaajiksi - käsipelistä konetyöhön," in Jussi T. Lappalainen (ed.), *Turun sataman historia* (Turku, 1999), 263-266; Teräs, "Modernisoituvat satamat," 138-141 and 170-177; Tapio Bergholm, *Kovaa peliä kuljetusalalla. Kuljetusalan ammattiyhdistystoiminta vuosina 1960-1990* (Helsinki, 2000), 332-338; and Kari Teräs and Tapio Bergholm, "Dockers of Turku, c. 1880-1970," in Sam Davies, *et al.* (eds.), *Dock Workers: International Explorations in Comparative History, 1790-1970* (2 vols., Aldershot, 2000), I, 99-101.

[15]Eero Pakkala (ed.), *Meri ja me* (Porvoo, 1962). See also Visa Auvinen, *Laivastoyhdistyksestä Meriliitoksi. Laivastoyhdistys - Meriliitto 1926-2001* (Uusikaupunki, 2001), 63.

[16]Jukka Parhiala, "Containerliikenne avannut uusia uria kuljetustoimelle," *Kuljetus*, No. 6 (1963), 60-62; "Helsingin satamapäivät," *Navigator*, No. 11 (1972), 35; and Timo Mikkilä, "Konttiliikennettä harjoitettu Suomessa kaksi vuosikymmentä," *Kuljetus*, No. 6 (1983), 20-22.

the full utilisation of the entire volume of the container. Confidence was inspired by the fact that specialised containers for various qualities of goods were developed, and their possible uses were increased by accessories. In principle, it was possible to transport nearly all cargoes in containers.[17]

A so-called Container Committee was established in Finland in 1966. It proceeded to conduct a study of the attitudes toward containers among companies engaged in foreign trade. A majority believed firmly in the potential of the new mode, even if containers were new and the public still had doubts. According to the Committee's estimates, the imbalance of imports and exports typical of Finland's maritime foreign trade was, however, likely to restrict the growth of container traffic. The Committee also feared that the transport of empty and less-than-full containers would cause problems because the regions of production and consumption were often situated far apart.[18] In the opinion of Finnish experts, all the Nordic countries were pioneers in the development of container traffic compared with the rest of Europe. Between 1956 and 1966, the impact was limited mainly to the American coastal trade. It was only in the late 1960s that they began to be used extensively in ocean-going traffic, after which their final triumph was never in doubt.[19]

Remote Finland had little ambition to lead the way in this development, and many considered it advantageous to observe events for a time. Finland aspired, in Alexander Gerschrenkron's words, "to enjoy the benefits of backwardness" while keeping as close as possible to the leading maritime nations.[20] Experts pointed out several times that in a country suffering from a lack of capital it was not worth "repeating the mistakes made by others."[21] The problem was that as long as containers came in several shapes and sizes, they would do little to reduce the total cost of moving freight. The risk of bad investments was diminished when the International Standardisation Committee in 1965 drafted the first ISO standard for containers, based on the American

---

[17]P. Mäkinen, "Yksikkölastit ja autolautta," *Kuljetus*, No. 4 (1965), 44-50; and Aarne Kaivola, "Katsaus konttikalustoon ja konttiliikenteeseen," *Kuljetus*, No. 3 (1975), 14-15.

[18]M. Valla, "Mitä mieltä maamme elinkeinoelämä on kontainerikuljetuksista," *Kuljetus*, No. 5 (1967), 27-30.

[19]Levinson, *The Box*, 201.

[20]Alexander Gerschenkron, *Economic Backwardness in Historical Perspective: A Book of Essays* (Cambridge, 1966).

[21]Jaakko Hemmi, "Kontainerikuljetukset – taloudellista realismia vaiko muotivirtaus," *Kuljetus*, No. 3 (1967), 35-39; and "Kontaineripäivä Helsingissä," *Kuljetus*, No. 9 (1967), 7-8.

ASA standard. The dimensions of containers were also defined in Finnish SFS standards. From the late 1960s, the Twenty-Foot Equivalent Unit (TEU) became the universal yardstick of containerisation. This was a huge advantage, since it enabled the easy compilation of statistics to be used in planning.[22]

Towards the end of the 1960s, the metaphor of "revolution" was increasingly used in Finland to describe the breakthrough of container traffic. This dramatic term referred both to the rapidity with which it was adopted and its all-embracing nature. Old structures seemed to be collapsing everywhere as containers piled into the ports. Contemporaries felt that they were involved in an important turning point, but at the same time they recognised that "revolutions do not only solve problems, they also create new ones."[23] Indeed, increasingly significant problems began to emerge as the effects of container transport beame clear towards the end of the 1960s.

Fears of the Costs

Containers were justified primarily by the anticipated savings. Rumours of savings from America soon reached Finland, although they were not backed by any particularly convincing data. The reason for this was that costs could be lowered only by making immense investments over the entire transport chain; the container system in its entirety was extremely expensive. An entirely new infrastructure was required at both the national and global levels. As one expert put it: "The new transport system has its drawbacks, however, the most important of which is the great need for capital."[24]

The state committees established to discuss port development emphasised the economic aspects of unitised cargo transport, which in public debate had been overshadowed by the technical aspects. Containers were a capital-intensive mode of transport compared to conventional traffic, and the question that needed to be answered was what share of the country's foreign trade would they be able to carry? The Southern Finland Port Committee, which played a significant role in the development of unitised cargo traffic, started work in 1967 and two years later published its recommendations. It argued that the aim of port development ought to be the "minimisation of the costs over the whole transport network or, in a wider sense, minimisation of the overall

---

[22]Broeze, *Globalisation*, 15; Levinson, *The Box*, 127-129; and Teräs "Modernisoituvat satamat," 136-137.

[23]Seppo Eerikäinen, "Huolitsijan tehtävät konteinerikuljetuksissa," *Kuljetus*, No. 9 (1967), 25.

[24]Mäkinen, "Yksikkölastit ja autolautta," 48; Vainio, "Lift-on-Lift-off," 27-30; and Hemmi, "Kontainerikuljetukset," 37.

transport costs of foreign trade relying on shipping."[25] This in a sense provided official approval for thinking about transport as a chain.

In the beginning, the costs of a "complete container transport system" in Finland were considered prohibitive in proportion to the volume of goods to be transported. For ports, the container revolution meant large investments in specialised equipment and a total reorganisation of functions. Of particular concern was the expected length of the transition; the shift to containers clearly could not take place overnight. There was a widespread consensus that ports would have to maintain dual facilities to handle both conventional and unitised cargoes for an extended period. The coexistence of container and conventional vessels was often described as an "unhappy marriage" that required new space allocations, technical equipment and working arrangements.[26] Even in the early days of the revolution, it was clear that the most efficient development of ports would only be possible on the basis of unitised cargo. Finnish experts travelled to both the US and Europe to visit modern "container ports of the future," many of which were already shipping containerised cargoes to the largest ports in southern Finland.[27] There was still an international disjunction, but it was obvious that this could not go on for long.

It was noted that in neighbouring Sweden, large sums had been invested in container traffic in the 1960s, while Finland was more cautious. In 1967 the Finnish transport magazine *Kuljetus* enviously described the new car ferry and container terminal at Gothenburg. In a new port built largely on land reclaimed from the sea were three large terminals equipped with modern cargo-handling equipment, including some large straddle carriers built in Finland. Gothenburg's new port followed in the footsteps of the recently-completed container ports in Rotterdam, Le Havre and Hamburg. The completion of the first large container port in Sweden sparked debate in Finland on the need for Scandinavian cooperation in container transport.[28]

The expansion of container transport in the late 1960s increased the pressure for global harmonisation. Many started to regard ports all over the world as part of a single network and came to believe that all should offer services of a similar standard if the anticipated cost savings were to be

---

[25]*Etelä-Suomen satamatoimikunnan mietintö* (Helsinki, 1969), 87.

[26]Rissanen, "Uusista suuntauksista," 10.

[27]Ma-Sa, "Tulevaisuuden konttisatama," *Suomen Merenkulku/Finlands Sjöfart*, No. 10 (1967), 233.

[28]Tauno Harama, "Götteporin uusi autolautta- ja konteinerisatama," *Kuljetus*, No. 4 (1967), 49-50.

attained.[29] In Finland, attempts were made from the mid-1960s to define a national strategy to cope with the new technology. The basic idea was to move as flexibly, economically and gradually as possible towards a complete container transport system. To minimise costs and disruptions, a consensus developed that a gradual revolution would be most suitable in the Finnish case.

The Southern Finland Port Committee tried to dampen the enthusiasm for containers and to find suitable forms of unitised loading for the products of the important forest industry which could "offer the same benefits as the container transport system with less significant economic sacrifices."[30] The Committee looked at containers as only one possibility, which is why measures were needed to develop other forms of unitised cargo loading, including large pallets, car ferries and trailers.[31] The financial arguments suggested the need for versatility: the price of an open large pallet in the mid-1960s, for example, was roughly one-third that of a container.[32]

In Finland, people started to refer to containers as only one form of unitised cargo traffic. According to many experts, the Scandinavian countries were more advanced than the US in the development of large units other than containers. This was because the large shipments of forest products had encouraged experimentation with other forms of unitisation. Since containers were not suitable for most forest exports from Finland, systems specific to their needs had to be developed. The revolution in Finland therefore could be based solely on containers, which were unlikely to achieve a dominant position. Although the Southern Finland Port Committee felt that the harmonisation of international transport would require more investment in unitisation, it was in no hurry to recommend massive infusions of funds.[33]

The ports strove to find solutions that would take the needs of the transition period into consideration. From the mid-1960s, transport magazines discussed with great enthusiasm large cranes manufactured in Finland, the

---

[29]Frank Broeze, "Containerization and the Globalization of Liner Shipping," in David J. Starkey and Gelina Harlaftis (eds.), *Global Markets: The Internationalization of the Sea Transport Industries since 1850* (St. John's, 1998), 401-404.

[30]*Etelä-Suomen satamatoimikunnan mietintö*, 2-3 and 56-69.

[31]*Pohjois-Suomen satamatoimikunnan mietintö* (Helsinki, 1972), 118-119.

[32]Mäkinen, "Yksikkölastit ja autolautta," 48; and Rissanen, "Uusista suuntauksista," 10.

[33]*Etelä-Suomen satamatoimikunnan mietintö*, 61-67; Erik Löfberg, "Eri yksikkölaivausmenetelmien vertailu ahtausnäkökannalta," in *Suuryksikkökuljetukset* (Helsinki, 1968); Bergholm, "Satamaliikenne ja yhteiskunta," 43-45; and Teräs, "Modernisoituvat satamat," 138-140.

performance and features of which were adequate for both conventional and container traffic. The country's largest ports all tried to procure at least one large multi-purpose crane to serve the increasing unitised cargo traffic. Leading Finnish engineering firms worked closely with shipping and stevedoring companies to develop a heavy truck fleet for ro-ro traffic, which expanded sharply in the late 1960s. The ro-ro fleet grew explosively in the early 1970s: during the ten years after 1966, more than twenty ro-ro berths were built at which cargoes were handled on a predetermined schedule.[34]

The first actual container crane in Finland started operations in 1969 in the port of Hamina.[35] Experts described the Finnish-built, forty-ton container crane that was completed in 1970 for the port of Helsinki as "magnificent," and it contributed to making Helsinki by far the most significant container port in the country. The special technical feature of this jib gantry crane was the great turning radius of the moving truck, which enabled the handling of containers that were not aligned with the edge of the quay. This was necessary because in some vessels containers were placed on the deck both fore-and-aft and athwart ship.[36] From the late 1970s, more fixed and moving cranes were procured by the largest ports, and their performance also improved.[37]

From the mid-1960s onwards, Finnish shipping companies strove to develop their vessels to allow cargo handling using various techniques for different cargoes. They optimised their design solutions as far as possible for the transport of wood products in close cooperation with the producers. Towards the end of the decade, *Kuljetus* ran a feature on the Bore Company's "revolutionary vessel types," which were able to transport units from containers to trucks on the ro-ro principle.[38] The Finnflow system, which was designed by the shipping company Finnlines in the early 1960s and implemented

---

[34]Teräs, "Modernisoituvat satamat," 143.

[35]"Ympyräkaupungin kuulumisia," *Ahtaajat*, Nos. 3-4 (1969), 18-20. The one-beam, twenty-five-ton container crane ordered by Oy Blomberg Ab was manufactured at the Hyvinkää plant of Kone Oy. The weight of the crane was 260 tons; the height, thirty-four metres; and the reach, nineteen metres. The properties of the crane allowed its use for the loading of all vessels serving Hamina. See also "Tehokkaita kotimaisia konttinostureita," *Kuljetus*, No. 1 (1968), 49-50.

[36]"Helsingin satamapäivät," *Navigator*, No. 10 (1972), 35; and Jukka Erävuori, *Helsingin sataman ja satamahallinnon historia* (Helsinki 1981), 184 and 344-346.

[37]Teräs, "Modernisoituvat satamat," 148-149.

[38]"Uusi Bore VI, käänteentekevä alustyyppi Suomen oloissa," *Kuljetus*, No. 9 (1967), 17-18.

in an advanced form in the vessel *Finncarrier*, was also an important technological innovation in the handling of various unitised cargoes. This system made use of ferry cars and large pallets, as well as special straddle carriers and truck tractors developed for handling large units and manufactured domestically. The vessel was designed to withstand the stresses of winter navigation since it would have to operate in ice conditions for at least three months each year.[39]

Terminal operations gave rise to great expectations in Finland in the 1960s. The Port Traffic Committee, which submitted its report in 1966, did not yet use the concept of a terminal, even though many of its proposals pointed in that direction by referring to export warehouses, which rather than merely storing goods would be able to sort them as well. Even in the trade magazines, the word "terminal" still conveyed a variety of meanings. Nonetheless, both the Southern and Northern Finland Port Committees defined the concept and discussed its role in an integrated transport chain.[40] The idea was to make cargo flow as smoothly as possible and to link the various modes of transport. A terminal referred to a section of the port that could work independently and was controlled by private companies. When vessels always arrived at the same time and place, it was possible to organise the loading and unloading effi-ciently, increase the utilisation of port equipment and handle more traffic. Terminals made cargo-handling independent of the weather and decreased turnaround times.[41] They could also serve conventional vessels, and for ro-ro traffic they were a necessity.

Terminals were seen as modern, self-contained enclaves in a port environment that otherwise retained its traditional character. The first terminals designated for specific shipowners or dedicated to certain destinations began operations in three ports in southern Finland ports in the late 1960s.[42]

---

[39]Pentti Mäkinen, "MS *Finncarrier*," *Kolmannen sukupolven lauttalaiva*, No. 3 (1969), 33-35; "*Finncarrier*," *Suomen Merenkulku/Finlands Sjöfart*, No. 12 (1969), 254; Mäkinen, "Lastausmenetelmät ja Superliner," *Kuljetus*, No. 1 (1972), 9-11; and Mäkinen, "Lastilauttaliikennettä," *Navigator*, No. 3 (1980), 10-13.

[40]*Kulkulaitosneuvoston asettaman satamaliikennetoimikunnan mietintö* (Helsinki, 1966), 54-59; and *Etelä-Suomen satamatoimikunnan mietintö*, 142. See also *Pohjois-Suomen satamatoimikunnan mietintö*, 118; and Erävuori, *Helsingin sataman*, 243-244.

[41]*Etelä-Suomen satamatoimikunnan mietintö*, 141-152; *Pohjois-Suomen satamatoimikunnan mietintö*, 118; Ulf Bergring, "Terminaaliliikenne Suomen merenkulun rationalisoimiskeinona," *Navigator*, No. 10 (1969), 7-8; and Eero Böök, "Rautatiet ja satamaterminaalit," *Kuljetus*, No. 9 (1972), 65-68.

[42]"Suurterminaali," *Suomen Merenkulku/Finlands Sjöfart*, No. 11 (1969), 244; and Teräs, "Moderni-soituvat satamat," 141.

Developing unitised cargo traffic and increasing the volumes, however, required more comprehensive solutions and a new type of port planning in which savings were sought in all links of the transport chain. The old harbour areas were cramped, poorly-equipped and inappropriate for handling large units. In the late 1960s, members of the maritime community in Finland started to become convinced that, as in the leading shipping nations, it was necessary to design totally new ports or sections of older harbours for container traffic with adequate field areas behind the quays and efficient equipment for handling large units.

The terminal for unitised cargoes on the island of Hietanen was completed in 1972 to serve Kotka, one of the most important export ports in the country, after four years of planning. The new port featured plenty of storage space, a shelter for ferry cars, large paved lots, two stern berths with hydraulic ramps and one conventional berth, as well as a massive fleet of specialised machinery, including two twenty-two-ton straddle carriers, one thirty-ton stacking straddle carrier and ten tractors, all of which had been manufactured in Finland.[43] The nation's other ports followed suit as quickly as possible. A separate container harbour was completed in Helsinki in 1976, equipped with a modern heavy-duty crane and straddle carriers.

Benefits of Cooperation

The large-scale investments required by container traffic involved great risks for everyone involved in the transport chain, even though such modernisation also created significant business opportunities. Conflicting interests had traditionally existed within and between the various modes of transport: each operated without much thought to the others. It was obvious that hauliers, port operators and shipping companies tried to make as large a profit from container transport as possible, and the first to introduce a new innovation was well placed to reap large benefits. Transport in general was characterised by unsynchronised development, which was one of the central reasons for inefficiencies.

The first signs of the logistic revolution in the 1960s produced a great deal of discourse about cooperation, the aim of which was to displace mutual competitors. Achieving a "close-knit co-operation" within the entire transport chain was justified more than anything by the potential savings. In Finland everyone had to pull together, and no mode of transport could afford inefficient investments that would not be supported by the others. Experts tried to

[43]"Ensimmäinen sopimus Hietasen terminaalisataman käytöstä," *Navigator*, No. 5 (1972), 39; and Teräs, "Modernisoituvat satamat," 146-147.

convince contemporaries that "costs will not be an obstacle if a sufficient degree of co-operation can be achieved."[44]

The transport chain concept required cooperation beginning with the planning stage. The representative of a large Finnish shipping company wrote in 1966 that the new ships "will be devoid of meaning if ports, manufacturers of equipment, and consigners and recipients of goods cannot be engaged in the co-operation."[45] It was necessary for the operators of various modes of transport to work together during the technically and economically demanding transition. In Finland, competing shipping companies had not done this during the introduction of the ro-ro system. To ensure that the same mistake was not repeated, a ro-ro rationalisation committee comprising representatives from shipping and stevedoring companies was set up in 1976 to discuss ways of harmonising and standardising cargo handling.[46] The aim of the publicly-funded port studies mentioned above was to promote cooperation between the state, ports and businessmen: in other words, to generate solutions that would work for all. There was no room for free riders, for if one link in the chain failed, all would suffer. Building mutual confience, however, was not easy.

Plans and investment were needed even before the volumes were sufficient to turn a profit. Participants had to try to anticipate the future, which also meant that the division of labour between various port actors had to be defined. From the 1960s onward, stevedoring companies in each port cooperated more closely, especially regarding the use of equipment and labour. In the next decade, concentration began to take place in the field as a result of sectoral rationalisations and ownership changes. A significant share of the ownership of stevedoring firms in the export ports was bought by companies in the forest industry, while in import ports, shipping companies bought into stevedoring firms. Stevedoring companies began to become port operators offering comprehensive services, and their investments in new technology and terminals increased dramatically. In an activity that had traditionally been labour-intensive, large sums of capital were needed to handle containers.[47]

Towards the end of the 1960s, proponents of the need for a national port policy became increasingly vocal. The state committees believed that port development should proceed from an "overall perspective," for only only the

---

[44]Rissanen, "Uusista suuntauksista," 4-10; "Kontaineripäivä Helsingissä," *Kuljetus*, No. 9 (1967), 7-8; and *Etelä-Suomen satamatoimikunnan mietintö*, 69.

[45]Westerberg, "Suuryksikkökuljetukset," 51-52.

[46]Teräs, "Modernisoituvat satamat," 143.

[47]Kari Jalkanen, *Suomen satamien toiminnallinen rakenne, työnjako ja kehitys* (Turku, 1996), 44-45; and Teräs, "Hampuuseista ahtaajiksi," 258-259.

state could mediate and guide the process.[48] Proposals included reducing the number of ports, increasing specialisation, rationalising labour policies and concentrating container traffic in the port of Helsinki. None of these gained wholehearted support, since nearly all the Finnish ports were owned by local authorities with their own agendas.

Because of local ownership, the national authorities could only influence ports indirectly, mainly through supporting individual projects. The tools the state had at its disposal included the construction of channels, the use of icebreakers, the level of shipping dues, the granting of subsidised loans for construction and the funding of basic research. While the state used these kinds of tools to create the preconditions for unitised cargo traffic, there was no centralised port policy in Finland in the 1970s. Decisions about ports were made by several ministries and administrative boards, along with the local authorities.[49]

Studies and reports financed by the state were also needed because of some special features of the Finnish port and transport system. In the early 1960s, there were two or three significant import ports but a wider range of export harbours because of the widespread nature of the forest industry. The most significant import ports operated year-round, whereas the operation of the export ports was interrupted during the winter. Moreover, the standard of technical equipment in the former was clearly better than in the latter. The division of imports and exports into different ports was a significant problem for container transport, which required continuous and balanced volumes of traffic. The state attempted to influence the development of the port system to achieve this.[50]

The worry was that in a small and remote country it would be impossible to enjoy all the benefits of unitised cargo to the same extent as elsewhere in Europe. There was a consensus, however, that cooperation among the various actors in transport was necessary if there was any hope of success. The need to develop unitised cargo traffic led to an increase in the icebreaker fleet, and from the early 1970s there was a determined effort to keep the northern ports open all year.[51] Although the groundwork was laid in the 1960s

---

[48]*Etelä-Suomen satamatoimikunnan mietintö*, 18-19.

[49]Teräs, "Suomen satamapolitiikka," 242-243. See also Evangelia Selkou and Michael Roe, *Globalisation, Policy and Shipping: Fordism, Post-Fordism and the European Union Maritime Secto*r (Cheltenham, 2004), 29-38.

[50]Bergholm, "Satamaliikenne ja yhteiskunta," 20-23.

[51]Helge Jääsalo, *Pohjoiset satamat auki* (Oulu, 1980), 118-215; and Teräs, "Hampuuseista ahtaajiksi," 238-240.

and 1970s, the dramatic growth in traffic volumes only occurred in the following decades.

Conclusion

While Finland was not in the vanguard of the container revolution, the new technology attracted a great deal of interest and prompted experiments early in the transition. Since it was dependent on shipping, Finland wanted to participate, even if a shortage of capital tempered enthusiasm. From the late 1960s, however, the introduction of unitised cargo traffic began to be regarded as a national task that required contributions both from the parties directly affected and the state. In the late 1960s and early 1970s, the first container applications were implemented in Finland, port equipment began to be improved and vessels were developed for unitised transport. Representatives of various modes of transport became convinced that cooperation in facilitating the use of containers and large unitised shipments was good business. For this reason, they took an active role in the debate. Although this type of dialogue was unprecedented, they seemed receptive to diverse opinions. The press also played a role, since writings about containers increased public awareness.

During the "container revolution," two basic types of discourse can be identified. One was basically internal, involving industry professionals, and was focused primarily on technical issues. The other was mainly external and took place in state-sponsored committees and various transport organisations; it emphasised the economic and social contexts of containerisation. Since the container revolution was such a broad phenomenon, however, there was little significant difference between the two: transport experts also discussed economic issues, while the state committees commented on technical solutions.

The move to containerisation was justified by discourse concentrating not only on the revolution but also on associated industries, savings and cooperation, all of which persuaded readers that since the logistic shift was certain to take place Finland needed a national strategy. The arguments found a receptive audience and built support that enabled Finland to reach a kind of transport parity with other industrialised countries. Thereafter, the containerised transport system began to revolutionise domestic industry and commerce within the context of an increasingly integrated global economy.

The Ports of Northern Chile: A Mining History in Long-run Perspective, 1880-2002[1]

Marc Badia-Miró

Changes in the distribution of economic activity in Chile between the late nineteenth century and the present have been quite substantial. The exploitation of a plethora of mineral resources in the north and central parts of the country, the development of an industrial sector and a strong trend toward urbanisation in the second third of the twentieth century have produced a complex commercial flow which combines foreign and domestic trade. Moreover, Chile's geography and topography have required a considerable amount of this commerce to be carried by sea.[2] For these reasons, an examination of the country's ports is a useful way to understand its trade.

In this essay I want to focus on the northern region of Chile where important mining deposits have led to particular production and commercial structures that in turn created a distinct population distribution. The export of nitrates and copper have drawn this area into a global trading system in which export earnings have been used to pay for the import of manufactured goods that arrive through the ports.[3] Indeed, shifts in world commodity markets have

---

[1]This paper is drawn from my forthcoming doctoral thesis, "La distribución regional de la actividad económica en Chile y su impacto sobre el desarrollo." It has been supported by Project SEJ2005-02498/ECON (MEC, Spain), supervised by Jordi Catalan, and also by BEC2003-00190 (MCYT, Spain), supervised by Albert Carreras. I am grateful for comments from Anna Carreras-Marín, A. Herranz, Lewis R. Fischer and the audience at the session on "Global and Local Connections: Historical Perspectives on Ports" at the Fifteenth International Congress of Economic History in Helsinki in August 2006. The usual disclaimers apply.

[2]Trade by rail usually went only as far as the closest seaport. See Marc Badia-Miró, "Evolución de la distribución de la actividad económica en Chile" (Unpublished MSc thesis, Universitat de Barcelona-Universitat Autónoma de Barcelona, 2004), 100-102.

[3]Nitrate production, which expanded rapidly at the end of the nineteenth century, dominated until 1930, while copper was the major export thereafter. Other minerals, such as silver and gold, were also important. For more information about export

had a direct impact on the fortunes of harbours; some have specialised in exports, others in transhipment and distribution, and some have disappeared.

Figure 1: Harbours of Northern Chile Engaged in Trade, 1880-2002

Note: Round dot indicates only coastal trade; triangle indicates both coastal and foreign trade.

Source: *Anuario de Comercio exterior*, various years.

---

cycles in Chile, see Daniel Lederman, *The Political Economy of Protection: Theory and the Chilean Experience* (Stanford, 2005), 33-67.

This study focuses on Norte Grande and Norte Chico (the provinces of Tarapacá, Antofagasta, Atacama and Coquimbo), which include thirty-four ports that engaged in coastal commerce, twenty of which also participated in foreign trade throughout the period (see figure 1). The data used to analyse maritime commerce comprise the total value of all entrances and clearances. For domestic trade we also have tonnage data. I have also examined the structure of this commerce for several years. While it is possible to analyse exports until the 1990s, we can only go to about 1960 for domestic trade (although tonnage data allow us to say something about this to the present). I also want to look at the impact of natural resources on industry and population. For this I have compiled evidence on industrial occupations by sectors and provinces and on population by province and by urban versus rural districts.

This region experienced many changes during the twentieth century. Before the Great Depression of the 1930s it had an export-led economy marked by uneven growth related to variations in the demand for, and price of, raw materials.[4] State-sponsored industrialisation thereafter relegated the region to a secondary role as a provider of essential inputs for mills and factories.[5] A protectionist tariff, introduced to spur regional development, and free-trade zones had important impacts on the location of industries.[6] The result was a mining industry oriented to the domestic market until 1973, when a new openness accelerated de-industrialisation, and the industry stopped being an engine of development. Exports of raw and semi-processed products reversed this.

The first section of this essay examines the evolution of commerce by products and ports in both foreign and domestic trade. The second part links these results with the evolution of industry and population throughout the twentieth century. A set of conclusions ties it all together.

The impact of commercial openness and the reduction in transport costs on the location of economic activity has been widely studied.[7] But the

---

[4]Victor Bulmer-Thomas, *The Economic History of Latin America since Independence* (Cambridge, 1994; 2nd ed., Cambridge, 2003), chapters 4-5.

[5]*Ibid.*; and Albert Carreras, *et al.*, *El desarrollo económico de América Latina en épocas de globalización – una agenda de investigación* (Santiago de Chile, 2003).

[6]The location of the automotive industry in Arica after 1960 was the result of the establishment of a Free Trade Zone and the desire by the government to foster regional development. See Robert N. Gwynne, "Geografía industrial," in *Geografía de Chile*, VII (Santiago de Chile, 1984).

[7]Paul Krugman, "Increasing Returns and Economic Geography," *Journal of Political Economy*, XCIX, No. 3 (1991), 484-499; Krugman, *Geography and Trade* (Cambridge, MA, 1991); and Masahisa Fujita, Paul Krugman and Anthony J.

effect this had on commerce has been less thoroughly examined. Did specialisation in production increase trade? Did the importance of a port (or indeed a region) change significantly? Did difficulties with exports redirect commerce? Did the greater capacity to export impact the ability to import? What about import substitution? There are many questions to answer.

The impact of foreign trade cycles is important for this analysis. For simplicity, I have divided the period into three parts. The first, which comprised the years before World War I, was marked by Chile's increasing participation in global markets due to increasing demand for natural resources.[8] The second, comprising basically the 1920s, was a period of readjustment from the economic dislocations of the Great War. A fairly weak recovery, exacerbated by the rise of chemical fertilizers, lessened the demand for nitrates, and the onset of the Great Depression struck Chile, like all export-dependent nations, especially hard.[9] The third period began after the Second World War and was more complex. It started with the initiation of "Industrialisation Guided by the State" (IGS), a set of policies designed to wean the country from a dependence on exports by providing domestic alternatives. Foreign trade became less important as industrial output, destined for domestic consumption, grew. To protect the domestic market, Chile came to rely on a policy of high tariffs that protected some sectors to the detriment of others. The institutional and economic crises of the 1970s, marked by inflation and high unemployment, convinced policymakers to change course, with the result that the 1980s were characterised by de-industrialisation and a reversion to encouraging the growth of export industries through a lowering of tariff barriers.[10] The debt crisis of the 1980s and severe balance-of-payments deficits drove the country to promote sectors that could earn foreign exchange. This

---

Venables, *The Spatial Economy: Cities, Regions and International Trade* (Cambridge, MA, 1999).

[8]On globalisation, see Kevin H. O'Rourke and Jeffrey G. Williamson, *Globalization and History: The Evolution of a Nineteenth-century Atlantic Economy* (Cambridge, MA, 1999).

[9]Chile and Cuba were the two Latin American countries most impacted by the Great Depression; see Bulmer-Thomas, *Economic History*. For the impact of foreign crises on the Chilean economy throughout the twentieth century, see Hernán Cortés Douglas, "El efecto de las recesiones internacionales en la economía chilena. Una visión histórica: 1926-1982," *El Trimestre Económico*, LII, No. 4 (1985), 1075-1095.

[10]On the changes after 1973 and the trade reforms, see Pilar Vergara, "Apertura externa y desarrollo industrial en Chile: 1973-78," *Colección de estudios del CIEPLAN,* IV (1980), 79-117.

renewed openness was reinforced in the 1990s by the introduction of a new development strategy.[11]

The next step is to analyse the evolution of trade. We may look first at coastal commerce, both entrances and clearances, by region and port in value and tonnage. The port data have been analysed by sector, but only when value data are available (data on tonnage only differentiate between solids, bulk cargoes and liquids). The second analysis will be of foreign trade data (exports and imports) by value. The benchmark points for coastal commerce are 1904, 1929, 1938 and 1953, while for foreign trade we also have 1982 and 2002.

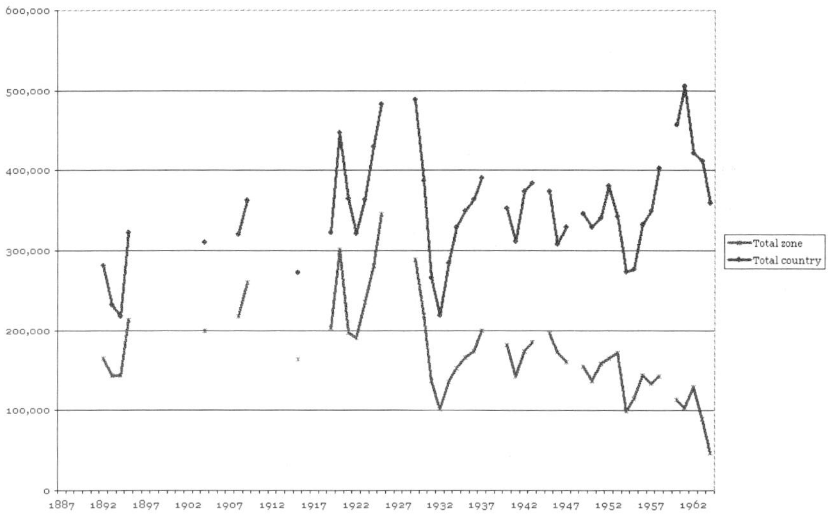

Figure 2: Percentage of the Total Value of Trade Provided by Coastal Imports in Northern Chile, 1880-2002

Note: Percentages calculated based upon the entire region in constant 1915 dollars.

Source: Chile, *Anuario de comercio interior y communicaciones*, various years.

[11]This is a commonly used time division in Chilean economic history. See Lederman, *Political Economy*; Simon Collier and William F. Sater, *A History of Chile, 1808-2002* (Cambridge, 1996; 2nd ed., Cambridge, 2004); and José Díaz, Rolf Lüders and Gert Walgner, "Economía Chilena 1810-1995: evolución cuantitativa del producto total y sectorial" (Unpublishd working paper No. 186, Universidad Católica de Chile, 1998).

The series on the value of entrances in coastal trade shows similar patterns for both the country and the region (see figure 2). Before the Great Depression the region's contribution to the national total was above sixty percent. Thereafter, it decreased by the 1960s to less than one-fifth. The total value increased strongly in the first third of the twentieth century but declined rapidly during the Great Depression; it took some twenty years before pre-1930s levels were attained again.[12] Tarapacá dominated through the first decade of the twentieth century, but as copper became a more important export than nitrates, Antofagasta became the leader. The pattern of coastal commerce was strongly linked to mining cycles.

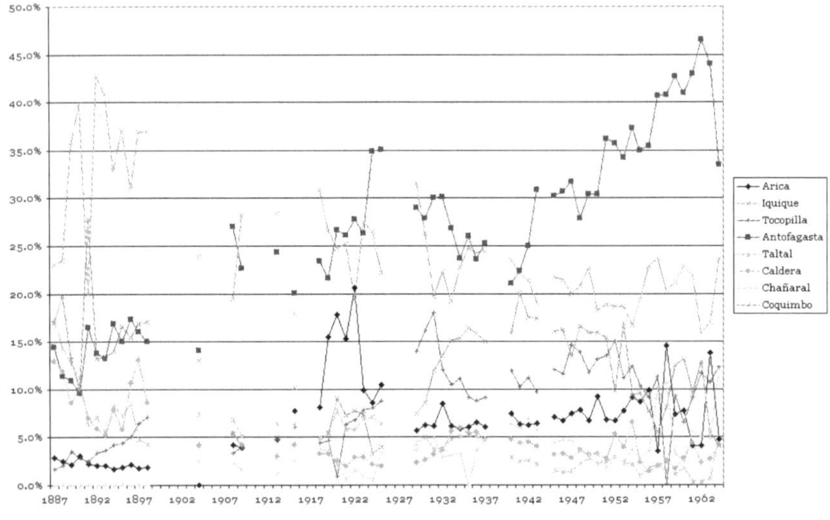

Figure 3: Percentage of Total Value of Trade Provided by Coastal Imports at the Main Ports of Northern Chile, 1894-1964

Note: See figure 2.

Source: See figure 2.

[12]The share of northern commerce in the clearances of coastal trade from Valparaíso was about a third of the total around 1870. Before the Guerra del Pacífico, total clearances to the north increased to two-thirds. This was the beginning of the great expansion of the north as a market for domestic products, a trend which increased at the end of the nineteenth and in the first part of the twentieth century; Julio Pinto Vallejos and Luís Ortega Martínez, "Expansión Minera y desarrollo industrial: un caso de crecimiento asociado (Chile, 1850-1914)" (Unpublished working paper, Departamento de Historia, Universidad de Santiago de Chile, 1990), 79.

The evolution of the larger ports - Antofagasta and Iquique (more than half of total entrances), Coquimbo, Arica, Tocopilla and, at the end of the nineteenth century, Taltal and Caldera - reflected provincial trends. Changes in coastal trade during the Depression caused similar shifts: half of the twenty-eight ports at the beginning of the century disappeared. Another six had a discontinuous flow after the 1950s and 1960s and disappeared later (see figure 3).

The commercial structure in 1904 showed that there were two different kinds of ports. First, there were the most important places (Pisagua, Iquique, Antofagasta, Tocopilla, Taltal and Coquimbo) with large entrances of foodstuffs and some of manufactured products. The second group comprised the mining ports, such as Tongoi and Guayacan, with no other trade. In 1913, the commercial structure was similar. There were large numbers of entrances of foodstuffs in the bigger ports near the centres of population with a greater movement of cargo (entrances in value grew by more than ten percent).[13] Gatico and Guayacan remained minor ports. By 1929 some ports ended their activity due to the stagnation of the 1920s (Carrizal Bajo, Pichidangui, Peña Blanca, Puerto Oscuro and Guayacán).[14] Entrances of manufactured products and equipment reflected economic integration.[15] In 1938, a decade after the crash began, while entrances stagnated, four ports (Junin, Caleta Buena, Gatico and Coloso) joined those with no commercial traffic.[16] Arica, Tocopilla, Antofagasta and Coquimbo were the bigger ports (also export ports), while Atacama's harbours did not show any noticeable hierarchy. The commercial structure was similar to what had existed previously with a predominance of foodstuffs and important imports of industrial products such as textiles, chemicals and other manufactures. On the other hand, several less important ports had high levels of entrances of different types of manufactures. While Punta Lobos and Guanillos had percentages of manufactured products that were similar to the more important ports (consumer goods, textiles and other manufactures), in Huasco and Guanillos intermediate goods (chemical products, tools and machinery) were more important. In 1951 four ports (Pisagua, Caleta Buena, Laguna Verde and Punta Lobos) had only minimal flows.[17] Elsewhere,

---

[13]This group includes Arica, Gatico, Antofagasta, Mejillones, Paposo, Carrizal Bajo and Peña Blanca. Iquique had few important manufacturing imports because many of these goods could enter through Arica.

[14]Some were minor ports even in coastal commerce.

[15]Pinto Vallejos and Ortega Martínez, "Expansion."

[16]The ports with no flows in 1929 were in Atacama and Coquimbo, but those with no flows in 1938 were in Tarapacá and Antofagasta.

[17]In these ports the entrances were of food and mining products.

the commercial structure changed little from the earlier period and was still dominated by foodstuffs and manufactured goods.[18]

To complete the study of coastal entrances, figure 4 depicts the data in tonnes. The problem is that data are scarce before 1930. Between 1930 and 1960 we have both value and volume. But even with these limitations it is clear that domestic entrances in this region declined despite overall growth elsewhere. The data also show stagnation in the 1990s. In the last years of the century we can see the importance of the province of Antofagasta and the decreasing roles of Tarapacá, Atacama and Coquimbo. By port, it is obvious that Tocopilla and Huasco were most important before 1995, after which Antofagasta became the leader.[19]

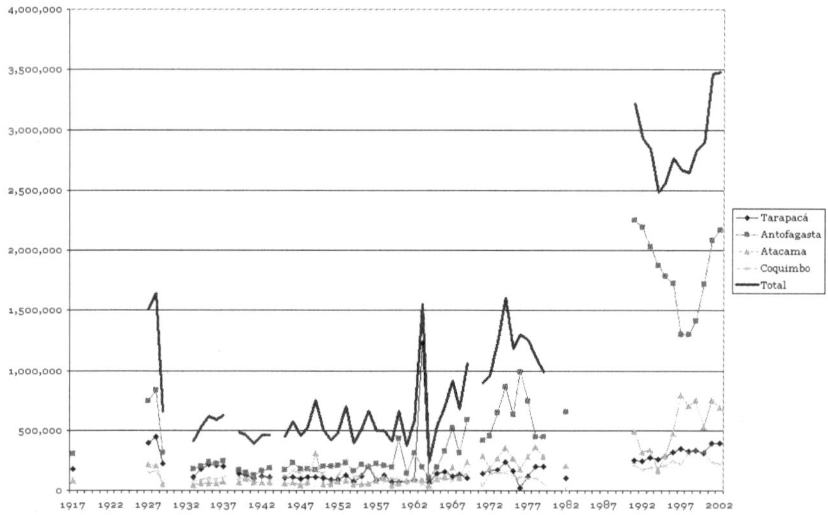

Figure 4: Total Value and Volume of Trade Provided by Coastal Imports in the Ports of Northern Chile and the Entire Country, 1917-2002

Sources: See figure 2; and *Anuario DIRECTEMAR*, various years.

For coastal clearances we see the same structure as before. The trend was more stable than for entrances because purchasing power was clearly affected more by mining cycles. Among the provinces, Tarapaca played an important role from the beginning of the twentieth century until the Great De-

[18]Only in Cruz Grande were manufactured products more important than food due to imports from the chemical and metallurgical industries.

[19]It should be noted that we only have tonnage data, which makes comparisons with other years difficult.

pression (later than in entrances) and in the 1950s and 1960s due to the special status of Arica as a Free Trade Zone (see figure 5). Clearances from Coquimbo were important for the entire period, comprising almost a third of the zone's total and on about the same level as Tarapaca in the 1930s and 1940s. Antofagasta became the most important in domestic commerce just after the Great Depression, at the same time that clearances from Atacama disappeared.

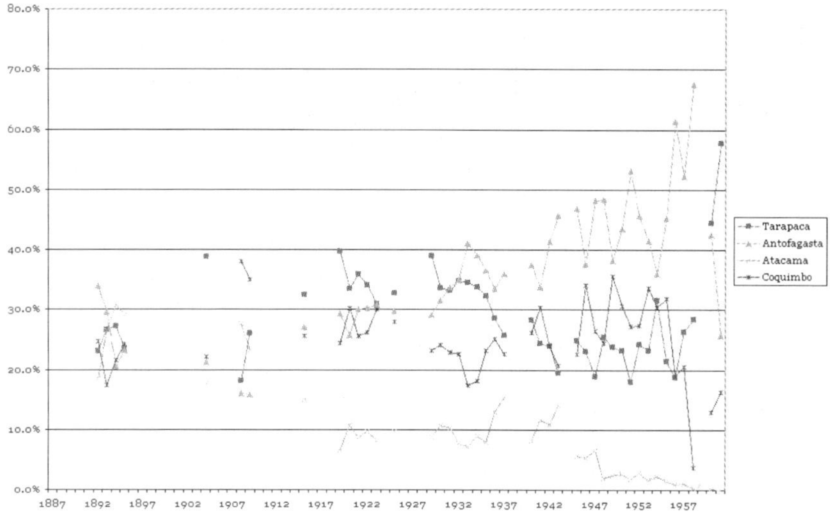

Figure 5: Percentage of Total Value of Trade Provided by Coastal Exports by Province in Northern Chile, 1892-1962

Note: See figure 2.

Source: See figure 2.

Among ports, Coquimbo, Antofagasta and Iquique were most important and were quite stable throughout the period. Antofagasta improved its position during the 1940s and the 1950s at the same time that the province became the leader (see figure 6). The importance of Coquimbo is remarkable because this was the first time a port not in Tarapaca or Antofagasta appeared relevant. It was the most important port in the region until the 1930s and remained significant until the 1950s. The evolution of Tarapaca's entrances was influenced by those of Arica due to its Free Trade Zone. The commercial structure of the ports in 1904 showed the importance of manufactured products, such as industrial oils and others, in Norte Grande; mining in some of the Atacama ports; and agriculture in Coquimbo. In 1913, the data are quite similar, with the exception of an increase of clearances of mining products for the domestic market. The differences between the provinces were large in 1929;

while the ports of Norte Grande specialised in manufactured goods and minerals, those in Norte Chico were dominated by agricultural products and foodstuffs for the domestic market. In 1938 mining was more important than manufactured products. As well, the commercial structure of the Atacama ports had a higher percentage of mining clearances, remained important in manufactured goods but fell in food and agricultural products. The ports of Coquimbo continued to specialise in agricultural products. In 1951 the impact of the Free Trade Zone in Arica was not apparent, but we can see the impact of the IGS policies over the previous twenty years in the commerce structure: a reorientation of clearances in Tarapacá toward chemicals, metallurgy and other manufactures. Antofagasta and Atacama had similar structures, being dominated by mining, foodstuff and manufactures.

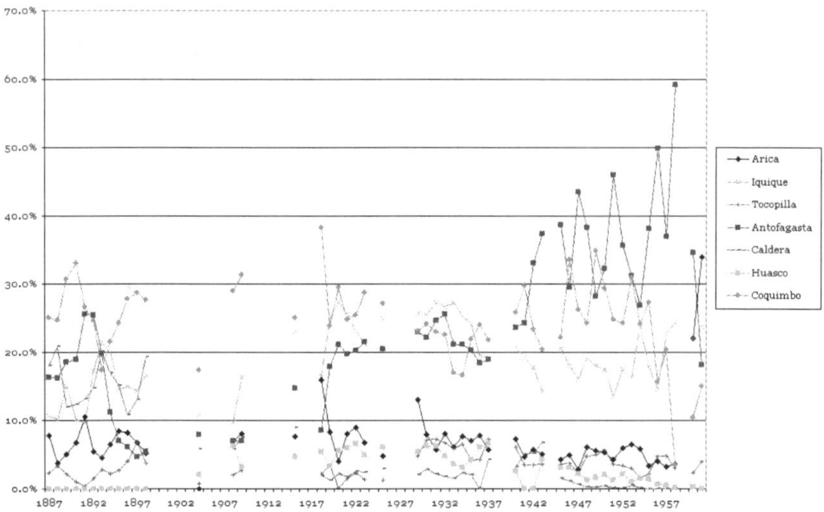

Figure 6: Percentage of Total Value of Trade Provided by Coastal Exports by Port in Northern Chile, 1892-1962

Note: See figure 2.

Source: See figure 2.

Finally, we have to resort to tonnage data to complete the last part of the period before the 1950s (see figure 7). We either lack data by product or by port, so the analysis is somewhat restricted. We can observe the stagnation of clearances, and the balance we observed in the analysis by value was severed in favour of ports in Norte Chico. After the domination of the Tarapaca ports during the 1960s, those of Coquimbo and Atacama reached the top during the 1970s, 1980s and 1990s due to the importance of these agrarian provinces as suppliers for the most populated areas, especially Valparaíso and Santiago. By ports, the predominance of Coquimbo disappeared in favour of places like Guayacan and Huasco in Norte Chico or Patillos and Tocopilla in Norte Grande. Those ports were highly specialised as suppliers of agricultural produce to the urban areas of the country.

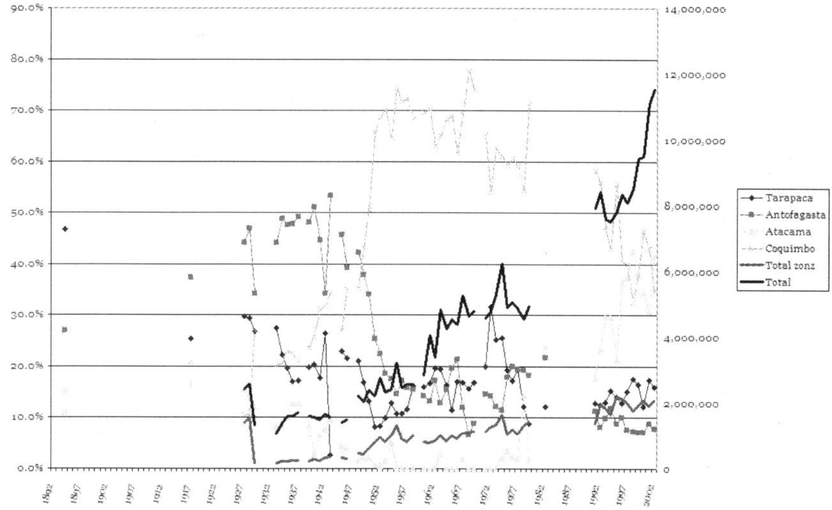

Figure 7: Percentage of Total Volume of Trade (Tonnage) Provided by Coastal Exports by Port in Northern Chile, 1892-2002

Source: See figure 4.

The absolute data on entrances shows a greater demand due to the higher purchasing power generated by exports, except during the 1960s when the Free Trade Zone in Arica changed the commercial flows and made the zone a net seller to the rest of the country (see figure 8).[20] By port, clearances exceeded entrances by far, with only a few exceptions: Mejillones, Arica (in the first part of the period), Huasco, Coquimbo and Los Vilos.[21]

---

[20]The importance of the export sector as a consumer of domestic production is broadly treated by José G. Palma, "Chile 1914-1935: De economía exportadora a sustitutiva de importaciones," *Colección de estudios del CIEPLAN*, XII (1984), 66-88; and Palma, "Growth and Structure of Chilean Manufacturing Industry from 1830 to 1935: Origins and Development of a Process of Industrialization in an Export Economy" (Unpublished PhD thesis, Oxford University, 1979).

[21]The three ports in Atacama and Coquimbo are examples of a differentiated structure in which some were guided by foreign and others by domestic markets.

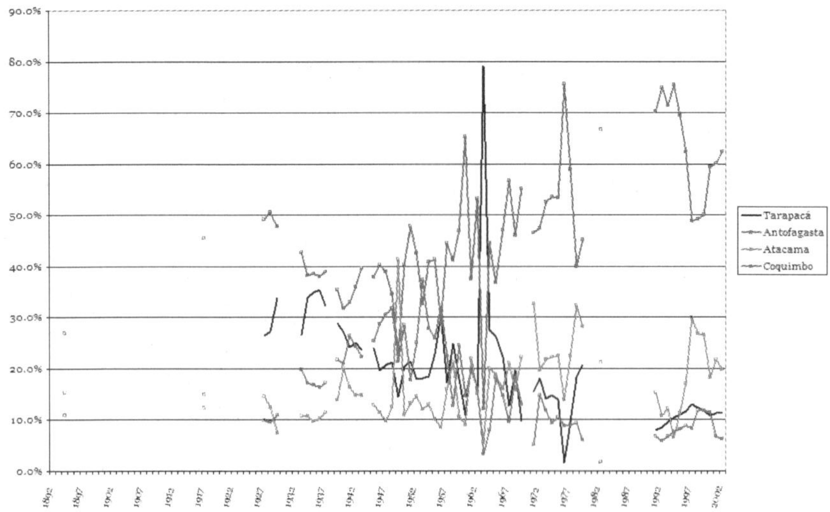

Figure 8: Percentage of Total Volume of Trade (Tonnage) Provided by Coastal Imports by Port in Northern Chile, 1892-2002

Source: See figure 4.

We can now turn to the export sector. We can see a strong correlation between the totals for the country as a whole and the zone. By province, figure 9 shows the impact of the mining cycles and the early predominance of Tarapacá, which was associated with the first cycle of nitrate exports that ended in the first decade of the twentieth century. The rise of Antofagasta as a main exporter was due to the second cycle of nitrates and copper mining (more than seventy percent in some cases).[22] Also, Atacama was important during the second mining cycle due to copper but disappeared as an important exporter during the liberalisation process of the 1980s and 1990s. By port, the tale is simple: three ports explain almost all the zone's exports.

Mining specialisation is a key to understanding the export sector. Minerals comprised more than ninety percent of total exports up to 1970s. Only Coquimbo, which was less important than the other ports, had relatively high exports of food products in 1929, although they decreased by 1938. After 1950, shifts in the market forced the copper industry to make changes to re-

[22]The nitrate era is discussed in J.R. Brown, "Nitrate Crises, Combinations, and the Chilean Government in the Nitrate Age," *Hispanic American Historical Review,* XLIII, No. 2 (1963), 230-246.

main competitive; these reforms were successful.[23] In the 1980 data, mining products remained stable but semi-manufactured goods grew in the ports linked with industrial cities, such as Arica, Iquique and Antofagasta. Other ports, like Tocopilla, Chañaral and even Coquimbo, which lost their specialisation in food products, also lost the trade in minerals.

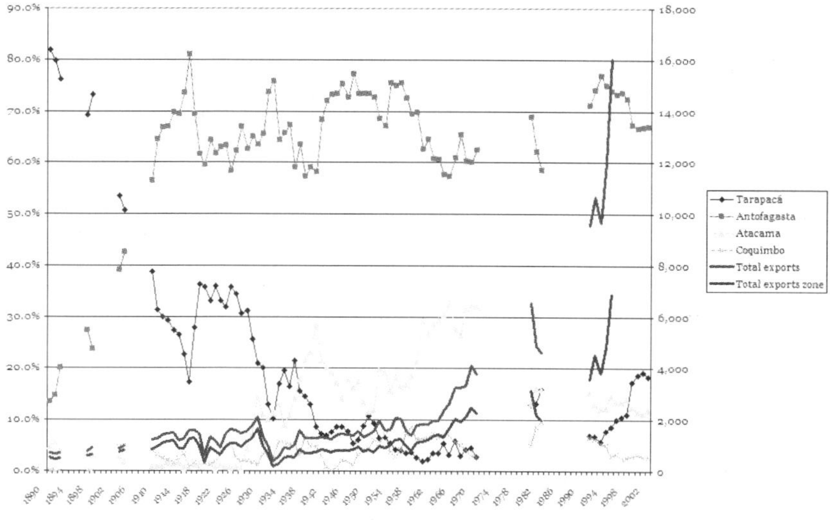

Figure 9: Value of Exports from Northern Chile by Province, 1890-2002

Note: US$ 10,000.

Source: See figure 2.

The pattern of imports was different. New regional development polices (the Free Trade Zone in Arica and the IGS policies during the 1940s, 1950s and 1960s) combined with shifts in global commercial policy strongly affected the region (see figure 10). The evolution of the provinces resembled total exports at the beginning: we can see the predominance of Tarapaca until the first decade of the twentieth century, coinciding with the growth of Antofagasta. This province became the leader of the zone during the 1930s and remained in this position until the creation of Arica's Free Trade Zone in the 1950s. Tarapaca became important until the 1970s, when liberalisation made imports through Arica less competitive. At the end of the century, Antofagasta

[23]For more on changes in the copper mining, see Ángela Vergara Marshall, "Conflicto y modernización en la Gran Minería del Cobre (1950-1970)," *Historia*, XXVII, No. 2 (2004), 419-436.

accounted for eighty percent of total imports. The Norte Chico ports never exceeded ten percent of total imports.

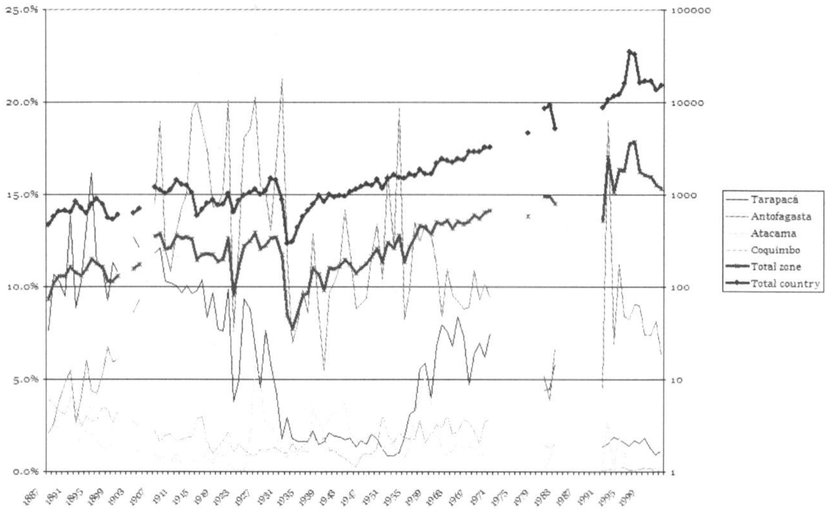

Figure 10: Value of Imports from Northern Chile by Province, 1890-2002

Note: See figure 9.

Source: See figure 2.

By port, the evolution was quite important. Iquique, Arica, Antofagasta and Tocopilla explained all the changes in imports into the north of Chile. Iquique disappeared at the end of the twentieth century,[24] while Arica grew substantially between the 1950s and the 1980s. The ports of Norte Chico, especially Coquimbo and Chañaral, became less important.

The commercial structure was modified significantly during the century. In 1904, an important part of Iquique's imports were concentrated in industrial oils, machinery and tools. Antofagasta and Coquimbo were similar, although both also had some imports of mining products and combustibles. Atacama's ports were different since their imports were concentrated in oils (about seventy percent of total imports). In 1914 industrial oils played an important role everywhere. By 1929 imports were more diversified, with important entrances of textiles in Norte Chico, whereas the machinery and equipment became dominant in Atacama. In Coquimbo, food products and transport equipment were more important, a trend that continued until 1951. In 1938,

[24]Iquique's imports decreased due to import substitution. Total imports of the province also fell.

the main imports everywhere were minerals. In 1951 chemical and food imports were strong in Tarapacá and Atacama. As well, manufacturing imports were higher (1950 marked the beginning of IGS and the flow of imports of intermediate goods to establish a domestic manufacturing industry). The North received direct aid for development, and the mining zone modernized part of its production system to increase productivity and to strengthen its links with other sectors of industry. In 1971, imports of machinery were a substantial component of total imports (up to thirty percent of the total), and a large proportion of entrances were accounted for by parts for the assembly of automobiles in Arica (the existence of the Free Trade Zone explained eighteen percent of car imports in the port). Finally, trade liberalisation in the 1970s affected manufacturing imports in the ports of Tarapaca, whereas in Antofagasta and Coquimbo imports were more diversified. The 2002 data show that a large share of imports was general cargo, but we cannot be more specific.

Exports were larger than imports in all provinces in the zone in all periods, except for three ports: Arica, where imports were inflated due to its role in transhipment to Bolivia and, after 1960, its position as the most important Free Trade Zone; Coquimbo, where imports rose due to the purchase power in the urban zone of La Serena-Coquimbo; and Mejillones at the end of the twentieth century as a result of garnering trade that had previously gone through Antofagasta.

The size of the industrial sector in the region has historically been far lower than the size of the population in the country and even farther below its share of domestic and foreign trade. The evolution of industrial employment in the zone had two different phases. Before 1950 it was quite similar to the development of the zone, but thereafter industrialisation, especially after 1973, led to some differences.

The employment structure by province at the beginning of the century showed the importance of the food, textile and chemical sectors in Antofagasta, Atacama and Coquimbo, as well as the metal trades in Tarapaca and Antofagasta (see table 1). Before the Great Depression, the metal industry increased in importance everywhere except in Tarapaca. During the 1930s deindustrialisation led to a decline in industrial employment, especially in the non-durable consumer sector. By 1968 textile employment disappeared, although it remained stable in the food sector and increased in machinery and transport. The great manufactured industries of the North were created at the same time that shifts to higher value-added exports occurred. In the 1970s the trade policy became more open, which led to a deindustrialisation. As a result, the role of the food sector became more important, especially in the fish and drinks industries in Tarapaca and Coquimbo. Less of an impact was observed in Antofagasta and Atacama, the provinces with stronger production; their industrial employment in metals, machinery and transport remained higher. In 1997, industrial employment was quite similar to the previous period; only

Tarapaca changed with an increase in employment in the metals sector in Antofagasta and Atacama and in the food sector in Coquimbo. Overall, employment in the chemical industry became more closely linked with mining.

Table 1
Industrial Employment in Chile and the Northern Provinces, 1911-1997

	1911	1928	1938	1951	1968	1979	1997
Total Chile	72,752	150,544	92,788	206,711	351,801	299,550	409,585
Total North	4282	7545	4116	6955	22,246	25,254	37,692

Source : Chile, Censos Industriales, various years.

Population increased in Norte Grande at the end of the nineteenth century due to increased migration from the central part of the country. On the other hand, population in Norte Chico stagnated along with the economy. From the 1920s until the 1950s problems in the mining sector constrained population in the North to roughly the national average (see table 2). Thereafter, expansion in the copper industry led to faster population growth than elsewhere in Chile. The IGS, however, did not lead to the kind of growth that might have been expected, except in Antofagasta.

Table 2
Total Population in the County, Northern Zone and Provinces, 1885-2002

	1885	1907	1930	1970	1982	2002
Tarapaca	54,314	120,527	113,331	174,399	273,427	428,594
Antofagasta	33,636	113,323	178,765	243,387	341,203	493,984
Atacama	64,143	63,968	61,098	149,758	183,071	254,336
Coquimbo	187,988	190,867	198,336	336,000	419,178	603,210
Total North	340,081	488,685	551,530	903,544	1,216,879	1,780,124
Total	2,479,085	3,184,610	4,215,021	8,382,463	11,108,535	14,922,250

Source: See table 1.

The distribution of the urban population shows two developments. Norte Grande had much higher urbanisation rates (up to ninety percent at the end of the twentieth century), while Norte Chico remained more rural. This was due largely to the degree of reliance on mining; when nitrates were important, population dispersion was more common, while copper tended to concentrate population. Climatic conditions also affected the population distribution.

The largest urban areas in the zone are concentrated in Norte Grande (Arica and Iquique in Tarapacá, Antofagasta and Calama-Chuquicamata in Antofagasta), whereas there are only two big cities in Norte Chico (Coquimbo-

La Serena and Copiapó). Except for Calama and Copiapó, all are port cities, reflecting the importance of commerce in the zone. Port cities of lesser importance included Pisagua (at the end of the nineteenth century), Mejillones, Taltal, Caldera, Carrizal Bajo, Chañaral, Huasco and Los Vilos. The other ports were only export ports without strong linkages to the economy.

Conclusion

The evolution of the Chilean trading system during the twentieth century has been influenced by the evolution of the Northern provinces. The higher purchasing power of these provinces, due first to nitrates and later to copper exports, has affected port structure, industrial development and population growth. But the results were very different in the two periods. In the nitrate era, labour-intensive industries needed a broad set of products (non-durable consumer products, food and beverages), which for the most part came from the central provinces of the country. The extraction centres were also dispersed, as were the number of ports with external links. In the copper era, however, this pattern changed, since copper mining was capital intensive and required mainly machinery and tools. The mines were concentrated in specific regions, and the resulting trading pattern required a different port system.

Exports were especially important in determining the evolution of this system. This is a central issue in Chilean historiography because of the influence of the North, which was not only local and regional but also national. State initiatives, such as the Free Trade Zone in Arica, had a profound impact on the domestic trade system. Tarapacá, for example, became a net exporter in domestic trade instead of a traditional importing province.

Globalisation and Privatisation of Ports in Turkey

Hülya Günaydin

Introduction

Globalisation has reduced the significance of territoriality. At the same time, the political environment has come to favour liberal economic policies, including privatisation, in many countries since the late 1970s. Though ports have mostly been considered "public goods" and are generally assumed to be owned and operated by the state, new patterns of governance in port operations and services have led to privatisation, liberalisation, commercialisation and competition. Turkey has been no exception and has initiated privatisation policies for ports through the Privatisation Law ratified in 1994, although the "public good" concept has not been eliminated entirely. Thus, methods of privatisation other than outright sales, including the transfer of operating rights, Build-Own-Operate (BOT) or similar methods, might be viable within this framework. The Turkish Maritime Administration (TDI) and Turkish Republic State Railways (TCDD) are the two state-owned enterprises that own ports in Turkey. Both have been included in the privatisation portfolio with the aim of increasing productivity and efficiency by developing competition through private sector investments and, most important, furthering Turkish integration within the European Union (EU) and the global economy.

The Impact of Globalisation on Privatisation

Privatisation can be broadly defined as the shifting of economic functions (mostly ownership) from the public to the private sector. This involves an increased reliance on private actors and market forces to perform functions that have previously been regarded as within the governmental sphere.[1] The state has a dual relationship between socio-economic structures and an international system of states which emphasises interdependence. The scope of economic activities has expanded as a result of globalisation, including new patterns of governance through privatisation. Within the transport sector, ports have been recognised for their role in economic growth and development. Just as global-

[1] Harvey B. Feigenbaum, Jeffrey R. Henig and Chris Hamnett, *Shrinking The State: The Political Underpinnings of Privatization* (Cambridge, 1999), 1.

isation has promoted the interdependence of nations, the volume of trade passing through ports has had significant effects on their wealth.

With the rise of globalisation, many have come to question the role of the nation-state. The range of economic activities that cross territorial boundaries has expanded, as have the ways that people view the world. Many of the challenges facing port operators arise from these phenomena. Transferring ownership or operating rights of state enterprises to private companies, and finding a new balance between the public and private sector, has been one of these, and ports have not been immune.[2]

Privatisation can be viewed narrowly as a reflection of the internationalisation of various economies. International trade has led to a new division of labour among states. Historically, the capitalist industrial system has increased the importance of trade and made international commerce more feasible, leading countries to make choices according to their perceived comparative advantage. Indeed, many consider international trade to be the driving force of the international economy, while world-system theorists consider it vital to the continued development of capitalism.[3] These approaches assume that globalisation is the key to the integration of national economies through trade, and it is clear that ports integrate economies through their distribution systems. Ports are crucial links between global and national systems. Shasi Kumar, in fact, has described globalisation in terms of maritime economics, noting that trade growth has outstripped the expansion of global GDP; since the fastest growing part of this is not in finished goods but rather in intermediate products and services, production has become a global process.[4] In the EU, ninety percent of foreign trade is carried by sea, a process which requires efficient and effective port operations and services. Total world international seaborne trade reached 4008 million tons in 1990, increasing to 5595 million tons in 2000 and 6168 million tons in 2003 (it was expected to reach 7138 million tons in 2006). World container traffic expanded on average by 10.6 per-

---

[2]E. Fuat Keyman, *Globalization, State, Identity/Difference: Toward a Critical Social Theory in International Relations* (Atlantic Highlands, NJ, 1997), 208; Walter C. Opello, Jr. and Stephen J. Rosow, *The Nation-State and Global Order: A Historical Introduction to Contemporary Politics* (London, 1999; 2nd ed., London, 2004), 232-233; and Jürgen Klenk, *et al.*, *Privatisation in Transforming and Developing Economies: Strategies, Consultancy, Experiences* (Wiesbaden, 1995), 4-7.

[3]Opello, Jr. and Rosow, *Nation-State and Global Order*, 233; and Keyman, *Globalization*, 18.

[4]Shasi Kumar and Jan Hoffmann, "Globalisation: The Maritime Nexus," in Costas T. Grammenos (ed.), *Handbook of Maritime Economics and Business* (London, 2002), 35.

cent per year between 1994 and 2004, reaching 359.7 million Twenty-foot Equivalent Units (TEUs) in 2004.[5]

The increase in the number, size and specialisation of vessels affects port infrastructures and operations, which has led to an increasing interest in private sector involvement. Ports are more than merely places to load or unload vessels; they also provide logistics, storage, processing and other services. According to the United Nations Conference on Trade and Development (UNCTAD), "Seaports are interfaces between several modes of transport, and thus they are centres for combined transport...An efficient seaport requires infrastructure, superstructure and equipment, adequate connections to the transport modes, a motivated management, and sufficiently qualified employees."[6] Moreover, ports act as interfaces between maritime and inland transport, such as railways, roads and river and canal boats. Containerisation and the development of intermodal transport systems have increased competition between ports.[7] The global utilisation of containers and electronic communications has also encouraged the standardisation of ports and carrier services. To have an efficient maritime transport system, ports must minimise costs and maximise the quality of operations.

These developments in seaborne transport have made it necessary for ports to invest in larger cranes, berths, storage yards, information technology and additional improvements in order to be competitive. Thus, ports have become more capital- than labour-intensive. Large investments in ports can provide savings in operations just as containerisation and intermodal systems have done. Such investments in infrastructure are expensive, however, and beyond the abilities of many governments, especially those with budget deficits. The participation of the private sector is increasingly seen as an alternative source of funds to modernise ports and increase their capacity. In addition, to improve efficiency many governments have concluded that the management and technological expertise of the private sector should be enlisted to operate and service ports in an increasingly competitive environment.[8]

---

[5]United Nations Conference on Trade and Development (UNCTAD), *Review of Maritime Transport 2004* (Geneva, 2004), xi.

[6]Deniz Ticaret Odası (Maritime Chamber of Commerce), *Deniz Sektoru Raporu* (Istanbul, 2005), 18.

[7]Lourdes Trujillo and Gustavo Nombela, *Multiservice Infrastructure: Privatizing Port Services* (Washington, DC, 2000), 4; and Ali Deveci, Guldem Cerit and Okan Tuna, "Determinants of Intermodal Transport and Turkey's Transport Infrastructure" (Unpublished conference paper, Antalya, 2003).

[8]Trujillo and Nombela, *Multiservice Infrastructure*, 4; and Adrian Smith, *The Privatized Infrastructure: The Role of Government* (London, 1999), 3.

The transfer of various assets and public goods and services to private owners is a multifaceted process affecting various groups in different ways. When we ask "who benefits from the privatisation of the ports" or "who pays the cost of port privatisation," we can better understand the multilayered affects on individuals and groups as well as the economic implications of port privatisation. It may help here to draw a distinction between public and private goods based upon their structural features. Ports have long been assumed to be public goods since their assets are non-divisible in crucial ways, and specific people can easily be excluded from their use. Private goods, on the other hand, are both divisible and contain excludable components. In this sense, post-World War II development policies mostly included state investments in port infrastructure and services as public goods. A fundamental transformation has taken place in the structure of public goods in today's global environment, however, making their provision problematic. As a result, private ports have become viable within the context of a global economy.[9] Many governments have implemented privatisation policies directed towards the effective and productive operation of ports in line with market conditions and to mobilise private resources to invest in their modernisation.

The liberalisation policies adopted in the early 1970s after the deregulation of US markets, followed by structural reforms, including a series of deregulation, liberalisation and privatisation measures in the UK, were soon followed by other states. The World Bank has also emphasised the importance of privatisation in the economic adjustment programmes it has prescribed since the early 1980s. With the collapse of the East Bloc in 1989, privatisation has become the guideline for the transformation of the former centrally-planned economies into market-based states. As Nicholas van de Walle has argued, "experiences show that unless it is accompanied by liberalisation measures, privatisation of state enterprises is unlikely to result in significant gains in the economic efficiency."[10]

Globalisation has recently been accepted by several international institutions as a process that can improve world welfare. But Dani Rodrik has noted a fundamental dilemma: while markets are becoming global, the related legal, social and political institutions remain mostly at the national level.[11]

---

[9]Philip G. Cerny, "Globalization and the Changing Logic of Collective Action," *International Organization*, IV, No. 4 (1995), 600-601 and 608; and Nicholas Spulber, *Redefining the State: Privatization and Welfare Reform in Industrial and Transitional Economies* (New York, 1997), 18-19.

[10]Nicholas Van de Walle, "Privatization in Developing Countries: A Review of the Issues," *World Development,* XVII, No. 5 (1989), 601-615.

[11]Dani Rodrik, *Four Simple Principles for Democratic Governance of Globalization* (Bonn, 2001), 1-2.

While the private sector has adapted flexibly to the global world, national laws, rules and regulations have been much slower to change. The creation of the World Trade Organisation (WTO) in 1995 to replace the General Agreement on Tariffs and Trade (GATT) is the latest multilateral step toward creating an environment conducive to the exchange of goods and services. The emphasis has been placed on the liberalisation of world trade based upon competitive market forces. Within the framework of the WTO's liberalisation and globalisation strategies, the privatisation of ports has gained increasing acceptance. International institutions like the WTO, UN, International Maritime Organisation (IMO), International Labour Organisation (ILO) and several others play an important role in the global functioning of ports by setting international rules, regulations and standards concerning operations and service quality, security, safety, training and other related subjects which enable ports to service international trade more efficiently and effectively.[12]

The paradox of privatisation lies in the fact that the state has to divest itself of some of its powers. In the case of the full privatisation of ports, the state has to cede both ownership and operations. Yet privatisation does not imply an end to the role of the state. On the contrary, privatisation provides the state with an opportunity to reformulate the functions of ports without being involved in commercial activities and enables it to focus on strategic and core responsibilities such as regulations, security, safety, order, education, training and taxation. National security and regional economic development are some arguments against port privatisation. But as governments become regulators rather than operators, new possibilities emerge.[13] Regulation has to be used to keep private operators under control and prevent them from exploiting their monopolies. Considering the public-goods nature of some services, ports need a suitable regulatory framework that uses market mechanisms to make socio-political requirements compatible with commercial goals. Thus, administration becomes even more important when ports are privatised.

All these shifts within a more competitive environment have also changed the concept of the monopolistic public ownership of the ports. During

---

[12]Ozer Ertuna, "Constraints of Privatization: The Case of Turkey" (Unpublished paper presented to the Public-Private Partnerships in the MENA Region Workshop, Mediterranean Development Forum, Morocco, 3-6 September 1998), 3; and Metin Ercan and Ziya Onis, "Politics within the State: Institutions and Dilemmas of Turkish Privatization in Comparative Perspective" (Unpublished paper, Bogazici University, September 2000), 3.

[13]Ercan and Onis, "Politics," 4; Pierre Guislain, *The Privatization Challenge: A Strategic, Legal, and Institutional Analysis of International Experience* (Washington, DC, 1997), 289-290; and Antonio Estache, "Privatization and Regulation of Transport Infrastructure in the 1990s – Successes and Bugs to Fix for the Next Millennium," World Bank Policy Research Working Paper No. 2248 (Washington, DC, 1999).

the 1980s and 1990s, the privatisation of ports has expanded around the world. During these two decades, more than thirty-six governments have privatised some or all of their ports. In 1983, the United Kingdom privatised the nineteen ports that comprised Associated British Ports by selling assets to improve efficiency, increase competition and promote capital investment. Malaysia began its privatisation by transferring the operations of the Kelang Container Terminal at Port Llang to a consortium in 1986 and continued to privatise in 1992 by transferring the second part of the same terminal for US $361 million. Among others that have privatised ports are Argentina (1992), Brazil (1991), Hong Kong, Mexico (1993-1995), Pakistan (1993-1995), New Zealand, Singapore and Venezuela (1991). According to the UN, such privatisation projects comprised fully one-quarter of the 325 global investment opportunities in 2004. Private sector involvement in ports has continued despite problems over concessions, labour, port authorities and other topics.[14]

The intensity of competition inherent in the global economy, along with the shift from single-activity to integrated service systems and the need to make large investments in modern technologies and facilities to increase efficiency and decrease costs, is leading many governments to consider some form of port privatisation. The main objectives include downsizing the role of the state; eliminating the financial burden of state enterprises; mobilising private sector funds for port infrastructure investments and operations; enhancing the efficiency and effectiveness of port operations and services; ensuring a competitive market; enhancing governance; including stakeholders in the decision-making and operation processes; raising social responsibility; increasing managerial and entrepreneurship capacity; and ensuring compliance with international rules, regulations, conventions and implementations.[15]

Who owns the ports and provides the facilities and services is of great concern in privatisation.[16] Port administration has the main responsibility of organising the flow of traffic in an orderly and efficient way. According to Lourdes Trujillo and Gustavo Nombela, ports can be divided into three groups depending on the role of the port authorities. "Landlord ports" are those in

---

[14]Trujillo and Nombela, *Multiservice Infrastructure*, 4; Guislain, *Privatization Challenge*, 38, 166, 226-227 and 249; David Haanmeyer and Peter Yorke, "Port Privatization: An International Perspective," Reason Foundation Policy Study No. 156 (1993), 5-8 and 10-12; and UNCTAD, *Review of Maritime Transport 2004*, 79-80.

[15]United Nations, International Trade, Transport and Financing Division, Transport Unit, "Port Modernization: A Pyramid of Interrelated Challenges" (3 April 1999), 21; Guislain, *Privatization Challenge*, 226-227; and Nur Jale Ece, "Privatization of Ports," *Turkish Maritime News*, 29 May 2006.

[16]Kevin Cullinane and Dono-Wook Song, "Port Privatization Policy and Practice," *Transport Review*, XXII, No. 1 (2002), 60.

which the infrastructure is owned by the port authority, which is also responsible for management. Port services are provided by the private sector, which owns the assets or superstructure, such as cranes and forklifts. This is the most common method of private participation. "Tool ports" are those in which the port authority owns both the infrastructure and the assets, which are rented by the private sector to provide services through concessions or licenses. Finally, there are "service ports" where the port authority owns the port as a whole, including the infrastructure and all the assets, and provides all the services.[17]

Table 1
Port Privatisation Models

Port Models	**No. of Ports**	**Port Elements or Activities**	**Port Regulator**	**Port Landowner**
Operator				
Public	7	Public	Public	Public
Private I	88	Public	Public	Private
Private II	2	Public	Private	Private
Private III	3	Private	Private	Private

Source: Alfred Baird, "Privatization Defined: Is It the Universal Panacea?" (Unpublished paper, Napier University, June 1999), 3.

Ports have been prime candidates for unbundling functions and improving competitiveness.[18] Alfred Baird's "port function matrix" is based upon three distinctive tasks of a port: the regulatory, landowner and operation (or utility) functions.[19] The first set of activities includes those duties defined by laws, regulations and statues enacted by local and national bodies and are mostly undertaken by port authorities. Some of the main responsibilities include implementing the laws, rules and regulations related to maritime activities; issuing licenses for port works; maintaining the facilities; managing traffic; and ensuring fair competition.[20] As such, port regulation has the sort of public goods nature that Cerny describes.[21] Thus, as Baird states, port regulation is the function that would least be expected to be transferred to the private

[17]Trujillo and Nombela, *Multiservice Infrastructure*, 18.

[18]Guislain, *Privatization Challenge*, 226-227.

[19]Alfred Baird, "Privatization Defined: Is It the Universal Panacea?" (Unpublished paper, Napier University, June 1999), 1.

[20]Alfred Baird, "Privatization Trends at the World's Top-100 Container Ports," *Maritime Policy and Management*, XXIX, No. 3 (2002), 272-275.

[21]Cerny, "Globalization," 600-601.

sector, yet it could well increase the efficiency of ports.[22] The landowning function is usually an important part of an urban place, with its economic, social, environmental and security dimensions. Some of the activities related to port land include the management of the estate; the development of municipal and road facilities; and the maintenance of physical assets. Finally, the operations function refers to the physical transfer of goods and passengers between sea and land, including stevedoring. There may also be some facilities like warehousing, storage and packaging. Baird defines the matrix for the privatisation of ports with respect to the fulfilment of these functions (see table 1).

Of the top 100 ports in the world analysed by Baird, only seven (in South Africa, Israel and Singapore) are totally owned by the state, and only three (all in the UK: Southampton, Liverpool and Thamesport) are fully privatised. Eighty-eight of the top 100 ports have adopted the Private I model, meaning that while port regulations and landowning continue to rest with the state, port operations have been transferred to the private sector. The Private I model also includes BOT, lease and joint-venture schemes in which the state retains authority as a regulator. Ninety-seven of the top 100 ports continued to have public authorities after privatisation.[23] As Jean Matons has noted, it has been necessary to retain a public authority to ensure that ports continue to operate in the public interest.[24]

Port Privatisation in Turkey

From its establishment in 1923 after the collapse of the Ottoman Empire, the Republic of Turkey has long relied on State Economic Enterprises (SEEs). From the 1930s up to the early 1970s, the SEEs grew rapidly. Turkey had a mixed economy up to the early 1980s with a policy of protection and import-substitution, which resulted in rapid development in the 1960s. The economic crisis of the 1970s, however, and problems with balance-of-payments deficits led to high inflation and economic recession thereafter.

Economic liberalisation has been the goal of Turkish governments from the early 1980s. The stabilisation and structural reform program decisions taken on 24 January 1980 were supported by institutions like the International Monetary Fund (IMF) and the World Bank. The main objectives were trade, fiscal and international capital liberalisation and a decreased role for the public sector by privatising the SEEs. At the same time, the Turkish economy experienced a shift from import-substitution to export-led industrial policies.

---

[22]Baird, "Privatization Defined," 2.

[23]*Ibid.*, 1-3; and Haanmeyer and Yorke, "Port Privatization," 5-6 and 10-11.

[24]Jean Grosdidier de Matons, "Is Public Authority Still Necessary Following Privatization?" (Unpublished conference paper, June 1999), 3.

Trade has grown rapidly - the ratio of imports and exports to GDP increased from 0.09 in 1980 to 0.30 in 2004 - and GDP reached US $302.8 billion.[25]

During the 1980s, Turkey's leader, Turgut Ozal, was greatly influenced by Thatcherite policies designed to reduce the state's role in the economy. In this context privatisation began as part of the economic reforms introduced in 1984 to minimise state involvement in industrial and commercial activities and to increase competition. The government believed that this would improve "critical success factors," such as efficiency, technology, management and quality.[26] The overarching objective has become economic integration with the rest of the world. Consequently, the privatisation of key institutions, including ports, has been an important issue.

Since 1984, the total value of privatisations has reached US $25.6 billion, of which US $17.4 billion was realised between 2004 and 2006, including the transfer of thirteen ports to the private sector for US $276 million.[27] Port privatisation began in 1995 with the transfer of operating rights in some ports. The IMF-sanctioned programme started in 2000, and subsequent agreements have resulted in large-scale SEE privatisations.

International Trade of Turkey

The volume of Turkish international trade increased more than 100-fold between 1970 and 2004. The value of this trade, which was about US $1.5 billion in 1970, reached US $160.4 billion in 2004, when the volume totalled 219.5 million tons (see appendix table 1). At the same time, Turkey diversified its foreign commerce. The country joined the GATT in 1950, signed the Uruguay Round treaties in 1994 and has been a member of the WTO since 1995. Turkey's foreign trade has been closely aligned with the EU since the negotiation of a Customs Union (CU) in 1996 covering industrial and processed agricultural products. Turkey no longer imposes quotas or tariffs on the imports of these goods from EU states, which has greatly increased trade volumes.[28] The CU has also played an important role in the institutional transformation of the Turkish economy. Following the Helsinki decision in 1999 to recognise Turkey as a candidate to join the EU, this trend has accelerated.

---

[25]Turkey, State Planning Organisation (www.spo.gov.tr).

[26]Turkey, Privatisation Administration (www.oib.gov.tr); and Ertuna, "Constraints."

[27]Turkey, Privatisation Administration.

[28]Merih Celasun and Dani Rodrik, *The Impact of Globalization on Turkish Economy* (Ankara, 2002), 10; and Bernard Hoekman and Subidey Togan, *Turkey: Economic Reform and Accession to the European Union* (Washington, DC, 2005), xvii.

Maritime Transport and Cargo-Handling in Turkey

Commercial and industrial services, including passenger and goods transport, vessel construction, port and auxiliary services and yacht tourism, are the main maritime sectors. The development of ports responds to changes in foreign trade since about eighty-seven percent of total Turkish foreign commerce passes through them (see appendix table 2).[29]

Turkey's merchant fleet has a capacity of more than 8.7 million deadweight tons (dwt); with about 576 ships over 100 gross registered tons (grt), it was the twentieth largest in the world at the end of 2003.[30] Turkish-flag ships recently carried nearly one-fourth of total Turkish maritime transport in both imports and exports; the rest was shipped in foreign-flag vessels, down from forty-two percent of imports and thirty-nine percent of exports in 1995.

Maritime transport in Turkey comprises 87.4 percent of the county's international cargo flows, whereas road transport has a share of 10.32 percent, while rail, air and other transportation facilities together only contributed 1.32 percent as of 2004. Maritime transport in that year accounted for ninety-one percent of the country's imports and 80.4 percent of exports. The EU was the biggest foreign trade partner, taking fifty-four percent of exports and contributing forty-seven percent of imports (see appendix table 3).

Turkey's maritime transport has fluctuated along with changes in global trade. Still, the volume of international cargoes that pass through Turkish seaports has increased by an average of approximately eight percent per annum between 1994 and 2004. The quantity of international cargoes transported in 1994 was 78.5 million tons, reaching 151.7 million tons in 2004, of which seventy percent was composed of import cargoes (105 million tons). Exports totalled forty-seven million tons in 2004 (see appendix table 4).

Domestic transportation is mainly the province of land-based modes (ninety-three percent), while the maritime sector handled only about 4.1 percent (14.7 million tons in 2004), which is low considering the country's long coastline.[31] The Cabotage Law (number 815) requires that all commercial shipping and related activities between Turkish ports be restricted to Turkish citizens (see appendix table 5).

In 2004, when total cargo handled at Turkish ports was 210.6 million tons, exports comprised 26.1 percent (54.9 million tons); imports, 57.1 percent (120.2 million tons); cabotage, 14.2 percent (29.9 million tons); and transit shipments, 2.6 percent (5.5 million tons). Over time, the change in the

---

[29]State Planning Organisation, *Transportation Expert Commission Report for the IXth Five-Year Development Plan (2007-2013)* (Ankara, 2006), 8-19.

[30]UNCTAD, *Review of Maritime Transport 2004*, 33.

[31]*Ibid.*, 18.

share of the various types of cargo has stemmed from an expansion of foreign trade and a decline in domestic and transit transport (see appendix table 6).

Turkey's Seaports and Operations

Turkey has a coastline of 8333 kilometres. It is located between Europe, Asia, the Mediterranean and the Middle East at the junction of a substantial amount of traffic. The coast faces four different seas and is bisected by two straits. The Marmara Sea, located completely within the national borders, connects to the Black Sea via the Bosphorous and to the Aegean and Mediterranean via the Canakkale Strait (Dardanelles). Turkish ports are an important component of a potential multimodal transport system and, along with railways, comprise a gateway to the Middle East and to a variety of landlocked central Asian countries. Turkey thus has a role both as a transit point and as an origin and destination for freight. Since large vessels ply the Europe-East Asia-Mediterranean sea route, Turkish ports are also important as feeders.[32]

Turkey has approximately 290 shore facilities, including ports, fishing harbours, docks and yacht basins, with more than 33,000 metres of quays, although most are small and designed for specific purposes. A total of 118 are seaports where ships over 500 grt can be docked and cargo handled. There are three categories of ports in Turkey: public ports belonging to the Turkish Republic State Railways (TCDD) and Turkish Maritime Administration (TDI); public/private ports owned by the state but operated by private enterprises with concessions running for as long as forty-nine years; and private ports, built and operated by private entities. A total of twenty small- to medium-size ports are owned by TDI, while TCDD owns seven ports with railway connections (Samsun, Haydarpaşa, Derince, Bandırma, Izmir, Mersin and Iskenderun). Both TDI and TCDD are SEEs. The overall capacity of the ports owned by TDI and TCDD is about fifty million tons per year; when the other ports are included, Turkey can handle about 200 million tons per annum.[33]

Container facilities are available at all the TCDD ports (see appendix table 7) as well as at two private ports located in Ambarlı and the Izmit Gulf. Fifty-four percent of maritime containers were handled at TCDD ports and forty-five percent at Ambarlı in 2004. The TCDD ports thus have about a ninety percent share of container traffic at state-owned ports, and Izmir is the leading port in Turkey, especially for foreign trade. Haydarpaşa is mainly utilised for import cargo, while Izmit is mainly used for exports. Mersin is the leading port for the Mediterranean, while container throughput is negligible at

---

[32]Ulker Yetgin, "An Overview of Existing and Future Turkish Port Infrastructure System within the International Combined Transport" (Unpublished conference paper, Antalya, 2002), 2; and Deveci, Cerit and Tuna, "Determinants," 2.

[33]Yetgin, "Overview," 1-5.

the Black Sea ports, unlike those on the Marmara Sea. Istanbul, Izmir, Mersin and Izmit are vital for foreign trade because they serve large industrial regions. According to the Nationwide Port Development Master Plan (2000), there will be a growing demand for containers, which will reach six million TEUs by 2020.[34]

Public ports in Turkey are "service ports" in which the port directorate provides all commercial services using its own labour and equipment. If the operating rights are transferred, they become "landlord ports." The state-owned ports provide a full range of services, such as pilotage, towing, stevedoring, mooring, demurrage, fresh water, solid and liquid waste removal, cargo handling, storage, weighing and equipment rentals.[35] Stevedoring and storage generate the most income. Since the tariffs for services are determined by TCDD headquarters, the charges for cargo handling are the same in all, but there are slight differences for some other services. At some TCDD ports, services such as pilotage and towing are provided by TDI.

The first private ports were established in the early 1990s after legislation in 1989 allowed ports that only provided specific services to handle third parties as well. Most of these private sector operators have become members of the Marmara Port Operators Association (MARLIM), which was founded in 1996. MARLIM, which now has members around the country, was renamed the Port Operators Associations of Turkey (TURKLIM) in 2006. For the purpose of this study, only the state-owned TDI and TCDD ports are included in the analysis of port privatisation in Turkey.

The state-owned ports at present labour under several disadvantages, such as obsolete technology, low degrees of modernisation and capital investment, inefficient and ineffective management, insufficient depth, and antiquated rail and road connections for intermodal transport. Both TDI and TCDD have had financial problems since the 1980s and have not had sufficient funds for modernisation. While the Ministry of Transportation has plans to develop the infrastructure, the necessary funds have been lacking.[36] Matons' comments on the inefficiencies of monopolistic port sectors in developing countries fit Turkey perfectly.[37]

---

[34]*Ibid.*; and State Planning Organisation, *IXth Five-Year Development Plan*, 38.

[35]Hulya Zeybek, "Ports in Turkey and Perspectives for Cooperation," *Turkish Maritime News*, 15 June 2006; and Shashi Kumar and Mahir Akarsu, *Turkish Container Ports: An Analysis of Problems and Potential Opportunities* (Izmir, 2004), 6.

[36]Turkey, Ministry of Transportation, State Railways, Ports and Airports Construction General Directorate (www.dlh.gov.tr).

[37]De Matons, "Public Authority."

Legislation Related to Port Privatisation in Turkey

The institutional development of port infrastructure and services concerned governments during the early Republican period. The first law to be enacted was the Law of Ports (number 618) on 14 April 1925; many of its provisions are still in force. Since ports were considered "public goods," article 1 stipulated that "the Government is responsible for the administration, cleaning, deepening and widening of ports, for the placing of buoys and their maintenance in good shape, and all the other activities related to ports."[38] Article 8, however, enabled the government to establish a joint-stock company to operate each port. Moreover, ports are also affected by the Turkish Constitution; Article 43 provides that "shores are under the jurisdiction of the State. In benefiting the sea, lake and river shores, and from shore strips bordering sea and lakeshores, benefit to the public is primarily sought."

Another major legal text on port regulation is the Seashore Law (number 3621 dated 4 April 1990). Article 4 defines ports: "Port means the coastal structures with sufficient water depth for the vessels to board and leave passengers, load and unload goods, moor and wait, that have technical and social infrastructure facilities protected from the wind and sea effects naturally or artificially." A law dated 29 April 1926 (number 815) concerns coastal shipping (cabotage) and restricts the activities of foreigners. Local Administration Authorities are responsible for the security and safety of the ports according to law number 2677. Port legislation today is being updated to take into account modern needs and to meet EU standards.

Although Turkey does not have an institution devoted to solely to ports, the Undersecretary of Maritime Affairs (UMA) within the Prime Minister's Office was established in 1993 to regulate maritime affairs. The UMA has seven regional directorates and sixty-eight Harbour Master Offices to implement rules and regulations. Some regulatory functions have also been implemented by the state-owned TCDD and TDI. As privatisation progresses, independent port authorities may take over some of these duties.

The Competition Law (number 4054) enforced by the Independent Competition Board stipulated many of the conditions that must be met for privatisation, and the Privatisation Law (number 4046, ratified in 1994) forms the institutional basis for the process. Furthermore, amendments in 1999 (articles 47 and 125) embedded the concept of privatisation in the Constitution and have allowed for international arbitration and direct foreign investment. Privatisation decisions are taken by the Privatisation Higher Council headed by the Prime Minister and composed of five ministers, and implementations are carried out by the Privatisation Administration (PA). Within this framework port privatisation can be accomplished by the transfer of ownership or by lease,

---

[38]Turkey, Undersecretary of Maritime Affairs (www.denizcilik.gov.tr).

although the transfer of port assets is somewhat restricted.[39] As a result, the privatisation of ports in Turkey is only partial, much like the Private I-type in Baird's schema, or the landlord port model, where operating rights are transferred to the private sector or methods like Build-Operate-Transfer (BOT) and leasing are utilised, while ownership and regulation is retained by the state.[40] A bidding process takes place to select private operators and is then ratified by the Privatisation Higher Council. If approved, a contract is signed between the PA and the selected enterprise.

Privatisation of Turkish Maritime Administration (TDI) Ports

TDI is an SEE active in the administration of several Turkish maritime services; it also owns and manages twenty mostly small- to medium-sized ports. Privatisation of this company was decided upon in 1993, but this could not be implemented due to legal problems. The Privatisation Law of 1994 clarified the concept of "public good" and explicitly included ports, allowing for the "transfer of operations rights" using BOT or similar methods for a certain period of time; ownership of the ports was retained by the state, while movable assets could be sold. Thus, the twenty ports owned by TDI were added to the privatisation portfolio.[41] Preparations for privatisation included land planning and registration; sectoral analyses to ensure competition; international supply-and-demand forecasts; and studies of investment requirements, global integration conditions, international standards, environmental issues, the training of labour and the valuation of ports.

Within this context, thirteen of the TDI ports have been privatised by transferring operating rights to private enterprises, while Gulluk, Gokceada, Canakkale, Lapseki, Istanbul and Kabatepe continue to be operated by TDI (see appendix table 8). The objectives for privatising these ports have been to increase efficiency, mobilise private-sector funds for new investments, develop competition and integrate the ports into the world economy. In 1997 six ports were privatised: Tekirdag (US $104.9 million); Hopa (US $4.4 million), Giresun (US $3.2 million), Ordu (US $1.6 million) Sinop (US $800,944) and Rize (US $5.6 million.) The next year Antalya (US $29 million) joined the ranks, followed in 2000 by Alanya (US $1.6 million), in 2001 by Marmaris (US $14.9 million) and in 2003 by Cesme (US $11.25 million), Kusadasi (US $24.3 million), Trabzon (US $20.16 million) and Dikili (US $4.25 million). All entailed the transfer of operating rights to the private sector for a period of

---

[39]Turkey, Privatisation Administration; and Ilhan Baytan, *Özelleştirme* (Ankara, 1999), 95.

[40]Baird, "Privatization Defined," 3.

[41]Turkey, Maritime Administration (TDI) (www.tdi.gov.tr).

thirty years; assets such as machinery, equipment, and vehicles were sold outright.[42] Among these ports, Trabzon, Antalya and Tekirdag were the largest with cargo-handling capacities of 3.9, 3.3 and 2.9 million tons per year, respectively. Alanya, Marmaris, Cesme and Sinop do not have container facilities, although some play important roles in the tourism sector.

According to the methods set out by Privatisation Law 4046, TDI ports have been valued and the bids assessed. Payments to the PA have two parts: a lump sum plus equal instalments and a share of the profits during the thirty-year period. A total of US $276 million has been generated as a result of the privatisation of the thirteen ports along with a TDI ship and other movable assets. Among the conditions stipulated in the contracts, those dealing with labour, investment, asset utilisation, international rules, caps on tariffs for five years and maximum idle periods are the most striking.

A post-privatisation analysis of the thirteen TDI ports show that some modernisation and increases in capacity have been achieved at a cost of US $30.6 million. But there has been no significant change in cargo handling, and the number of personnel decreased in all ports except Hopa, Ordu and Rize. On the other hand, the volume of business increased significantly in most ports (see appendix table 9). Despite privatisation, TDI still recorded losses of about US $65 million at the end of 2005.[43]

TDI's Salipazari port (also called Galataport) in Istanbul was included in the privatisation programme by the Privatisation Higher Council in 2004; the method chosen was BOT. This differed from the previous privatisations not only in the method but also in that the plan included a complex containing a marina for big ships, five-star hotels, shopping centres, fair and congress centres, museums and other commercial and tourist attractions. The project is expected to cost about US $4.3 billion. The Galataport tendering process began in 2005 with an invitation to bid to both domestic and foreign investors. The procedure was completed by the PA, although it was cancelled on 2 February 2006 due an injunction over land. To further the process, the PA has prepared a new plan to be submitted to the Privatisation Higher Council for approval. Galataport is expected to be an integrated commercial centre serving not only shipping but also the needs of the entire region.

Privatisation of Turkish Republic State Railways (TCDD) Ports

TCDD is an SEE established specifically to own and manage the state railways, but it also owns and manages seven ports connected directly to the railway system. The total wharf length is 16,000 metres, and together the ports

---

[42]Turkey, Privatisation Administration, December 2006.

[43]*Ibid.*

have a capacity of 17,800 cargo and passenger ships.[44] The total capacity of cargo handling was 36.8 million tons in 2005, which constitutes approximately ninety percent of the entire container capacity at state-owned ports.

The financial condition of TCDD has been poor for several years, which resulted in deferred maintenance and investment in the infrastructure of both railways and ports. TCDD has recorded losses for more than a decade, and these stood at about US $140 million at the end of 2005 (they were much higher in previous years). Thus, there were no increases in capacity or modernisation, and by 2005 it was estimated that it would take approximately US $5.5 million to accomplish this, which is not a significant amount compared with the scale of the infrastructure. Even though the Ministry of Transportation has been planning new infrastructure investments to be financed by the state, most have not yet begun. The seven TCDD ports, however, have been operating at a profit, at least according to the financial statements. Indeed, their total profit was about US $235 million in 2005.[45] It is not clear whether this is due to the TCDD's monopoly over container operations in most regions of Turkey.

In accordance with the privatisation objectives laid down by the PA, Izmir, Mersin, Iskenderun, Derince, Bandirma and Samsun have been included in the privatisation portfolio since 30 December 2004.[46] Haydarpaşa is excluded since it will be part of a tourism complex. These six ports are the most important in the country considering their location, investments, infrastructure/superstructure and railway and highway connections. Container traffic at these ports is forecast to increase by about twenty percent per year, whereas the average increase in Turkey is about eight percent.[47] The main reason for privatising TCDD ports is to meet this increasing demand and to generate sufficient capital to finance the necessary investments.

The privatisation strategy entails a transfer of operating rights in which the ownership of the ports and their infrastructure (including land) will remain public. Operating rights will be transferred to the private sector for a period of forty-nine years for Izmir and thirty-six years for the other ports. TCDD will be responsible for the post-privatisation performance monitoring of private-sector operations, such as maintenance and repair. The policy enhances competition in that no operator can control more than one port. As well, private operators will have to invest to accommodate traffic increases. About 1100

---

[44]TCDD, TCDD Statistics, December 2006, 75 (www.tcdd.gov.tr).

[45]*Ibid.*, TCDD Statistics, 90 and 93; and Ministry of Transportation, State Railways, Ports and Airports Construction General Directorate (www.dlh.gov.tr).

[46]Privatisation Administration, Privatisation Higher Council Decision number 128, 30 December 2004.

[47]State Planning Organisation, *IXth Five-Year Development Plan*, 27.

civil servants (out of 4200 currently employed at the ports) may be transferred to other TCDD operations after privatisation, thus reducing the burden on the operators. Even though TCDD has increased labour productivity within the last five years, an increase of about fifty percent in employment expenditures over the same period has had a negative impact on operating income. Cargo-handling has almost doubled to about 8400 tons in 2005.[48] The capacity utilisation ratio of the TCDD ports is around fifty percent, which is expected to increase after privatisation to meet the increased demand.

Within this framework, the bidding process for Mersin and Iskenderun began in 2005. These two ports are located close to each other in southern Anatolia, and both serve an extensive hinterland connected by rail and roads. Mersin has the second highest cargo-handling capacity among the TCDD ports; in 2005 it handled 10.2 million tons, mostly liquid bulk cargoes like petroleum. In the same year Iskenderun handled one million tons and generated an income of US $4.2 million. Container traffic is expected to increase by eight percent per year, a level that operators are expected to meet immediately after obtaining the rights. The highest bid for both was submitted by the Akfe-PSA Joint Venture Group: US $755 million for Mersin and US $80 million for Iskenderun.[49] The Competition Board is currently analysing the impact on regional competition. Mersin will be transferred after the legal formalities and final contract details are completed, while the continuation or renewal of the privatisation procedure for Iskenderun will be decided after the decision of the Competition Board.

Privatisation preparation studies of Izmir have recently been concluded by the PA, and tenders have been called with a deadline at the end of the first quarter of 2007. Privatisation will be implemented by granting operating rights for forty-nine years. The private operator is expected to have a minimum level of financing, such as a minimum worldwide turnover or a managing fund of US $100 million and net assets of at least US $75 million, as well as successful operating experience.[50] Izmir is located on the Aegean Sea and is the largest container port in Turkey, with a twenty-nine percent share of Turkish container cargo. Compared to other TCDD ports, exports comprise a higher share at Izmir. The port has a significant agricultural and industrial hinterland supported by an extensive highway and railway network. Izmir also plays an important role in tourism due to its proximity to historical and cultural centres.

---

[48]Privatisation Administration, Privatisation Outlook, December 2006; and TCDD Statistics, December 2006, 87-90.

[49]State Planning Organisation, *IXth Five-Year Development Plan*, 39; and Privatisation Administration, December 2006.

[50]Privatisation Administration, December 2006.

Operating revenues of US $87 million were earned in 2005 through services like cargo handling, terminal and storage services.[51]

Other TCDD ports are being prepared by the PA for privatisation, and as long as market conditions are appropriate this will occur. The TCDD ports are structured as service or tool ports but will become landlord ports after the operating rights are transferred to private companies.

Besides TDI and TCDD, other small ports serving specific SEEs are also being privatised. One is Tasucu, for which the bidding process began in 2006. There are also the yacht ports that belonged to SEEs. With the privatisation of TDI, TCDD and the privately-owned ports, port services in Turkey will be totally liberalised.

Conclusion and Lessons from the Turkish Experience

Privatisation should not necessarily be thought of as the full withdrawal of the state; on the contrary, it can take a variety of forms. It is an extension of the ideology of neo-liberalism within the globalising world economy. The expansion of global corporations, organisations, institutions, unions and trade, as well as a variety of social relations, has affected the privatisation of ports and the way they are managed. Since every state has its own unique conditions, the method of port privatisation is likely to vary from country to country.

Port privatisation in Turkey has been implemented by a transfer of operating rights – Alfred Baird's Private I strategy – which has become the most common technique globally. In this method, the ownership of land and assets remains with the public, but management and operations are undertaken by private entrepreneurs. Indeed, current Turkish law does not allow for full privatisation. Since the late 1990s, the Privatisation Higher Council has proceeded with the privatisation of the ports owned by the two main SEEs, TDI and TCDD, using the transfer of operating rights, BOT or similar methods. TDI ports are rather small compared to those of the TCDD, which are container ports connected by rail to a large domestic hinterland. Since all these ports need investment and modernisation, the mobilisation of private-sector funds, along with economic liberalisation, has been the main aim of government. The privatised ports are expected to reach international standards and to play important roles in the global integration of the Turkish economy.

Post-privatisation figures for TDI and ongoing privatisation analyses for TCDD show that liberalisation has had a positive impact on Turkish integration with the EU and the global transport sector. This suggests that Turkey has begun to become a global actor in shipping and trade.

[51]TCDD, TCDD Statistics, December 2006, 79.

Appendices

Table 1
Development of International Trade in Turkey, 1995-2005

Year	Exports ('000$)	Imports ('000$)	Total International Trade ('000$)	Change (%)	Total International Trade ('000 tons)	Change %
1945	21,637	35,709	57,346	12.5	92,406	14
1996	23,224	43,627	66,851	16.6	108,113	17
1997	26,261	48,559	74,820	11.9	130,972	21
1998	26,974	45,921	72,895	-2.6	118,134	-10
1999	26,587	40,671	67,258	-7.7	124,748	6
2000	27,775	54,503	82,278	22.3	133,463	7
2001	31,334	41,399	72,733	-11.6	130,362	-2
2002	36,059	51,554	87,613	20.5	143,465	10
2003	47,253	69,340	116,593	33.1	160,113	12
2004	63,075	97,362	160,437	37.6	219,458	37
2005	73,476	116,774	190,250	40.0		

Source: Turkey, State Institute of Statistics (DİE), 2006.

Table 2
International Maritime Transport in Turkey, 1994-2004 ('000 Tons)

Years	Exports	Imports	Total International Maritime Transport	Change (%)
1994	24,034	54,498	78,532	
1995	22,064	62,791	84,855	8.1
1996	19,818	65,391	85,209	0.4
1997	21,062	72,643	93,705	10.0
1998	25,019	73,691	98,710	5.3
1999	28,287	71,961	100,248	1.6
2000	29,821	86,758	116,579	16.3
2001	35,178	66,579	101,757	-12.7
2002	39,069	90,027	129,096	26.9
2003	41,045	98,098	139,143	7.8
2004	47,058	104,697	151,755	9.4

Source: DIE, 2005.

Table 3

Main Seaborne Export Trading Partners of Turkey, 2004 ('000 Tons)

Country	**Exports 2004**	**Share (%)**
Italy	7842	16.7
US	4407	9.4
Spain	3529	7.5
Israel	2013	4.3
UAE	1818	3.9
UK	1525	3.2
China	1092	2.3
Germany	927	2.0
Russia	791	1.7
Portugal	721	1.5
Others	22,394	47.5
Total	47,058	100.0

Source See appendix table 2.

Table 4

Main Seaborne Import Trading Partners of Turkey, 2004 ('000 tons)

Country	**Imports 2004**	**Share (%)**
Russia	24,793	23.7
Ukraine	8194	7.8
Iran	5416	5.2
USA	5125	4.9
Libya	5140	4.9
Romania	3317	3.2
S.Arabia	2602	2.5
Brazil	1927	1.8
Italy	1898	1.8
Others	46,285	44.2
Total	104,697	100.0

Source: See appendix table 2.

Table 5

Turkish Domestic Seaborne Trade (Cabotage), 2004

Years	**('000 Tons)**
1998	21,529
1999	21,229
2000	20,848
2001	12,634
2002	16,430
2003	18,716
2004	14,678

Source: Deniz Ticaret Odası (Chamber of Maritime Commerce), 2005.

Table 6
Turkish Cargo Handling by Trade, 1990-2005 ('000 tons)

Years	Exports	Imports	Cabotage	Transit	Total
1990	15,239	43,878	47,114	42,950	149,181
1991	20,343	49,892	32,409	974	103,618
1992	21,915	50,245	34,242	1030	107,432
1993	18,102	64,875	36,244	471	119,032
1994	22,113	52,631	34,004	187	108,935
1995	20,175	64,007	34,535	315	119,692
1996	18,846	72,834	36,162	899	128,741
1997	37,010	75,364	41,716	14,669	168,759
1998	24,773	79,303	38,715	13,043	155,834
1999	32,923	77,978	38,658	20,865	170,424
2000	32,291	85,957	37,328	30,770	186,346
2001	40,634	72,781	26,281	28,724	168,420
2002	39,065	86,180	32,300	23,436	180,981
2003	41,477	98,674	28,500	n.a.	n.a.
2004	54,935	120,260	29,881	5492	210,568
2005	54,494	126,169	28,069	5621	214,353

Source: Turkey, Undersecretary of Maritime Affairs, 2006 (www.denizcilik.gov.tr).

Table 7
Container Cargo Handling by the Public and Private Sectors in Turkey, 2003-2004 (TEUs)

Owner	Port Name	2003	Share (%)	2004	Share (%)	Change (%)
I. TCDD (public)						
	Samsun	0	0	0	0	
	Haydarpaşa	244,467	9.79	316,982	10.29	29.66
	Derince	1936	0.08	1509	0.05	-22.06
	Bandirma	0	0	36	0	0
	Izmir	700,795	28.07	804,563	26.11	14.81
	Mersin	467,111	18.71	532,999	17.30	14.11
	Iskenderun	1745	0.07	607	0.02	-65.21
	Subtotal	1,416,054	56.72	1,656,696	53.77	16.99
II. MARLIM (private)						
	Kumport	439,993	17.63	483,831	15.70	9.96
	Marport	250,126	10.02	462,009	14.99	84.71
	Sedefport	31,731	1.27	34,180	1.11	7.72
	Borusan	80,909	3.24	82,806	2.69	2.34
	Mardas	85,914	3.44	132,566	4.30	54.30
	Gemport	172,806	6.92	204,893	6.65	18.57
	Subtotal	1,061,479	42.52	1,400,285	45.44	31.92
III. Others						
	Antalya	11,196	0.45	18,387	0.60	64.23
	Trabzon	3661	0.15	1549	0.05	57.69
	Akport	4000	0.16	4434	0.14	10.85
	Subtotal	18,857	0.76	24,370	0.79	29.24
TOTAL (Turkey)		2,496,390	100.00	3,081,135	100.00	23.43

Source: TCDD and Marmara Seaports Operators Association (MARLIM) (www. tcdd.gov tr) and (www.marlim.org).

Table 8
Physical Capacities and Facilities of TDI Ports

Ports	Length (metres)	Depth (metres)	Annual Cargo Handling Capacity ('000 tons/year)	Ship Service Capacity (ships/year)
Gulluk	358.9	(-10,-12)	3750	240
Gokceada	500.0	(-6.5)	312	104
Canakkale	100.0	(-6,-6.5)	300	104
Lapseki	200.0	(-6,-6.5)	100	100
Istanbul	1120.0	(-6,-10)	-	5250
Kabatepe	320.0	(-6,-8)	-	-
Total	2598.9		4462	5798

Source: TDI (www.tdi.gov.tr).

Table 9.1
Comparison of TDI Ports before and after Privatisation
Number of Ships Serviced by TDI Ports

Ports of TDI	As of Privatisation Date	After Privatisation (as of 2003)
Alanya	302	465
Antalya	2207	1263
Giresun	834	281
Hopa	439	296
Marmaris	226	1007
Ordu	77	223
Rize	443	282
Sinop	259	39
Tekirdag	1551	868

Source: Turkey, Privatisation Administration, June 2006 (www.oib.gov.tr).

Table 9.2
Comparison of TDI Ports before and after Privatisation
Number of Employees by TDI Ports

Ports of TDI	As of Privatisation Date	After Privatisation (as of 2003)
Alanya	25	9
Antalya	212	105
Giresun	63	20
Hopa	6	102
Marmaris	10	12
Ordu	5	15
Rize	13	20
Sinop	1	1
Tekirdag	68	57

Source: See appendix table 9.1.

Table 9.3
Comparison of TDI Ports before and after Privatisation
Volume of Services by TDI Ports ('000 tons)

Ports of TDI	As of Privatisation Date	After Privatisation (as of 2003)
Alanya	1	224
Antalya	1874	1513
Giresun	251	218
Hopa	418	374
Marmaris	1	0.1
Ordu	81	200
Rize	292	580
Sinop	10	7
Tekirdag	862	994

Source: See appendix table 9.1.

Table 9.4
Comparison of TDI Ports before and after Privatisation
Total Revenues from Port Services by TDI Ports (US $)

Ports of TDI	As of Privatisation Date	After Privatisation (as of 2003)
Alanya	604,832	773,022
Antalya	4,500,000	6,540,000
Giresun	641,250	768,362
Hopa	311,110	1,855,957
Marmaris	1,740,682	2,663,861
Ordu	0	526,347
Rize	312,296	3,464,068
Sinop	0	41,320
Tekirdag	4,410,450	3,734,300

Source: See appendix table 9.1.